JOYCE BLOCK, PH.D.

FAMILY MYTHS

LIVING OUR ROLES, BETRAYING OURSELVES

SIMON & SCHUSTER
NEW YORK LONDON TORONTO SYDNEY TOKYO SINGAPORE

SIMON & SCHUSTER
Rockefeller Center
1230 Avenue of the Americas
New York, New York 10020

Designed by Songhee Kim
Manufactured in the United States of America

1 3 5 7 9 10 8 6 4 2

Library of Congress Cataloging in Publication Data

Block, Joyce
Family myths: living our roles, betraying ourselves / Joyce Block
p. cm.
1. Family—Psychological aspects. 2. Parent and child
3. Identity (Psychology). 4. Self-perception. I. Title.
HQ518.B633 1994 93-33058
306.874—dc20 CIP

ISBN: 0-671-75909-4

To my elusive but beloved sister,
whose life inspired these reflections

ACKNOWLEDGMENTS

Between the time when I began this book and the time of its completion, I had moved halfway across the country, given birth to my daughter Vera on a living-room chair, and learned, with unaccountable difficulty, how to drive a car. Each experience required me to revise my image of myself and my life, stirring up feelings of loss and awakening me to new possibilities. As I committed myself (sometimes fervently and other times wistfully) to creating a new life and shaping a new identity (I was to become a Midwesterner, a second-time new mother, and my family's live-in chauffeur), fragments from my past—people, places, sensations that could not be put into words—became ever more precious to me. And so it was particularly timely to be writing a book about holding on to and letting go of childhood images of the self; my writing informed my life as much as my life informed my writing. Each day in my new home, I spent my spare time riveted to my computer and discovered there that the stories I had heard in my "former life," the ones I was trying to make sense of now, were my stories as much as anyone else's.

In my own personal trajectory through space and time, strains from the past (songs of childhood) resonated inaudibly within, and, like the "characters" I was writing about, I plunged ahead boldly and then looked back longingly, labored patiently and then defiantly stalled out, expanded and then contracted and then expanded once again. And as my "new" life began to cohere (my daughter Vera grew, and my beloved book assumed a form that I and my editor could live with), I knew that I too was struggling to sift apart the essential from the nonessential aspects of my identity, and that, in this state of temporary disequilibrium, I, like the people I was writing about, found it hard to resist humming those old familiar melodies that have the power to rock me to sleep and lull me into forgetting who I really am.

I am indebted to all those people who confided in me their stories, which doubtless were always a blend of fact and fiction, dream and memory. This includes my psychotherapy patients, my friends, and members of my family. Their impulse to unearth that which had been carefully buried for so long, nourished my own desire to understand.

Although the stories I relate refer to real people, they also incorporate my interpretations of what these people told me about themselves and their lives. Therefore, although I always tried to remain true to the spirit of the material, it is by no means free of my own vision of what it all meant. For good or bad, this is the nature of writing a history, be it the history of an individual, a family, or a nation, and I claim no objectivity. In order to protect the confidentiality of the people I present, all identifying features have been changed.

There are innumerable influences on my thinking, and though I refer to various writers throughout the text, they are by no means exclusive; it would be futile to try to mention all. Let me note, however, that psychoanalytic and family-systems theories have together been very important in shaping my ideas about the genesis and maintenance of identity, and that my conversations over the years with Amos Gunsberg are and always will be with me.

The fairy tales and ancient myths I have been reading to my daughter Saralena for the past couple of years have given me untold pleasure and have convinced me of the universality of our secret fantasies of transformation and transcendence. If I had not been curling up many an evening with my daughter and sharing in her delight at these classic dreams, I am certain that this book would have looked quite different.

I wish to thank Sharon Friedman, my literary agent, whom I consider a dear friend as well as a loyal advocate. Oddly enough, she is both wonderfully diplomatic and refreshingly honest: able to strike a compromise but incapable of mincing words. These qualities continue to be an inspiration to me.

Because this book has been a labor of love and I have been endlessly fascinated by the people whose stories I relate, I needed (though initially resisted) the steadying influence of Dominick Anfuso, my editor. Tactfully he encouraged me to pare down material that threatened to be limitless and potentially overwhelming. By means of his helpful comments, I was able to sharpen my focus, and I believe that as a result my readers can better share in my enthusiasm. For this I thank him gratefully. I also wish to thank my copy editor, Terry Zaroff, whose ability to balance meticulousness with unobtrusiveness was impressive.

I have dedicated the book to my sister, with whom I shared my childhood and my earliest fantasies, but my dear friend Ruth Saada has also been a sister to me in the true and most beautiful sense of the word. Ruth has always been someone I could talk to about my ideas and my adult fantasies; and because she was interested and her responses were thoughtful, she helped me decide which dreams were worth pursuing and which I would be better off leaving behind. Her faith in me and in the value of our imaginative meanderings together has been an endless source of nourishment.

Finally, my husband, Henry Weinfield, my stepson, Paul, my daughters, Saralena and Vera, have had to live with my sometimes obsessive involvement with deciphering and telling other families' stories. Their love and their irritation helped me put it all in perspective; I hope I can learn from them and will tolerate their imperfections as well as they have tolerated mine.

CONTENTS

PART ONE

MYTHOLOGICAL IDENTITIES AND REAL-LIFE DRAMAS

1

An Introduction to the "Self-Fulfilling Prophecy"

O body swayed to music, O brightening glance
How can we know the dancer from the dance?

—William Butler Yeats, "Among School Children"

IMAGINATIVE PLAY AMONG CHILDREN

When my daughter Saralena was three years old, I would have occasion to watch her and her friends play at being all sorts of characters—fairies and princesses, big sisters and mothers, Cinderellas and Sleeping Beauties. Although my daughter and her friends obviously took great delight in creating an imaginary world in which they could pretend to be anything they wanted, it was clear that they took their play very seriously. It was "make-believe," but somehow it was also very real. No wonder none of the girls at that young age wanted even to *pretend* to be one of Cinderella's ugly stepsisters or Prince Charming. ("I'm not a boy!") A couple of years later maybe, but not at three, when fantasy and reality still blended too easily into each other, and playing at being a character almost made it real.

Swept away by their own powerful imaginations, these little people seemed momentarily to forget that they were merely actors in a drama that they themselves were constructing, and that their "characters" bore no relationship to their actual identities. And so, when I watched one girl vehemently insist on "being" her favorite character, the Little Mermaid, and heard another girl *plead* with her companions to be the mommy or the big sister but not the baby, it was clear that, in their minds at least, something very critical was at stake, something that could not be explained away by adult logic.

After some musing, I came to the conclusion that these girls "made believe" so well that they almost believed in their "make-believe," and so experienced their play characters as natural extensions of themselves. When they insisted on playing one role rather than another, it was not because they wanted to be the star or the center of attention (play was never done for an audience). More fundamental than that, it was a question of self-definition and self-esteem—nothing less! Dressing in rags like Cinderella was just a leap of the imagination away from being the most loved and most special of sisters, marrying the prince, and living happily ever after.

What I found particularly intriguing was that my daughter would become terribly upset and frustrated when one of her playmates declared that *she* was the character they both aspired to, whereas Saralena was to be her less favored counterpart. If my daughter had been simply angry at her friend's unilateral decision, I would not have been surprised, for why shouldn't she challenge a perceived injustice? But what startled and unnerved me was that my daughter responded to her friend's pronouncement *as if* it represented the Truth and she were fated, against her will, to *be* someone she did not wish to be. Her pitifully unhappy demeanor expressed the feeling that, unless she could persuade her friend to change *her* mind, she was consigned either to be someone she did not wish to be or else to be nobody at all!

This was some difficult choice for a child to have to make, and this was "only play." When we are conscripted into playing a role in our family dramas, we face a similar dilemma, and then it is not supposed to be just for "pretend." Children's imaginative play comes to an abrupt halt when the mothers arrive and the play date is over; imaginative play within families may actually be interminable.

As I impotently watched my daughter grapple with her dilemma (explanations and reassurances did little to allay her anxiety), I realized that at three years old she was not yet clear that nobody, let alone another child, has the power to define who she *really* is—in play or in real life. At that early stage of development, other people's ideas are treated as if they have substance and magical power over us. They are not easily dismissed as false or simply fantastical. Consequently, even at three we have indeterminate identities, subject to the idiosyncrasies of other people's imaginations. This universal experience is bound to be unsettling. It is no wonder that as children we need the reassuring jingle: "Sticks and stones can break my bones but names can never hurt me." The three-year-old in all of us is unconvinced.

IMAGINATIVE PLAY AMONG ADULTS

> The child was faced with the dilemma of whether to believe the parent or his own senses. If he believed his own senses he maintained a firm grasp on reality. If he believed the parent, he maintained the needed relationship, but distorted his perception of reality.
>
> —P. Watzlawick et al., *The Pragmatics of Human Communication*

How thin is the line that separates fantasy from reality! Imagine then, for a moment, how difficult it would be for a child to dispute his parents' vision of who he is. He might just as well argue that night is day and day night as argue that he is not the kind of kid his parents think he is. His cries of protest fall upon deaf ears.

Children learn about themselves through the eyes of their parents, and their parents' representations of them are taken for real. The image in the family mirror, however distorted, becomes part of their subjective reality, coloring their own (perhaps more accurate) perceptions of who they actually are. (Sometimes it boils down to a question of who is crazy: the child who sees things one way, or the parent who sees them another? Most of the time, the child has to conclude that it is his judgment that is wanting—after all, wouldn't it be far worse to think that his parents were out of their minds?)

To a small child it is inconceivable that those powerful parental figures upon whom he depends for his very survival have needs, fears, and wishes of their own which they hope to satisfy through their offspring. It would never occur to five-year-old Diana that her father is a disappointed and frustrated man and that this is why *he* depends upon *her* to brighten up his day and confer meaning on his life. She only knows that he calls her "a human dynamo," "a raving beauty," that he named her Diana, after the Roman goddess of the hunt, and that his eyes glow with adoration and longing whenever he looks in her direction.

And Laurel—how could she have guessed at seven that her mother loathed herself and needed *Laurel* to be her false mirror, her confidante, her faithful disciple? She only knows that her mother talks incessantly but rarely listens, as if she, Laurel, were invisible, and calls *her* "cold" and "selfish" and "ungrateful" when she dares to break the trance.

Normally egocentric, young children cannot put themselves in another person's shoes, let alone imagine the inner workings of their parents' minds. Instead, they are mesmerized by their own reflected image, be it beautiful or hideous, and so they fail to realize that the image may be out of focus and not at all a faithful rendition of the original. They do not know when modifications in contour and shading are made so that their faces will blend nicely into the family landscape. How can a child guess that his very own self-portrait is tailored to fit snugly into the empty space within the family album?

Of course, as a child develops a more sophisticated understanding of his parents' limitations, he may challenge the image set before him, or discover that, if he embellishes upon it, it feels more like his own, and this makes it palatable. But in either case he will not be able to ignore it. That would mean being left out of the family play entirely, and such psychic exile is too much to ask of any child when the family drama seems to be "the only show in town."

But why, you might ask, would the average, nonpsychotic, well-intentioned parent see a distorted image of his child and not the actual child that is before him? And why would he choose to weave an elaborate mythology with mythological figures substituting for real people when there are true stories to be told and real people to experience? Is our discussion relevant only to those "pathological" few who, unlike the rest of us, cannot distinguish clearly between reality and fantasy? Or does it apply to most families and therefore to you and me and those we think we know most intimately? It is my thesis that we are all implicated, to a greater or lesser degree. When we consider what seems to be a universal human impulse to create myths and fairy tales, expressed as it were in the literature of all peoples, the tendency to mythologize our own lives and members of our own families is not all that mysterious.

As a culture and as individuals, we externalize our inner dreams, desires, and conflicts, projecting what is going on inside ourselves onto real or imaginary beings, hoping in this manner to discover ways to express and resolve our personal dilemmas. Psychologist Jerome Bruner explains the impulse toward "mythmaking," by referring to "the human preference to cope with events that are outside rather than those that are inside. . . . An internal plight is converted into a story plot ("Myth and Identity," p. 277). When we invent characters who then act out our desires for us, we can live vicariously, watching the drama, which is really our own, from a pleasingly secure position. The anger, the despair, the love, and the losses are ours but not ours, and as audience to a "drama," even if it is our own, we feel as if we cannot really suffer any permanent harm or censure.

In fairy tales and myths, the various characters fight our battles for us, each representing an aspect of our personality which we might otherwise hesitate to acknowledge. We deplore the Envious, the Spiteful, and the Lazy, and heave a sigh of relief when we can locate them *outside* ourselves, pointing our fingers at them and shaking our heads; in art we reaffirm the ideals we have failed to live up to in life and feel virtuous.

Real life may be frustratingly limited, and real people may be forever outside of our control, but in our fairy tales and myths we are suspended in a space that exists "once upon a time." There we can transcend life's limitations and create for ourselves the happy illusion that there is a method to the madness we are daily witness to. It is comforting to think that our pain is always meaningful and that our individual lives are part of some grand scheme. As we enter into a mythological world, we leave behind us the doubts and the terrors of our own.

Our myths—in literature *and* in families—reflect the world as we would have it. It is a world that is orderly, uncomplicated, and coherent, where conflict is built right into the system, and life's ambiguities are systematically ignored. Passions rage, lives are shattered, miraculous transformations occur, but all is ultimately predictable. Moreover, in the world of the myth, we the mythmakers are omnipotent, and who can resist seizing the chance to play at being God? Real life cannot offer such an opportunity, only art!

The fairy tales we tell ourselves add the finishing touch, reassuring us that, in the final analysis, there is not only order but also justice—if not in this world, in the next. The Good are sure to be victorious (in the end), the Bad are destined to suffer defeat, and all those who lie somewhere in between Good and Bad receive their Just Deserts. The first become last and the last become first, and all those who are unfortunate, unappreciated, or misunderstood are compensated in the end. Who among us, rich or poor, male or female, cannot identify with one or another of these experiences? Who would not like to believe that his life conforms to such a pattern?

As the scholar Max Luthi points out in his analysis of the fairy tale "Sleeping Beauty": "one instinctively conceives of the princess as an image for the human spirit: the story portrays the endowment, peril, paralysis and redemption not of just one girl, but of all mankind. The soul of man again and again suffers convulsions and paralysis, and, each time—with luck—it can be revived, healed, redeemed. With luck! . . . It fills its hearers with confidence that a new larger life is to come after the deathlike sleep" (*Once upon a Time: On the Nature of Fairy Tales*, p. 24).

Personal myths and personal fairy tales serve similar psychological functions: the stories that we read in books capture our imagination because they resonate with the unwritten stories we silently tell ourselves. One need not have read Grimm's or Perrault's or Walt Disney's version of "Cinderella" to live as a Cinderella-like figure with all the trimmings, including an array of jealous stepsisters, a handsome prince, and a magical fairy godmother. And for every Goliath in business clothes or uniform there are ten Davids of varying size, shape, and strength who are eager for the chance to vanquish the powerful forces of evil against all the odds. We can all be heroes and heroines in the world of our imaginations, stars in our private theaters.

Regrettably, the family serves as the "natural" arena in which to stage our dramas, since in even the most psychologically sophisticated homes children are frequently mistaken for extensions of their parents, and as such become the "natural" repositories of their parents' dreams, fears, and desires. Where else but in families are the boundaries separating one individual from another so blurry? And in what other relationship but the parent-child relationship is there such an imbalance of power right from the start? (And such potential for "well-meaning" abuse of that power?) When identifications and projections are rampant (as they tend to be among intimates), there is fertile ground for the cultivation of mythological identities.

Freud spoke with brilliant insight of how children can become "narcissistic objects," as their parents attempt to assuage their own egos and salvage their own tattered illusions of perfection by projecting them onto their offspring. In describing such a parent's relationship to his child, he writes that "illness, death, renunciation of enjoyment, restrictions on his own will, shall not touch him; the laws of nature and society shall be abrogated in his favor; he shall once more really be the center and the core of creation—'His majesty the Baby,' as we once fancied ourselves. The child shall fulfill those wishful dreams of the parents which they never carried out—the boy shall become a great man and a hero in his father's place, and the girl shall marry a prince as a tardy compensation for her mother" ("On Narcissism," p. 91).

Of course, the idealization of a child is just one of many possible mythological scenarios. We shall see later, however, that, despite the pretty gloss, this form of distortion can be as limiting to the child's development as a parent's devaluation. Suffice it to say at this point that, when children are caught in the net of their parents' mythologies, whatever they are, and enlisted to play out their parents' fantasies for them, children's mythological identities are conceived and sustained at the expense of genuine self-consciousness, and the commitment to mythmaking is passed down from generation to generation.

In literature one myth feeds on another, so, for example, in the biblical story, the figure of David, the diminutive shepherd boy turned king, assumes mythic proportions only in conjunction with the figure of Goliath, the brutish Philistine who is himself bigger than life. And in the fairy tale "Beauty and the Beast," the character of Beauty, the innocent, self-sacrificing daughter whose love is transformative, is interesting only in relation to the character of the Beast, the handsome prince cast under an evil witch's spell.

Similarly, in families one person's mythology buttresses up another's, and eventually everyone holds shares in the family's creative-arts business. There are mergers, conglomerates, and competing factions, but mythmaking and myth-breaking becomes a family affair.

In my role as a family therapist, I have encountered many a quiet, diligent, and self-sacrificing couple seeking psychological help on account of one extraordinarily brutish, irresponsible, and selfish child. To all appearances, these parents are innocent victims of their child's "flawed character," which seems to be the embodiment of every bad quality that they themselves do not possess. But although there is no denying that these "gentle" parents are being abused by their not-so-gentle offspring (outrageous incidents are enumerated in vivid detail), I cannot help wondering how these "monsters" were conceived, how veritable angels could give birth to such alien creatures.

Careful not to be seduced into taking sides in what could easily be mistaken for a clearcut battle between Good and Evil, I remind myself that these beleaguered parents might yet, in some circuitous fashion, be at the bottom of all this, working behind the scenes. In contrast to their offspring, such parents are often painfully diffident and lead colorless and uneventful lives. Indeed, if we are to believe the narrative they tell, their existence would be *perfectly* harmonious, and entirely devoid of any conflict or passion, were it not for their "aberrant child."

Yet, as parents, these mild-mannered folks catch a glimpse of unbridled passion, raw emotion, and all the other frightening experiences they have managed, up until now, to insulate themselves from. Through their hedonistic and egotistical children they have a chance to see how the "other half" lives and still retain their own impeccable reputations!

In some of these cases at least, it seems reasonable to assume that the "monstrous" children were conceived in that form for the express purpose of a family drama, which has now gotten out of hand. As the Forbidden Idea becomes flesh, the parents/dramatists lose control of the action and live in *real* terror of the drama, which has now taken on a momentum of its own.

In such extreme cases, a family begins to resemble a collection of stock vaudeville characters; however, I would argue that even in so-called ordinary households family life often becomes a repetitive series of "routines" that are no more than variations upon a consistent theme. Brothers and sisters and mothers and fathers represent diametrically opposing human tendencies which only when added all together make up a satisfying whole. In exchange for the privilege of participating in the family drama, each individual is condemned to live as a fragment of himself, and never develop into the whole human being he could have been.

Psychoanalyst and pediatrician D. W. Winnicott speaks about the "false self," which he believes develops when a child discovers that he must stifle his spontaneity in order to live comfortably with others. Rather than feeling free to discover and express his unique personality, the child devotes himself primarily to the careful monitoring of the responses of those upon whom he depends. As he disregards his own inner realities and invests his time and energy into molding himself to conform to other people's needs, the true self is divided from the false self, and the schism between appearance and reality, inner and outer experience, has its origin. (R. D. Laing refers to similar ideas in his books, *The Divided Self* being one.) As I see it, the family mythology, whatever form that mythology takes, is the home and breeding ground of this same false self, which we then perfect over the course of a lifetime.

With a minimum of encouragement, most of us can paint colorful though admittedly caricatured portraits of each and every member of our family, including ourselves. And even when we are committed to the idea that each of us is a unique and complicated individual, our family portraits are often striking for their absence of nuance and their simple-minded vision. Far from being distinctive, each member of the family easily corresponds to one of a number of familiar stock characters that we encounter in literature as well as real life, characters who are more personifications of certain human qualities than complete persons who think and feel.

The family Brain and the family Comedian, the Wild Child and the Sensitive Plant, the Responsible Daughter and the Prodigal Son are but a few common examples of the characters families create and then enlist for the purpose of enacting a particular family drama. The Black Sheep plays opposite the self-sacrificing Martyr, and the Free Spirit/Rebel plays opposite the Upstanding Citizen. Brothers and sisters, husbands and wives, parents and children play complementary roles, and though the content varies, and over the course of a lifetime the characters may exchange places with one another, the steps are carefully choreographed and the dramatic "dance" remains essentially unchanged.

Some families imbue one or another member with superhuman powers—one son is a Prince who can (and must) do no wrong, while another is the Ne'er-Do-Well, doomed to bring shame and misfortune on himself and his family. Other families are more modest—one daughter is cast as the Intellectual while another is cast as the Charmer, one son has his "feet on the ground," while the other has his "head in the clouds." But in all cases the mythological identities that have been constructed prescribe what lies in store for the future. The Prince must get his bride (and she must be a venerable princess, because nobody else is good enough). The Ne'er-Do-Well must end poorly (and/or repent his evil ways). The Intellectual must never be too frivolous (if only her friends/children/husband wouldn't always pull her away from her work . . .). And the Charmer must never presume to think too much ("You look beautiful when you're mad"). The pattern is set, and the prophecy must be fulfilled; otherwise, the story, which is the story of life, would no longer make sense in the same way.

Our family portraits are ageless; they hover over us throughout our lives, casting shadows which obscure our features so that we are no longer recognizable. These portraits are so colorful and appear to us so vividly that, despite our numerous disclaimers, we frequently mistake them for true reflections of ourselves. Consequently, although these images of who we are originate within the context of our early-childhood relationships, they have far-reaching implications for how we live our lives long after we "grow up" and leave home. When we think through these images, and feel through these images, we live them, and that becomes our life.

As adults, many of us may feel, on occasion, as if our lives have taken on a momentum of their own, and that we are careening down a path that is both familiar and also somewhat alien to us (a path that we feel compelled to take without knowing fully why we don't just choose to take another). It is as if we are on a merry-go-round ride, strapped onto one horse, and unable to dismount. The music is hypnotic, but the scenery is monotonous as we circle endlessly. This is because we often assume that these mythological figures (and that is how I shall refer to them) are the *essence* of what we identify as being "me." We fail to realize that we act out our characters so meticulously and fulfill our destinies so faithfully simply because we have come to *believe* in the inevitability of a particular story line. It is our *belief* in the vision that makes it so difficult for us to wend our way back to our true selves.

Although "fate" is not part of our modern vocabulary, and as ordinary people we hardly resemble the epic characters in Greek mythology, most of us unconsciously make predictions about our own and other people's futures, and as in the case of the ancient oracles, it is uncanny how often these predictions come to pass. Myths, fairy tales, and choreographed performances are not limited to literature and the fine arts, and this may serve as an explanation. Most families tell stories in some form or another—funny stories, sad stories, tragic stories, and inspiring stories—and in these tales are hidden messages about the meaning of life, the nature of relationships, the prospects for the future, and the basis of identity. Family stories have significance for each member of the family, even those who are not included in the action as described. Being excluded from a favorite family story is as significant as being cast in the starring role.

The compilation of stories, memories, myths, and experiences that evolve over the years constitutes the family lore. Through this narrative, which has no apparent organization but which is nevertheless "overdetermined," we all discover and then rediscover who we supposedly are and what we are valued for. (Freud speaks of the "overdetermination" of symptoms, maintaining that there are always many factors that converge in the formation of a symptom. Therefore, there is no single cause, no one meaning, but several, none of which are mutually exclusive. When I use this term, I mean to imply that there are many motives for constructing and maintaining family myths, and that no single person is responsible.)

The power of the family lore lies not in its truth value; indeed, we may protest that the stories misrepresent our experience or are even patently false. The family mythology, (and myth is what it often is) has the power to shape our images of who we are (and who we are not) and what we are destined to become. Whereas some mythological roles are flattering, even inflating, others are demeaning, even debasing. All are, however, unreal, and therefore represent a betrayal of the self.

In contrast to staged dramas, whose actors shed their costumes and resume their ordinary lives and identities once the curtain has fallen to give a clear signal that the performance is over, family dramas are rarely acknowledged as dramas at all, and the actors are mistaken (and mistake themselves) for the characters they play. Because there is no circumscribed stage, life itself becomes the stage for the ongoing drama, which can resume at any time or place.

Often the "favorite" family stories have been repeated so many times that everyone in the family knows the punch line by heart. There may be new embellishments introduced to enliven the tale, or a new story may surface that is a variation along a well-known theme, but there will be few surprises as the plot unfolds over Thanksgiving dinner. A story may secretly tickle our insides or inexplicably gnaw away at them; it may be a signal to launch into an age-old family battle, or it may enable us to smooth over differences so that new battles are not waged and the illusion of family harmony is preserved. Family mythologies are created with a purpose in mind; they are not simply memories but metaphors. Consequently, it would be as futile to argue about the "truth" of a particular incident as it would be to argue over whether Snow White's stepmother *actually* spoke to her mirror, or whether Athena *actually* was born from the head of Zeus.

In Greek mythology, Oedipus does not placidly submit to his fate as it is decreed, and neither do we. Rather, each of us wrestles with his or her "destiny" as it has been prophesied within our families. Indeed, sometimes, instead of allowing our lives to unfold as expected, we, like tragic heroes, consciously defy our "fate" and, yearning to be free, struggle to disentangle ourselves from the web of ideas in which we are our own prisoners.

But as we challenge the fictional self we were handed, we often create a new fictional self to take its place, who is not more "real" than the mythological figure he is substituting for. When the schlemiel feels compelled to become the *exemplary* corporate executive, or the model student/model child "drops out" and feels *obliged* to inveigh against the "establishment," the curse of living unspontaneously—that is, "in character"—continues to haunt us. The reaction, the antithesis, which on the surface appears to be quite revolutionary, is in reality only a devious variation upon a consistent theme. The schlemiel as corporate executive feels "as if" he is an impostor at the board meeting, and as such he is driven to prove again and again that he is in fact a smooth operator and not a fumbling idiot; at all times his performance must be impeccable, or else he is in danger of reverting to his previous identity. The model student turned model "hippie" excels in whatever she does and is driven to be the "best" revolutionary just as she was driven to be the "best" pupil in her high-school class. She repudiates all forms of competition but is anxious to be the *most* noncompetitive person in her circle. And if her parents do not recognize their daughter now that she has shed her pumps and tailored shirts to apply herself painstakingly to the job of becoming a social outcast, *we* can identify the thread linking one mythological figure to the other—the family Star to the family Dropout.

The "negative identities," identities constructed in reaction against the prophecies, inadvertently fulfill the prophecies they hope to circumvent. Beginning with Freud, psychoanalysts have maintained that, at least from the perspective of the Unconscious, opposites are paradoxically equivalent, and this is never more apparent than when one mythological identity is momentarily obscured by another, very different one. As one mask substitutes for another, the masquerade takes on different forms, and it becomes increasingly difficult to distinguish what is "pretend" from what is real.

Sherry, a young woman who alternates between binging and self-starvation, is a perfect example. Sherry *feels* fat and out of control with her eating even though she is pencil-thin. She came to perceive herself as Insatiable (substitute "fat") because her family defined even a normal amount of anger and neediness as "too much." So now, though she counts every calorie by day, refusing to be the Pig she felt she was destined to become, at night she compulsively *forces* herself to consume more than her stomach can comfortably hold, insisting that she *is* as she was led to believe she was, and that nobody is going to hold her back! Her friends think she looks like a model, her boyfriend says that she "eats like a bird," and she, like her family, knows better. But does she really?

Even when real change does occur, and life as we have actually lived it challenges the mythic identities we have adopted as children, we do not always digest the new information available to us. The childhood images of the self and of others stubbornly endure and continue to distort our perceptions and constrict our lives. Psychiatrist R. D. Laing, famous for his analyzes of pathological forms of communication within families, describes the process by which we come to live our myths in this way:

> If I hypnotize you I do not say "I order you to feel cold." I indicate it is cold. You immediately feel cold. I think many children begin in a state like this.
>
> We indicate to them how it is: They take up their positions in the Space we define. They may then choose to become a fragment of that fragment of their possibilities we indicate they are.
>
> (*The Politics of the Family and Other Essays*, p. 62.)

As early unarticulated memories (psychoanalyst Christopher Bollas speaks of the "unthought known"), images of the self are imprinted in our minds, and because as children we are not equipped to question them or understand their origin, they are preserved in their original form—fantasy blended with reality (*The Shadow of the Object*).

If as children we are hypnotized, so to speak, as adults we become our own hypnotists, and give ourselves suggestions which we follow religiously and subsequently forget. Spellbound, we wait for the fairy-tale ending in which we are miraculously rescued and restored to our true form. But as we repeat the early betrayal of the self again and again (as if the self were our antagonist), the true self becomes more and more elusive and difficult to recognize. Polonius' facile injunction "To thine own self be true" raises more questions than it resolves: which self should we be true to—the one we have buried, or the one we have adopted, cultivated, and lived with for most of our lives?

Once we have constructed a coherent identity around false or partial images of who we are, we become attached to these fragmented images, which we have woven into a personal story line or life narrative, and as a result we are loath to give them up. After having made a virtue of necessity, we cling to our personal mythological identities as if they were our special magic, an infallible camouflage that has protected us and will continue to protect us against assaults to the self.

In the fairy tale "The Emperor's New Clothes" by Hans Christian Andersen, everyone treats the ridiculous emperor and his impostor tailors with the utmost respect until a courageous little boy innocently declares that the emperor really is parading naked and that his magnificent garments are only imaginary. But, rather than welcoming the truth, everyone is embarrassed by it—the vain and foolish emperor who would prefer to deceive himself than squarely to face up to the fact that he has been duped, his cunning tailors who depend for their livelihood on other people's insecurity, and the spectators who didn't dare to trust their own perceptions but instead allowed the "authorities" (in this case the nobility) to dictate to them their beliefs. As the fairy tale concludes, the royal parade continues, even though it is now obvious to all that it is nothing more than a farce. Apparently, continuing the sham is the only way for all of the characters to save face.

Once we have taken a similar step and exposed our mythic identities to the test of reality, we are also apt to feel uncomfortable and uncertain of how to proceed. Like the emperor and his entourage, we can continue as we always have and—accidentally on purpose—fail to assimilate the insights we have gained. Alternately, we can admit that for years we have been operating under false pretenses and that it is up to us alone to cut our losses now and move on.

But if we defy our "fate" and declare once and for all that our prophets were false and that we have been misled, we must live with the knowledge that the past is the past and there is no undoing it and no compensation for lost time. All we have now is a present, like anyone else. Nothing more or less, and in this world, unlike the world of myth, there is no guarantee of what lies in store for us in the future—the end of *our* story has not yet been written.

Before the spell of the self-fulfilling prophecy can be broken, we must begin at the beginning and explore the origin of the "mythological identities" that we mistake for real as they emerge within the context of the parent-child relationship. As we work our way back to the present, which is after all the only thing we can ever hope to change, we shall see how inadvertently we carry the tattered family banner with us everywhere and deny ourselves access to our actual potentialities. Paradoxically, by acknowledging our helplessness as children, we can finally admit to our responsibility as adults as we identify why and how *we* perpetuate the past and set limits on our future. Only when we recognize our motivation for continuing to live incognito (in a kind of fairyland) can we attempt to write a new and original conclusion to the narrative of our lives.

2

The Parent-Child Relationship and the Art of Mythmaking

"To look at me now, you'd hardly believe I was really a happy and satisfied sort of person—would you?" And indeed, Mr Turvey looked so melancholy and distressed that it seemed quite impossible he could ever have been cheerful and contented.

"But why? Why?" demanded Michael, staring up at him.

Mr Turvey shook his head sadly.

"Ah!" he said solemnly. "I should have been a girl." . . .

"You see," Mr Turvey explained, "my mother wanted a girl and it turned out, when I arrived, that I was a boy. So I went wrong right from the beginning—from the day I was born you might say."

—P. L. Travers, *Mary Poppins Comes Back*

The most important task for a child is to "crack his mother's love code."

—Jules Henry, *Pathways to Madness*

Frequently, children are conceived and then fashioned as vehicles through which to express the conscious and unconscious needs of their parents. This is one, perhaps unfortunate, consequence of our uniquely human capacity for symbolic thinking. Even though we are limited by reality, we, unlike animals, are able to imagine that which is not real and through fantasy transform our subjective experience to suit our purposes. We "displace" our love and our anger onto objects that are safe for us to love or hate, we create idols so that we can share in their glory by first worshipping and then identifying with them, and we purge ourselves of our basest feelings and impulses by projecting them onto others, whom we distance ourselves from and self-righteously condemn. Because parents are only human (though young children are not aware that this is so), they are as likely as anyone else to give in to the temptation to distort reality, and so it is not uncommon for them to see their children as they would have them be, which is not necessarily as they really are.

So, for example, a parent who has always shouldered his responsibilities without indulging in a single word of complaint may vicariously rebel against his stoicism by producing an extraordinarily sensitive or impractical child. This Poet/Dreamer satisfies his parent's desire to escape the drudgery of the life he has boxed himself into. And as long as the mythical child acts out his parent's wishes, "sways to the music" that has been carefully orchestrated for his performance, nobody has to know whose feelings are whose (the parent's and the child's all blend together), and nobody will be able to distinguish the "dancer from the dance."

By superimposing a mythological identity onto a child, a parent may feel, moreover, that there is a special and indestructible bond between them. After all, the imaginary child is a kindred spirit and, unlike a real human being, he is entirely his parent's very own creation. A piece of art has no mind of its own, and a statue cannot run off and abandon its creator, at least not without his consent. For these reasons, inventing mythical children is one method by which a parent can stave off feelings of anxiety and despair, deny his separateness and even his mortality.

In most family mythmaking, each child represents a different aspect of a parent's personality. One may embody what her mother fears or despises and hence is eager to disown, while another embodies this same mother's idealized self—the person she would like to be. Or, as in the case of Julia, a patient of mine, the same child may serve both functions, and live a life that alternatively expresses and repudiates her parent's forbidden desires.

BEAUTY (AND THE BEAST)

The Beast had vanished; instead, a handsome prince was kneeling at her feet thanking her for breaking the spell on him. Though the prince was worthy of all her attention, she could not help asking him what had become of the Beast.

"You see him here at your feet!" replied the prince. "A wicked fairy condemned me to stay in the shape of a Beast until a beautiful girl would agree to marry me. . . . Thus you were the only person in the world good enough to let your heart be touched by my good nature, and though I offer you my crown I can never repay all I owe you."

—Madame de Beaumont, "Beauty and the Beast"

On first impression, Julia appears to be the embodiment of innocence and self-sacrifice, of selfless devotion and Christian humility. The mental image I retain of Julia, one that has stayed with me over the years even though it has proved unfaithful to the person I have come to know, is the image of a very sweet, very pretty, and very earnest young woman. Julia's only obvious fault, if it could be construed as such, is that she seems to love too much and to demand too little. Her natural, unadorned beauty and her ingenuous but all the same intelligent expression is entrancing, and, were I to allow my critical faculties to be lulled to sleep by her gentle singsong voice, I could have almost believed that Julia was a fairy-tale character who had slipped off the page of a book. She resembled the archetypal "Youngest Daughter," who is always the most virtuous and the most deserving of her sisters, a figure many of us wish we could be.

Actually, the character of Beauty in the story of "Beauty and the Beast" corresponds most closely to the image Julia projects and the life she attempts to lead—Beauty, who offers up her life to save her father and ends up rescuing a prince (and herself) with her transforming love.

Julia's aspirations to be pure and unselfish, a Ministering Angel whom anyone and everyone must love, are surely not unique to her but epitomize the feminine ideal that many women in this culture adhere to and many other women uneasily resist. The women's movement of the 1960s, and the current movement to be "codependent" no more, testify to the extent to which the fairy-tale Beauty figure (sometimes labeled "masochistic," more recently described as an "enabler") has infiltrated women's fantasies and seduced them into unholy alliances with the most beastlike of men.

As is common in some families and to most myths, Julia's brother is described as her opposite—an impulsive and reckless troublemaker, a Wild-Eyed Motorcyclist who, killed in a motorcycle accident, met with a fitting if tragic end. We shall see how Julia's story, and all the characters that play their variegated roles in her ongoing life drama, has resonance beyond her particular family. Her relationships with her Beautiful mother, her Crazy Destructive brother, her Wishy-Washy stepfather, and her natural father, who is dead but who lives as a Romantic War Hero in her imagination, form the basis for her image of herself. However, the drama she enacts as a substitute for living reflects universal conflicts about the soul and the body, aggression and love, reality and appearance, and the nature of male-female relationships; that is why Julia's myth is a myth for us all.

Although first impressions are inevitably partial, they are also quite revealing, if only because they tell us what qualities a person wishes to present for the purpose of public consumption. And since Julia looked like a peculiar combination of Pollyanna (long hair, knee socks, denim skirts) and your typical 1940s movie-star image of the nurse "on the front lines," I gather that this is the mythological identity she was intent on living. Softspoken and tentative when addressing me, quick to agree with any suggestion or interpretation that I offered, she seemed as open as a child, as trusting as one who is too innocent to know not to trust, and as pleasing as a little china doll whose only purpose in life is to sit demurely on a shelf and look pretty. Of course Julia turned out to be someone altogether different, but it was no accident that my fantasies of who she was took this form. She painted the picture for me and made every effort to hide her real, more complicated self behind this simple mask.

Gradually, over the course of treatment (which she sought *only* on account of her alcoholic boyfriend, Peter's problems with intimacy), the early-childhood antecedents of her mythological identity came to light. Julia's innocence and virtuousness, all that made her a kind of Beauty figure, was inextricably linked with her brother's "bestiality" and her mother's ambivalent relationship to her own and her daughter's complex emotions. In her everyday life, Julia's mother, Katherine, shied away from intense feelings of any kind, and lived "as if" they were foreign to her. And yet Katherine was clearly fixated on the memory of her long-defunct passion for Julia's dead father and passed this contradictory attitude toward life and love on to her daughter.

Katherine was a war widow; a fact sure enough, but one that was used to promulgate an image that then assumed mythic overtones. She had met Julia's father in her hometown in England when he had shipped overseas as an American soldier during World War II. When he died shortly before the war was over, he left her with a three-year-old daughter, and nine months pregnant. Whereas some women suffer similar losses and move on, Katherine's tragic circumstance became her identity, an identity that allowed her to indulge in her fantasies of love and devotion without the distracting influence of reality. (Of course, her preference for a fantasy lover over one made of flesh and blood may have already been firmly established before she became a widow; if so, circumstance only served as a convenient hook to latch on to; but this we can never know.)

Bereft and uncertain as to how to cope with the unanticipated changes in her life, Katherine created a world in which Julia served as her consolation, her Ministering Angel, her chance to regain her own lost innocence and to soothe her own psychic wounds. Julia's younger brother, Brendan, served as a counterpoint, representing the other side of her experience: he was the embodiment of his mother's regrets, the child conceived on the impulse, the one who more closely resembled his daredevil father, who had abandoned the family in death; Brendan was the one she loved fervently and spoke of with passion, but also the one she would have been better off not having. This is the story line as Julia remembers it, a compilation of fragments and innuendos over the years.

Although Julia's mother remarried a couple of years after losing her first husband and left her home in England to join her new husband's family in Florida, life with the living never really resumed; true love and happiness had supposedly been buried years back, along with the children's father.

Julia's mother idolized her first husband and spoke nostalgically, if bitterly, of his valor and her loss. In private, she would confide to Julia about her loyalty to her first husband, to the Romantic Hero he had become through the magic of memory. Katherine's love for her dead husband was kept alive by her storytelling, and in the process he himself was transformed into a mythic hero. This made her a heroine and allowed her to feel special when she did not really feel special at all. But, having once lived with a dashing officer in military uniform, she would not deign to love an ordinarily successful man who ran his family's bakery business. Her own self-esteem was at issue. Moreover, her dead husband's remoteness made him all the more alluring, and with him gone there was nothing to stop her from inventing the most fantastical stories. Julia's tame and all-too-present stepfather was a comfort, a security blanket, but he just couldn't compete.

Indeed, in contrast to her father, Julia's stepfather was described by her as kindly but colorless. As she recalls it, he may as well not have been in the picture at all. Although in reality the family would not have been able to stay afloat without Martin's practical know-how and unfailing good nature, the consensus was that he was peripheral and essentially uninteresting, that he was lucky to have joined this illustrious family, not the other way around. Again, this is the family myth Julia lived and breathed.

In Julia's experience, marriage and family life generally was a study in muffled disappointment and pretense. Nobody touched, nobody argued, and there were no strong emotions expressed whatsoever—except, of course, for her bothersome brother, but he too managed to commit his "crimes" far from the sacred domicile. All was serene, superficially cheerful, and carefully manicured, and nobody dared to openly question that version of the truth.

It is in this setting that Julia constructed her personal philosophy of life and love with an identity to match. According to her philosophy, appearances are all-important and yet, at the same time, are never to be taken at face value. They are valued for what they hide, and should not be mistaken for what is *really* essential. *That* lies beneath the prettily polished surface, which, for safety's sake, must be preserved at all costs.

But if "beauty" is only an illusion that camouflages a cruder but more compelling reality (as it was in her mother's "lovely" home), then perhaps the converse is also true: what appears bestial and crude on the surface is actually the seat of *real* beauty. If her Good and Responsible stepfather is emotionally vacuous and of little value (as her mother implied) and her Bad and Impulsive brother is troublingly intense, seductively mysterious, and the focus of attention (just like her dead father), then what are Julia's options? Wouldn't a respectable identity have to encompass both elements—the Good and the Bad, the domesticated and the wild? And then who *really* was her mother's favorite? The Good Child or the Bad? And where did her allegiance *really* lie? With the husband who was absent or the one who was present? Because no clear answer was given and messages were always mixed, Julia learned to double as Beauty *and* the Beast—in her imagination, she needs both in order to survive.

A therapist learns about a patient's experience of herself not only by listening carefully to her descriptions of life outside the office but also by observing how she conducts herself within the context of the therapeutic relationship. Although Julia and her boyfriend, Peter, came to therapy as a couple, (he sulkily, she naively hopeful) and presumably each of them had an equal part in their relationship problems, Julia regularly deferred to Peter whenever he voiced an opinion, and insisted, without having to say scarcely a word, that his and not her problems be the primary object of our interest and concern. As they both agreed that he needed help, not she, that his psyche was cloaked in mystery but hers was crystal clear, I got a glimpse of how Julia transforms herself into a Ministering Angel, committed to saving everyone's soul, unearthing everyone's hidden talents but her own.

Initially, it was very frustrating working with Julia in therapy, because she had difficulty identifying anything in her own experience that even approximated conflict. Acknowledging turmoil would have been inconsistent with her identity as a self-effacing Beauty figure. Indeed, as if she had no substance of her own and no personal history to speak of, Julia offered nothing about her life apart from Peter, who, at the time, was absorbing all of her psychic energy. Although without Peter's collusion Julia would have never been able to be so Selflessly Devoted (he seemed perfectly content to be the sole object of analysis), Julia demanded, without appearing to demand anything, that Peter take up all the space in the office and leave her with very little room to expand.

But then, as might have been expected, Remote and Mysterious Peter precipitously withdrew from couples counseling after only three sessions, leaving Devoted Julia still earnestly denying that she had any internal conflicts of her own, and Julia's sweet, diffident smile began to show signs of strain. Our sessions were filled with long periods of awkward silence, which were relieved only by clichéd formulations that Julia offered as substitutes for genuine emotion or insight. This is because Julia was committed to giving me only an image to work with, not a real person. Without anything to grab hold of, the therapy began to flounder, and I began to wonder whether Julia was actually a patient or was merely going through the motions.

Unlike a fairy godmother, I was incapable of transforming Peter—or Julia, for that matter—into what Julia wanted, and as a consequence I had proved myself to be a grave disappointment to her. Of course, it would have been completely out of character for Julia to have told me this directly (anger is not part of the myth), but her polite shrugs, her soulful expressions, her wide-eyed reticence said it all. They were her revenge for my failure to give her what she wanted. They also served as a masterful resistance to delving any deeper into her psyche. Indeed, at this stage Julia was trying her utmost to find a safe way to disappear from sight. Peter had absconded and was no longer there to hide behind, and Julia's mythologically sweet identity as Beauty was in imminent danger of turning rancid from overexposure. I was the last person she could trust to help her reconstitute it!

With a sincerity that was nearly persuasive (I do not doubt that Julia persuaded herself), Julia repeated monotonously that her family was really very "normal," whatever that meant, and that her childhood was entirely free of complications and happier than most. But as Julia's family portrait came into sharper focus, I realized that there were big empty white spaces where emotions, positive or negative, are ordinarily found. Indeed, what was *missing* in her stories was as critical to understanding her experience of herself as what was included.

It turned out that Julia's most vivid memory of her mother was of her mother's quietly horrified reaction to any open display of emotion. Apparently, Katherine was repelled by Julia's adolescent moodiness and winced whenever she saw her daughter sad (or too exuberant), let alone when she was red-eyed and blotchy-cheeked from crying. Instead of softening in response to Julia's normal upsets, Katherine hardened herself and froze off all channels of communication, leading Julia to conclude that there was something fundamentally repulsive about her. Where was Beauty now?

Gradually, Julia complied with her mother's implicit demand to hide her less pretty feelings, and, more significantly, internalized her mother's attitude toward them. Not only was she careful not to let her mother see when she was upset about anything, but she also began to feel ashamed of herself and to suspect that she was perverse, even crazy. Whenever she felt angry or happy, jealous or triumphant, Julia would quietly retreat into her room and act as if there were nothing at all on her mind. Resolved to keep a pleasantly blank expression permanently plastered on her face, she was able to fool nearly everyone, but she couldn't quite fool herself.

In complete solitude, Julia would enter what retrospectively she describes as an enormous "black hole." There in that other space, she would silently yell out her guts, convulsing on the bed as if possessed by the devil. Julia sheepishly let me know that she still did this sometimes, hastily adding that she really didn't want to find out what it was all about, because "I know it's insane."

In Julia's family, in order to feel secure, a person had to be Good (just like her mother), but this also meant being untrue to oneself and invisible to others. Consequently, Juila was perennially faced with the dilemma of whether to uncover the "ugly" truth about herself, whatever it happened to be, or to seal over her feelings with yet another pretty if disingenuous smile. Since Julia's mother worked so hard at pretending that she, Julia, was like the fairy-tale figure Beauty, Julia could only conclude that there was good reason for dissembling. If she were to stop pretending to be what her mother wanted her to be, she would, in all likelihood, be condemned to being some awful creature instead; maybe even one who was obliged to self-destruct, as her Tempestuous brother had done, and then to live on only in memory.

Ironically, as she matched her mother's idealized image and assumed the identity of a Ministering Angel, Julia began to resemble her kind and self-sacrificing stepfather, whom everyone depended upon to "hold up the fort," but whose virtuousness went largely unappreciated, earning him more contempt than respect. Some crucial element was missing!

I believe that it was probably at this juncture, during Julia's adolescence, that a complementary mythological identity of Julia the Untamed Nymphomaniac was conceived. From that time on, she was simultaneously her mother's Beauty and the Beast rolled into one.

Once Julia's mythological innocence was turned inside out, her mythological perversity sought material expression—the idea searches to substantiate itself. So, during her young adulthood, Julia was not only a Ministering Angel to various fallen young men but also a sexually promiscuous young woman who spent time working as a topless go-go dancer, inspired by her own sexual prowess, her high-risk behavior, and her risqué life-style, of which her family suspected nothing.

Ironically, as the nymphomaniac/go-go dancer, Julia expressed opposite sides of the same mythological identity, never really rejecting the mythological system of her family. She used her body and abandoned her soul to please *and* manipulate an audience, and in the process she imagined herself to be a "lost soul" who was only disguised as a whore (like the handsome prince in the fairy tale who is only disguised as a beast). By obeying her mother's implicit message that she should stifle her feelings so as not to interfere with other people's fantasy images of her, Julia became a Ministering Angel who, having sacrificed herself in the service of others, desperately needed to be rescued and ministered to. Julia as the go-go dancer is like Beauty's mythological Beast: she must find someone who will see beneath the surface, love her, and in the process restore her to her rightful form.

Both Julia and her brother played an essential part in their family drama, because, just as in the fairy tale, there could be no Beauty if there wasn't also a Beast, and their prematurely widowed mother wanted terribly to feel Beautiful. As a mother of mythological figures, Katherine could condemn her despised child without knowing that there were really aspects of herself and her dead husband that she feared and hated, and she could identify with her idealized one without having to admit that she and her children's father had fallen far short of her ideal.

Although in families (unlike in the theater) only the actor who plays the part of the favored child is audibly applauded for being what his family needs him to be, the less favored child plays just as important a part in the mythology, as he soaks up his parents' anxieties or self-loathing by embodying the Forbidden. His reward for doing a good job is less obvious. Without having to say a word, he is promised that he will never be abandoned. As long as he matches his parents' image of him, he will always have a part reserved for him in the drama, and in this he finds some consolation. Within the world of the imagination, Brendan the Beast and Juila the go-go dancer/Sex Queen will never have to confront their essential aloneness, any more than Julia's mother did when she played at being Beauty. This is the illusion of power that a mythological identity offers each one of us, albeit at great cost.

PANDORA, THE TROUBLEMAKER

> If life is just a play or an image on a screen, its pain as well as its pleasure is unreal. . . . Walking about, a prima donna on the stage, the pain is forgotten in the stimulation of the performance and the noise of the applause—or the imagined applause.
>
> —Jules Henry, *Pathways to Madness*

Sometimes when I listen to Laurel's misadventures, I am reminded of the Greek myth of Pandora, who is the epitome of the Irrepressible Troublemaker. Pandora is too curious, too impulse-ridden for her own good (or so goes the myth), and because she does not heed her husband's warnings she foolishly opens the box in which all the evil of the world was hitherto safely contained, letting out all the misery that plagues mankind along with "delusive hope." Like Eve (our Judeo-Christian counterpart), Pandora is the mirror image of that other mythological character Beauty, whose virginal purity requires that someone play the whore. We shall see how Laurel's position within her family prompted her to gravitate toward this spoiled identity of the Guilty Rebel; however, stories in the Bible and in literature make us aware that Laurel's images of herself are grounded in tradition. They correspond to images of Woman that men and women have held for millennia. Laurel has her own personal reasons for latching on to this mythological identity and in the process abandoning herself, but she is one of many; this image expresses universal conflicts, fears, and desires. Just as in the case of Julia, Laurel's mythological identity as a Free Spirit/Messmaker has meaning for us all.

Not unlike Julia's mother, Laurel's mother needed her children to bolster her shaky self-esteem and deflect her attention away from her disappointment with herself. Laurel, her eldest daughter, was selected to do the job, one way or another. After serving faithfully for years as her mother's favorite mirror image, her invisible confidante and adoring disciple, Laurel betrayed her mother's trust and reflected back to her an image that was distinctly unflattering. Thus her expulsion from the Garden of Eden.

It seems that, after years of colluding with her mother by pretending to be her shadow, a captive audience to her mother's dramatic accounts of her adulterous love affair and unfulfilled potential, Laurel began to feel as if she really had no substance of her own and, panicking, set out to prove otherwise. At first this simply meant speaking her mind. "Mom, why don't you stop complaining all the time about men and go back to school, or just do something with your life?" But after being dragged to a therapist at age twelve for her "fresh mouth" and selfish attitude, Laurel began to compete with her mother on her mother's own terms. She, Laurel, was to outdo her mother and become the tragic heroine, par excellence, whose life was chaotic, and whose passion was unrequited even if it meant being the most miserable and guilt-ridden character in the entire family.

And this was how Laurel the Flattering Mirror was almost instantly transformed into the family Troublemaker, the clumsy and disfigured "stepchild" who, understandably, was barely tolerated by her "charming" mother, her "erudite" father, her "artistic" sister, and her "responsible" and "successful" younger brother. Recall how furious Snow White's stepmother was when *her* beloved mirror did not tell her what she wanted to hear. Perhaps the moral of her story is that we should all beware of trampling on a parent's dream!

Laurel's identity as Troublemaker/Black Sheep is what is manifest; it is what Laurel hopes to eradicate by coming for psychotherapy. We shall see, however, that within Laurel's imagination contradictory self-images continue to coexist: the image of herself as her mother's "favorite" co-conspirator, and the image of herself as the family's disreputable "outcast." Each represents one moment in her variegated relationship with her mother, though *neither* one affords her the freedom to become a person in her own right.

Laurel is an attractive, exceptionally articulate woman of thirty-four, who, despite her hangdog expression and self-deprecating remarks, has a dry sense of humor that is both captivating and thoughtful. When I first met her, her life and her emotions were in a tumult. She had been recently fired from her latest job as a managing editor of a scientific publication and was in the throes of an on-and-off relationship with a married man. But as I was to find out later, this state of affairs was nothing new. The panic, the anger, the air of defeatism that I witnessed in my office constituted just one scene in a lifelong drama, a corner piece in an elaborately reticulated design for living. Laurel, the Troublemaker, was by definition *always* steeped in trouble of one form or another. Her circumstances and her emotions were natural extensions of her self-image.

Given that she was unemployed, unmarried, and purportedly without any close ties to friends or family, Laurel's claim to hopelessness was difficult to argue with. Her savings were steadily dwindling down to nothing, her lover was interminably vacillating as to whether or not to leave his wife and two kids, and tensions were mounting between them with no possibility of a happy end in sight. But what was most significant was that periodically Laurel would throw more fuel on the fire consuming her life, and seemed intent on convincing anyone who cared to listen that she could do nothing except make a royal mess of her life.

Triumphantly she informed me during one of our early sessions that she had missed the deadline for filing for unemployment insurance and, just as her financial situation was becoming desperate, she was no longer eligible to collect the money she needed to help tide her over. With a guilty gleam in her eye she confessed, moreover, that she was spending most of her free time smoking marijuana (something she hadn't indulged in since her college years) and reading trashy science-fiction novels, though her job search was at a standstill with her résumé buried beneath the pile of unopened mail and unpaid bills that crowded her small apartment. Having presented what she believed was an open-and-shut case against her character, Laurel waited expectantly to see whether I would join in her attack on herself.

Although, from one perspective, Laurel had a lot going for her—a sharp intellect, a pretty face, an impressive résumé, and an inexpensive apartment in a lively urban neighborhood—to hear her talk one would think that Trouble and Unhappiness ran through her veins and that a black cloud followed her everywhere, signaling danger and threatening destruction. Sensing my skepticism about her unhappy "fate," Laurel once demanded angrily whether I too wouldn't feel doomed if I were in her shoes.

According to Laurel, despite her superficially attractive qualities, she manages *somehow* to foul things up and become alienated from nearly everyone. Out of one side of her mouth Laurel pleads innocent of any crime and insists that she is mystified by her unhappy life, but out of the other side she is anxious to characterize herself as *the* universal Misfit, the obnoxious loudmouth who deserves scorn, pity, but also admiration. Both arguments are fundamentally flawed, based on distorted images of herself as either an empty vessel (her mother's Flattering Mirror, who merely reflects back other people's self-serving fantasies) or a perennial Instigator, the courageous Free Spirit who is the source of all the trouble in the world. The constant shift in position from being the one who is loved and depended upon to being the one who is rejected and abandoned echoes her experience in her family, an experience that has generated a self-fulfilling prophecy but which allows her to feel magically connected and specially endowed.

Laurel has waffled back and forth between these two opposing identities since her revolt during adolescence. Having for years been expert at anticipating her mother's needs for comfort and support (her marriage was a grave disappointment, she had no career to speak of, and *her* married lover wouldn't make a commitment after ten years), Laurel made an about-face and became an exemplary social disaster, who consistently put her foot in her mouth and "innocently" antagonized family, friends, and colleagues. Every boss has squirmed under her "honest" criticism, and every "unavailable" lover has been made to suffer for his callousness and neglect.

But Laurel's identification with the image of a selfish and willful Troublemaker is as much an expression of her mother's fantasies as her submissive adulation. As a Pandora figure, Laurel overtly defies her mother's wishes, and salvages a modicum of self-esteem, thinking that at last she is speaking "the truth" and being *real*, yet she does not sever the invisible cord that binds them together as one unit. Because she is caught within the myth, Laurel's rebelliousness is steeped in guilt and her inflammatory behavior leads to her own self-destruction. Laurel the Free Spirit is inextricably linked to Laurel the Failure, the spoiled promise, the bittersweet end to an unfulfilled life. As these mythological figures, Laurel lives out her mother's unconscious despair, so that when her mother looks at herself in the mirror she does not need to recognize that the despair is her own.

Consider next a father who identifies strongly with one child but insists that the other is the "spitting image" of his wife. His responses to both can hardly be objective. There is too much at stake, in terms of his own identity, for him to see either of his children clearly. Moreover, this is a perfect channel through which he can express feelings about himself and his wife (and possibly his mother and women in general) that may otherwise be inadmissible. And who could possibly accuse him of indiscretion? Nobody will decode the cryptic messages he sends, mostly to himself.

And so this father, who could be any parent, may seize the opportunity to do what is ordinarily impossible, to live two lives simultaneously. As he responds to the one child as he would to himself were he starting all over again (with love, with pity, or with anger), he feels more in control than he ever has before. He will look to this child for confirmation of his own identity, so that he can proclaim once and for all who *he* is, where *his* value lies, and why *his* life has taken the form that it has. Again, in the extreme case, the child as a child no longer exists except as a means by which his parent can prove his point or elaborate upon his own personal mythology. The child is there to win an argument in a case that is being tried in the realm of his parent's imagination.

Now, a father's myth may include an image of himself as the Youngest Son (a popular figure in fairy tales). Noble in spirit but heretofore unappreciated, he may be overindulgent toward his identified alter-ego, and deny his actual child's shortcomings, and demand special privileges for him. He may urge his child to amass the trophies that he himself never claimed, and be anxious that his child become a hero at any cost. If this closest child, this object of identification, fails to achieve glory (as his father failed in his time), this too is grist for the mill. Depending upon the father, his child's perceived failure may serve as a peculiar kind of consolation ("I told you that it's only the s——t that rises to the top in this world"), or it may figure as one more reason to feel that life has treated *him* unfairly; his bitterness is thus justified. Perhaps there is a further claim to martyrdom, another front upon which to wage his battle against his fate.

Indeed, if a parent's personal mythology includes the image of himself as the Loser or the Failed Promise, he may actually *need* to see this selfsame image reflected back at him from his closest child. If he is hypercritical, if he magnifies his child's faults and minimizes his accomplishments, then, miracle of miracles, he will have the child he wanted and fulfill his dream. The person he'll see before him will be the one he needs to see, the one whose destiny mirrors his own, the perfect target upon which to deflect his own self-hatred or self-pity.

On the other hand, a parent may see one of her children as her complete opposite, the embodiment of everything that is alien to her. She is introverted, unathletic, and bookish, but finds, to her astonishment, that her daughter is a virtual "social butterfly," a jock, and only a B- student. Maybe the child reminds her of one of her own brothers or sisters, or of one of her parents, the one she never felt she had much in common with or the one she longed to be. Memories are stirred up and connections are made.

Under any circumstances, the differences and similarities that presumably exist between a parent and child are bound to elicit feelings, be they curiosity and admiration, or envy and competitiveness, and then, depending on the parent's hidden agenda, these differences may be exaggerated or denied. But whether it is a child's difference or his similarity that reminds his parent that there are old scores to be settled and closet dramas to be resuscitated is ultimately not what is most significant. Whatever the trigger happens to be, once we have entered the realm of the symbolic, the child's actual qualities are distorted under the aegis of "poetic license," and the mythmaking begins.

DIANA, ONE FAMILY'S GODDESS

The anti-narcissist looks into the pond and sees a resplendent reflection that is indeed endowed with a wealth of talent. But he sees in this reflection a figure so beyond his true inner state. . . . He does not feel his inner nature, but sees that if he lives out this talent he will indeed be constantly fed with praise and admiration; or to be more accurate, that "it"—the reflection—will be the object of such idolatry. . . . The anti-narcissist casts a stone in the pond to shatter the image.

—Christopher Bollas, *Forces of Destiny*

When, at birth, a child is given a name, it is his very first identifying feature, and Diana's name is prophetic, as perhaps many are, though not usually in such obvious terms. In the process of naming a child, we sometimes send out messages that tell of our secret hopes and expectations. She may be named after a relative, a historical or literary figure, or even a human quality. I know one child who was named Orion after one of the constellations in the sky! His parents apparently have very high aspirations for him.

Though it is not difficult to derive meaning from names like Hope, Faith, Joy, or Charity, and in some families children are named Abraham or Ruth, Jesus or Mary because of the obvious religious associations, most of the time the language that we use to convey our message is cryptic and may never be decoded, particularly since names go in and out of fashion and have different connotations in different sociohistorical contexts. Nevertheless, despite the insurmountable problems of interpretation, I am of the opinion that, when there is a message being sent and the child is the unwitting vehicle of that message, there is bound to be some translation into real life, and that this is the self-fulfilling prophecy at its most primitive level.

It was Diana and her life story that first prompted me to think about mythological identities, and specifically about the plight of the idealized child. (Psychoanalyst Alice Miller in *Prisoners of Childhood* and psychiatrist Hilde Bruch in *The Golden Cage* discuss the ramifications of such idealization, which both authors argue implicitly places on the child a demand to be perfect.) As a young girl about six years old, Diana was told that she was named after the chaste but beautiful Greek goddess of the hunt, the one she saw a statue of on a family visit to the museum, the one her father liked to read to her about from vividly illustrated story books.

Through her name, Diana was sent the implicit message that she was to become her *family's* goddess, her father's alter-ego, a mythological female figure too self-contained, too perfect ever to let herself fall passionately in love. Since Diana's character and way of life came to bear an uncanny resemblance to that of her mythological namesake, we can only assume that her family's subliminal message was received, digested, and then acted out.

We shall see that, although Diana initially basked in the glory of her father's adulation as she fulfilled his dream of giving life to a being who stood head and shoulders above the common man, in the long run she suffered for having carried the weight of her parents' inferiority complex on her back. All idealized children suffer, because not only do they feel responsible for the parents' well-being but also they feel guilty for their own unhappiness, having been led to believe that they have been given everything. Diana's ambivalent relationship with her father will illustrate how confining it is for a child to be glued to a pedestal, turned into a museum piece so that her parent can vicariously relive his life—this time in heroic terms. By examining her life, we shall see how, paradoxically, being loved *too* much is psychically equivalent to not being *really* loved at all.

Diana's father, George, had told her of her namesake as soon as he thought that she was old enough for him to read her the magical stories he loved so much. They were stories of passion and courage, heroism and trickery that transported *him* to a far more thrilling universe than the one he actually inhabited. He needed a companion there. An exceedingly unheroic kind of figure himself—thin, nervous, envious, and openly self-deprecating, in his words a "failure" and a "weakling" who, with a law degree from an Ivy League university, was painfully overqualified for his civil-service job—George was entranced by the myths of the Greek gods and goddesses, heroes and heroines. Feeling diminished by his own life, George found consolation in hearing tell of the exploits of those who were "bigger than life," the Strong, the Courageous, and the Beautiful. Real flesh-and-blood heroes and heroines—great men and women of the past or present—were only painful reminders of his own failures, but George could admire the gods and goddesses unstintingly, free from crippling jealousy or envy.

Whereas George's own mythological identity crystallized around the image of Buried Potentiality, Diana his first born was to embody his grandiose dreams of Resurrection and Ascension. The first to proclaim himself an *incurable* physical and emotional "wreck," George delighted in imagining that *his* very own daughter—his flesh and blood, as he frequently called her—was a physical "dynamo" and an intellectual "marvel," desired by all, possessed by none. Diana guesses that George felt himself exalted by her presumed radiance; she knows that she felt stripped naked by his piercing look, which seemed to be saying to her, "You are mine." If she let herself feel, it made her skin crawl.

As peculiar as it sounds, Diana believes that her father considered her name a sign of destiny, but in case the Fates needed some help in accomplishing what was prophesied, George was at hand to carry out the decree. Frequently he would compliment her for her strength, her beauty, or her brilliance, and talk to her as if she were an adult when she was only eight or nine years old. He spoke about religion, politics, literature, and the follies of ordinary people, confiding in her his disappointments with women and his contempt for most men. Implicit in his confidences was the assumption that the two of them shared a mutual and exclusive understanding, and though she and she alone was worthy of his admiration, he was not worthy of hers. Only George's mother was Diana's equal, (she also assumed mythological stature), and part of the family lore was that Diana looked exactly like her grandmother, who was of course a "raving beauty" and from all accounts a terrible social snob.

During their intimate conversations, George would interject warnings about the sexual obsessions of men and the petty jealousies of women. And at night, hidden in the shadows of his daughter's darkened bedroom, George would sing Diana to sleep and confess to her his own craven impulses. Diana remembers him telling her that he could barely contain his desires to rape women he encountered on the street or in his office, and she recalls how, even as a child of ten, she felt obliged to purge him of his feelings of guilt and applaud him for his self-control. "Good Daddy, for not giving in to temptation," was what he needed her to say, and she complied.

George's personal confessions only prodded Diana forward in the direction she was already headed, underscoring the importance of holding herself aloof from mankind in general and from the male sex in particular. Ironically, George's untempered love for her only reinforced in her an attitude of suspicion and contempt toward the world at large. The myth of Diana the Goddess complemented the myth of George the Snake in the Grass; she was fated to sneer as he was fated to grovel at her feet.

So, as the virginal Greek goddess separates herself from the intrigues that dominate the lives of other women, even other goddesses, Diana also learned to insulate herself from unruly passion, becoming a kind of statue—admired for her grace and strength but out of reach and forever frozen in space and time.

Before I go on with Diana's life story, I must note that it is no accident that I have not as yet mentioned Diana's mother; her role in her daughter's life, and in the family drama as it is described, is a supporting one. Whereas Diana's father dreamed in vivid color of glory and conquest, her mother, Luba (which means "love" in Russian), emptied herself of intense emotion and preferred to live colorlessly, inconspicuous almost to the point of invisibility. Deferring to her husband, who, feeling minuscule, always spoke with a tone of conviction, Luba failed to provide Diana with a positive alternative identity; her vacant expression and passive submissiveness were at least as threatening to her daughter as the father's invasive adulation. So, by default, George was given license to whisk Diana away to a castle in the skies (Mount Olympus perhaps) and after a day of adventures and debacles father and daughter would return to earth, where her mother and later her younger sister were busily doing what ordinary mortals do. Each night, over the dinner table, Diana and her father noisily recounted their various exploits to their awestruck audience.

Diana's stories mostly confirmed the prophecy that she was destined to live an extraordinary life. She excelled in grade school, was reasonably popular (for a know-it-all), and was all around the object of admiration—particularly, but not exclusively, her family's. Her classmates' parents would point to Diana when they wished to offer their own children an example of maturity and achievement, and if this attention made her diffident mother avert her eyes with embarrassment, it only made her father glow with pride. Diana says that she wasn't certain what to feel: she felt both special and guilty because of it.

It is told that Diana's sixth-grade teacher predicted that Diana, one of her favorite students, would become the first woman president of the United States; after all, she was not only brilliant but also unusually self-confident and articulate for a girl her age. This prediction became a permanent story in the family repertoire, and Diana would hear it in front of friends and relatives over and over again.

At the top of her class throughout primary school, high school, and college, Diana skipped three grades—one at the advice of elementary-school teachers who were impressed by her precocity, the other two at her own promptings. And so, like her father, who was also an "early bloomer," Diana graduated from yet another Ivy League college at the young age of nineteen. Wasn't her life proof, then, that the family myth was no myth at all? George was amazed at his progeny but gloating, Luba didn't know what to make of it all (by some miracle she had conceived a genius!), but Diana was quite miserable (also like her father). She was trapped in a "charmed life" that insidiously cut off the possibility of her loving or being loved.

Like the mythological figure Narcissus, Diana could not fully participate in real life, with real people. She felt different in some intangible way, and could not bridge the psychological gulf that she felt separated her from her peers. Only her reflected image was perfect enough for her to love, and only an image could be so devoted to her as to follow her every movement, as her "loving" father had so slavishly done.

The men who sought her out always seemed to lack something. They proved to be clumsy or boring, homely or inarticulate, or else simply ordinary, nothing exceptional, and in the end that was the most damning. These men invariably diminished her, their idiosyncratic personality tics were irritating, and their limitations cast a shadow over her face.

And so, like Narcissus, pursued by everyone, Diana was "destined" to suffer from feelings of isolation and loneliness. Because she was addicted, as it were, to an image that could never satisfy her yearning to be real, Diana's romantic affairs always ended in bitter disillusionment after a brief period of mutual infatuation. (In the myth of Narcissus, it is significant that the nymph who falls in love with Narcissus is Echo, one who has no voice of her own.)

Though George expected Diana to be forever grateful to him for having transformed her into a goddess, and counted upon her to transform him into a god by association, his idolization backfired. Inadvertently, George had created a kind of Frankenstein monster who ultimately turned on him, a goddess who, like her namesake, would have contempt for men and keep them at a distance—and that would include her father. George's contempt for humanity had rubbed off on his daughter, who grew to believe in her mythological identity and fulfilled her father's prophecy by becoming a lesbian and a political revolutionary. Then she disappeared from sight altogether (no forwarding address) to become a legend in her own right—a character whom I can write about, but not a person I can know.

A parent may actively condemn or heartily applaud his offspring for being what he himself never was, depending on whether he feels primarily envy or admiration for the "not-me" aspects of his personality that have resurfaced in the form of his child. (In *The Interpersonal Theory of Psychiatry*, psychiatrist and psychoanalyst Harry Stack Sullivan described how the small child gradually discovers those aspects of the self that are unacceptable within the framework of his interpersonal relationships. He learns to dissociate himself from these forbidden qualities, so that they begin to occupy a category within his psyche designated "not-me.") But whether a parent criticizes or praises his child for being a particular kind of person, what is ultimately *more* significant is his unchallenged determination that this is in fact the kind of person the child is and must be. Such is the power of the self-fulfilling prophecy: loved or hated, the child of a mythmaker learns to live as a myth and in the process puts himself on hold and his life on automatic pilot. Diana's self-imposed exile—her radical rejection of society and her emotional withdrawal from her family and friends—is but her version of her father's myth of his child the Chaste Greek Goddess of the Hunt.

THE JELLYFISH VERSUS THE SNOW QUEEN: A BULIMIC'S MYTHIC BATTLE

Jack Sprat could eat no fat,
His wife could eat no lean;
So 'twixt them both
They cleared the cloth,
And licked the platter clean.

—*Mother Goose*

When a parent's fantasies are superimposed on a child, the child is caught in that never-never-land in which fantasy and reality overlap, and a kernel of truth serves as an excuse for an elaborate lie. Under these circumstances, the only choice a child has if she is to preserve some semblance of self-esteem is to reshape her parents' fantasy to suit herself; to enter the mythic battlefield and fight magic with more magic. Experience has shown that reason does not have the power to debunk a myth. (It is futile to argue with family dogma.) Only a fairy godmother or a Prince Charming or a secret potion can break an evil spell once it has been cast.

Sherry is a good example of someone in the midst of a battle of opposing images which correspond to caricatured portraits of her parents. It is a battle *she*, a person in her own right, can ultimately never win. Bulimia is the magic weapon Sherry uses as she attempts to transform the unflattering image of herself that was reflected back to her from the eyes of her parents. When, late at night, Sherry gorges on leftover pasta (which she refused to touch at dinnertime) and then subsequently forces herself to vomit up all she eats, she affirms her childhood mythological identity, only to deny it afterward. She is *not* going to allow anyone to see her as softhearted and weak-willed, though this is the image she sees in the mirror and mistakes for a true reflection of herself. Behind closed doors, she will live the myth of Sherry the contemptible Jellyfish and fulfill her parents' prophecy, thinking all the while that she is expressing her "real," despicable self. But in public she will emulate her mother's sangfroid, and live instead the myth of Sherry the imperious Snow Queen. In either case, however, whether she is binging or purging or starving herself so that she resembles a skeleton and not a shapeless blob, Sherry is trapped within the frame of her early-childhood experience, and the terms her family used to define one another remain her terms.

Sherry describes her mother as cold and unexpressive, a woman whose self-esteem hinges on her abhorrence of the sentimental and the sensual. She is proud of her ascetic relationship to life, and through it she stakes a claim to superiority. Sherry's father, the complete opposite of his wife, is continually subjected to humiliation for his open displays of affection and insatiable appetites (he is always in heat and always hungry). In this family's mythology, only the weak express their feelings, and the impenetrable Snow Queen is justifiably repulsed by those around her.

As Sherry's mother contemptuously rebuffs her husband's sexual advances in full view of all the children, Sherry's father shamefacedly confides in her, his older daughter, his frustration at being married to a beautiful woman with a heart made of stone. This is the backdrop for Sherry's own personal mythology, her unending struggle to find both self-respect and love through restricting and indulging her appetite for food.

During her adolescence, Sherry's mother kept a safe distance from Sherry, refusing to acknowledge her daughter's untidy emotions and developing sexuality just as she refused to acknowledge her husband's feelings or her own. Uncomfortable with Sherry, she was explicit about her dreams for her daughter. She fantasized that Sherry would become a competitive swimmer, maybe even qualify for the Olympics, which was something she had always wanted to do herself and never had. Unabashedly, her desires for her eldest daughter were indistinguishable from her desires for herself, and, unconsciously repudiating all signs of "weakness" in her own person, she consciously shamed Sherry into similar forms of self-denial.

Children are naturally eager to ally themselves with their parents, even if, from the point of view of the self, it is against their own best interests. So Sherry colluded with her mother and internalized her mother's dreams, ideals, and prohibitions. Despite her widening hips, her full breasts, and her perversely insatiable appetite for junk food, she affected an air of little-girl innocence and aspired to become a Bodiless Spirit, if not an Olympic swimmer. By the age of fourteen, Sherry had a ruthless campaign of self-starvation well under way as she attempted to deny what to her were undeniably repulsive aspects of herself that prevented her from reaching her ideal. It was as if her body were the source of her defiled identity, and if she could only ignore its urgings, put mind over matter, then she (or at least her mythological self) would emerge victorious. But no matter how thin she became, she was unable to undo her image of herself as weak, spineless, and ever hungry for more.

When Sherry's mother discovered one day that her far-from-perfect but nevertheless dutiful daughter would sneak away from her daily swim practice to take solitary refuge in the neighboring park, guiltily eating bags of potato chips until it was safe to go home, she recoiled in horror. From that time on, Sherry despaired of ever being able to win her mother's approval on her own terms. And as her belief in her mythic identity as a repulsive Jellyfish became ever more entrenched, her commitment to undo it became her obsession.

But if Sherry's mother grew ever more distant from her as she became a young woman, her father increasingly sought her out for exchanges of intimacy. As he cried on her shoulder and hinted broadly of his unsatisfactory sexual relations with her "frigid" mother, he assured Sherry that he loved *her* more than anyone, and promised her, his favorite child, the world. (Jewelry, clothes, her own car were hers without even asking.) As I said earlier, mother and father were opposites, the one withholding, the other oozingly sentimental and intrusive, and Sherry had no choice but to oscillate between these two extremes. Since she was unable to please her exacting mother and unable to avoid being her father's favorite, the choice as to which parent she would lean toward was made for her. And then again, Sherry could not help feeling a special affinity to her father, as he did to her; at least he seemed to be made of flesh and blood! However much Sherry would have liked to be made of ice, she knew she wasn't, even if her very own mother appeared to be.

But Sherry paid a high price for being "Daddy's girl." Her mother's revulsion toward her overly emotional (as she put it "slobbering") husband spilled over onto Sherry, and Sherry began to experience herself as her mother experienced her father: she was too soft, too needy, too emotional, and far too obtrusive. She was a Jellyfish, and she nauseated herself. This distorted self-image was to be the basis for a life-threatening eating disorder.

After years of self-starvation and compulsive exercising, Sherry arrived at a compromise with herself (and her internalized parents). This is the origin of the binge-purge cycle that consumed her life. During the day, she would emulate her mother, and devote herself to the elimination of all desire. She ate nothing and thought obsessively about being thin. Sherry believed that, if she could exercise enough control, even more control than her emotionally constricted mother must have exercised, she could never be accused of being just like her father—a repulsive and weak-willed little pig. She too could look down her nose at ordinary folks bound by flesh-and-blood realities. She could live the myth of the Pure Spirit/Snow Queen.

But at night, her mother's projected image of her reigned supreme; after all, that was who she believed she *really* was. Sherry would gorge herself and prove the myth she had struggled all day to disprove. By careful subterfuge—induced vomiting, daily exercise, restricted eating—Sherry managed to live as her mother's despised self and yet appear quite different. Who would ever guess that this slim, fashionable, and pleasantly sardonic young woman, who regularly arrived at her office a half-hour early each morning just to get a head start, experienced herself as a needy, dependent, and contemptible mush. Her parents were certainly instrumental in shaping her debased and false image of herself, but she was an excellent pupil and learned very well how to use the art of deception for her own purposes. She created her own private drama and fought lies with lies.

THE WILD ANIMAL AND HER TAMER

Every "fight over nothing" is a fight against nothingness, a fight against becoming nothing, which may sometimes be a fight because one is nothing.

—Jules Henry, *Pathways to Madness*

Maia dresses as if she were a cross between an East Village bohemian and a high-class call girl—hair stylishly tangled, jeans torn in all the right places, and psychedelic-colored tank tops. She is only sixteen, but she is already a master in the art of provocation. Maia disappears for hours at a time without informing her agoraphobic mother where she is; she goes off the innumerable diets her skinny mother is forever putting her on; and though she scores well above average on all the standardized tests, she plays hooky from school and manages to fail English and math, frustrating her teachers, who plead with her to try to live up to her "potential."

When Maia informs me that she is contemplating having sex with the local drug dealer, she is well aware of the shock value in her statement. It seems as if Maia can't resist any opportunity that comes her way to be Bad. If she weren't caught and reprimanded for being just that, how could she continue to believe in her mythological identity as a Wild Undomesticated Animal? And without that identity, what would happen to the Animal Tamer who remains loyally at her side through thick and thin? Maia is Irresponsible, Incorrigible, and Boldly Outrageous as a complement to her mother's Responsibility, Compliance, and generalized Fear of the Unknown.

The relationship between Maia and her mother shows yet again how a child's identity can be seen as an expression of some aspect of a parent's personality that needs to be camouflaged. When a parent ascribes characteristics to a child that are really aspects of his or her own personality, and then proceeds to respond to the child as if he were actually the projected image of the parent, psychoanalysts refer to the defensive maneuver as "projective identification." The interpersonal drama that ensues is an external analogue of an intrapsychic conflict originating in the parent, and though there are now two players—parent and child—the boundaries separating the one from the other are intentionally fuzzy, so that it is as if there were only one. Maia was brought for therapy by her adoptive mother when, one evening, feeling lonely, floundering, and angry at herself and everybody else because she was feeling this way, she made superficial cuts on her wrist. Several months earlier, Maia had become depressed and irritable after breaking up with her steady boyfriend in order to "play the field"; she had felt confined (Wild Animals do not belong in cages) and wanted her "freedom." But, according to all accounts—Maia's as well as her mother's—Maia had *always* been a difficult and tempestuous child, continually flirting with danger and courting disaster. Affectionate and kittenish one moment, Maia can shut down and take flight the next, systematically inducing terror and rage in everyone who cares about her.

Almost immediately during our first session together, Maia's mother offered me her definitive explanation for her daughter's behavior, defending her own now routinized responses to her: "She was *always* doing crazy things, and I could *never* safely let her out of my sight, even for an instant." In order to prove her point, Maia's mother described the first in a long series of crises that, according to her, culminated in Maia's recent suicide attempt. One day when Maia was only two and her mother was in the other room cleaning up, her mother returned to find that Maia had "disappeared into midair." "Of course I panicked," she related breathlessly, not pausing in her narrative a moment to see whether I would agree that this had been the only thing to do. But, the story goes, when she was just about ready to call the police, Maia's mother caught sight of "the little rascal" out on the fire escape, having a picnic, seemingly oblivious to her mother's cries of distress! "I was terrified, and beat her in fury, but she really couldn't have cared less. She thought it was amusing." That is the way Maia's mother perceives her daughter, who has always run out on her, gotten herself into life-threatening situations, and left her a nervous wreck and a martyr. Surely she cannot be blamed for Maia's demonic personality, or for her frantic pursuit of her daughter down every blind alleyway.

Whether or not the incident Maia's mother describes is true in all its detail is less significant than the fact that it has become the emblematic story of Maia's character. It is used to explain the mother's anxiety, her overprotectiveness, and her dire predictions for the future. (Because Maia *cannot* stop running, her mother *cannot* stop chasing, and then how can she possibly have any peace of mind, any life of her own?)

Needy, but fundamentally suspicious of others and uncomfortable with her dependency, Maia reluctantly agrees that her mother is the only person capable of penetrating the wall with which she surrounds herself. Indeed, her mother has devoted her life to doing just that. That invisible wall is a necessary prop if their two-person show is to continue to run, and in order to keep the action going, and to prevent each character from drifting off the stage, it must go up and come down again with every new scene. As Maia withdraws behind it, she mumbles a tantalizing "You can't catch me" out of the corner of her mouth, and then the chase is on. Her mother responds to her provocations by battering down the fortress—which exists in order to be battered—and she wages a brutal but successful attack.

When Maia's mother has forced her way in, she proceeds simultaneously to envelop and disparage her daughter. And it becomes clear after a while that the verbal abuse she heaps on this most "ungrateful child" has a very important function: it clears the path to a peculiar kind of intimacy that both mother and daughter mistake for love. They are inseparable in their mutual antagonism. Bad, self-destructive Maia, and her Good, well-meaning mother are inseparable, and as long as they live in a mythological universe they need not confront their separateness.

Maia is not only her mother's alter-ego but also her nemesis, her reason for not being able to return to work or "find herself" now that her children are past the age when they need her to remain at home. So the myth goes, and so history is made. Without the myth of Maia, what terrors would her mother have to face? And as daughters are wont to do, Maia has learned well from her mother; she has created her own mythology to avoid facing her own demons. According to Maia, her mother is *her* nemesis, the obstacle in *her* path to individuation. In a way, they are both right, but they conspire to maintain the status quo and to "convert an internal plight" into an external one.

But if Maia is her mother's cross to bear (a punishment for the untold acts of rebellion she wished to commit herself but never did), she is also the vehicle through which her mother expresses the forbidden. Maia's mother is afraid of using the subways and rarely ventures outside of her immediate neighborhood, while Maia knows no boundaries at all and defiantly throws caution to the wind; her mother appears to be verging on anorexia, while Maia eats compulsively and brazenly breaks all the dietary rules; her mother is Sensitive and her life revolves around the needs of her family, while Maia is Cold and Inconsiderate. They are mirror images of each other, and together they make up a total person.

A DAVID IN SEARCH OF A GOLIATH

To defy Power, which seems omnipotent . . .

—Percy Bysshe Shelley, *Prometheus Unbound*

Howard, who was forty-eight years old when I first met him, is a physically powerful man, well over six feet tall and weighing about two hundred pounds. Yet, having been audience to his dramatizations of his ongoing struggle with the Powers That Be, I gather that Howard still sees himself as a quavering runt of a boy with learning problems, the favorite target of the school bullies. Having characterized himself as a "nebbishy" kind of child, a kid who didn't have the gumption to stick up for himself, Howard lives so that he might now prove himself to be the opposite—an Underdog Soon-to-Be-Hero. His marginality and lonely isolation are to be reinterpreted as signs of his secret superiority, like that of the Lone Ranger or Zorro, the figures he admired most as a boy.

Although Howard served as his family's scapegoat, and thus became the embodiment of frustrated idealism, envy, and compensatory self-aggrandizement, his experience of himself as an innocent victim who is determined to turn the tables on his oppressors and make the world a better place, is something most of us can identify with. At one time or another, all children are confronted with their own powerlessness in relation to authority; consequently, the fantasy of the Underdog Soon-to-Be-Hero has universal appeal. The prototype is the biblical story of David and Goliath, and though on the surface Howard bears no resemblance to that idealistic shepherd boy who by his daring and refreshingly childlike self-confidence easily wins our hearts and our allegiance, internally his experience of himself is not that different; his myth is David's myth without the happy ending.

Howard was identified as a Problem Child, a source of misery, a cursed specimen of masculinity, from the day he was born. Paradoxically, the images his parents projected onto their eldest son include that of a pathetic sap as well as spiteful alley cat; either way, Howard was, to use his father's term, their "little bastard."

According to the story his mother, Caroline, tells, Howard was so big at birth that he literally ripped her apart, permanently damaging her. Thus, according to family lore, it was he who was responsible, albeit indirectly, for the decline in his parents' sex life. Significantly, Howard appears, at this point in his career as a Rebel and an Outsider, to be quite eager to assume the burden of guilt for his parents' diminished sexual relations, and for the divorce that followed a few years afterward. Surely it is one further sign of his tremendous subversive power that he got between the sheets of his parents' bed and successfully disrupted their lovemaking! According to Freud, this may even be every young boy's unconscious fantasy!

And never mind his father's alcoholism and physical abusiveness to Howard, his younger brother, and their beautiful "aristocratic" mother. Never mind his father's unwillingness to apply himself to ordinary work after his brilliant career in the navy reached a crescendo and then came to a sudden halt. Howard alone was to blame for all his own problems, in school, at home, with his younger brother. The fault lay within him; he had a perversely troublesome character, or so he came to believe.

Nevertheless, when his parents finally did divorce, Howard felt that it was up to him, as the elder son, to compensate his mother for her loss, to make amends for his father and take his place by her side. Then maybe he could be reborn as the legitimate elder son. Predictably, he failed; it was predestined. He could not have been his parents' son and succeeded in rescuing his mother from her chronic state of unhappiness. That would have been a betrayal of the myth—his success would have upset the apple cart! Nevertheless, though it was all carefully choreographed beforehand, Howard's failure was seen as further proof of his inadequacy, and evidence of his similarity to his despised father—that unheroic figure who only dreamed of heroism but never lived heroically for any extended period of time. Indeed, years later, during one of our sessions, Howard told me that he felt like the mythical King Arthur's illegitimate son whom everyone wanted to forget about. "I've been deprived of my birthright; I feel like I should have been the prince of Wales, and instead I have been treated like I don't belong anywhere."

One of Howard's earliest memories, one that foreshadows his life as he has lived it, is of when, as a little boy of five or six, he was walking down the street with his mother on a trip to the big city. He recalls staring up at the towering office buildings all lit up amid the evening darkness. Standing outside in the cold wintry air, he was fascinated by the silhouettes of people moving mysteriously behind the glittering windows. As he gazed in awe at the fabulous world stretched out before him, he had a vague and overwhelming feeling of being left out. He remembers distinctly asking his mother how there could be any room for him in those office buildings when he grew up, since they already seemed to be filled to capacity. Even then, before there was a logical basis to do so, Howard doubted that he could ever be included in that wonderful and elusive adult world that was so close yet so far beyond his grasp. This is his memory, no doubt distorted retrospectively, as memories tend to be, to create a sense of consistency in what was to become a lifelong identity as an Outsider.

By the time Howard was ten, he had reached the conclusion that his mother's constant criticisms of him, his schoolwork, even the way he made his bed in the morning or mowed the lawn, were justified, and that she was right to wish for something more than what he could give her. He was a skunk and he knew it better than anyone else, and he continually invented new ways of proving it. He lied ineffectively, he squealed on his younger brother and his fellow classmates, and he wallowed in the punishments that the authorities meted out—egging them on with his unrepentant grin until someone finally lost patience and exploded with frustration: "That little bastard thinks he can get away with murder." Actually, Howard didn't want his "crimes" to go unnoticed, for then how could he sustain his identity as the fearless Rebel?

Howard's identity as a kind of scruffy alley cat who lives by rifling through other people's garbage was not limited to his home—identities of this kind generally spill over. Because he had difficulty concentrating on his schoolwork, Howard was considered by his teachers, whom he characterized as uniformly unsympathetic and narrow-minded, as either lazy or stupid. The memory, be it true or false, is what will be significant, and the image Howard carries with him into adulthood is of himself as a disappointment and a misfit. Sometimes he felt like an abused child whom nobody understood, and sometimes like a defective child whom everybody understood too well!

Of course, there might have been more possibilities for Howard, had he been able to establish a positive image of himself in relation to his peers. But this too was not to be. As he describes it, his family were never integrated into the suburban community in which they lived, and relations between his parents and the neighbors were characterized by mutual feelings of contempt tinged with envy.

His classmates' families were second-generation immigrants who had recently moved to the suburbs of Long Island, and, in his recollection, they were all True Believers in the American Dream. They liked to live extravagantly, drive fancy cars, and frequent fashionable country clubs. Smugly, Howard informs me that conspicuous consumption was the new religion in those days, and since his family were conspicuously *not* consumers, they were viewed with suspicion. Howard, being a loyal member of his tribe (despite his reputation as the family Ne'er-Do-Well), took it upon himself *not* to fit in with his peer group, and at this he was a smashing success.

Howard's mother prided herself on her ability to live abstemiously, and to remain aloof from the mainstream of American life. Her fantasies were no less modest than those of her neighbors, however, but of a different genre—old European nobility. Her dreams were bitter dreams of unfulfilled majesty, not of American-style affluence. They foreshadow Howard's similarly lofty fantasies of martyred heroism.

Whereas the neighbors believed in the "work ethic," Howard's father chose, after the war, to drink and collect his navy pension instead. Having had claim to heroism, he found little appeal in pursuing another career, which was bound to be less glorious. Apparently, Howard inherited his penchant for the Heroic from both parents: each aspired to glorious marginality and "on principle" refused to blend in.

Paradoxically, as Howard echoed his parents' feelings of alienation and contempt for "middle-class society," he cut off any possibility of achieving "success" but edged his way closer to his family. Accordingly, Howard learned to transfer his feelings of outrage at being assigned the role of family Bastard onto the outside world, and his longing to depose (and expose) his powerful parents became a mission to poke fun at and deflate the Powers That Be "out there," whoever they were. Like David in the story of David and Goliath, he would surprise everyone and someday reign victorious.

And so Howard stood out, perhaps even more than he had to. He was the poor, scruffy kid on the block who walked around with a chip on his shoulder, the one whose clothes looked secondhand and who in junior high school had to earn his allowance by running a paper route. A formidable social critic by thirteen, Howard had a verbal facility that made him a master of ridicule, and nothing was safe from the sting of his venomous tongue. He made it a point to look down his nose at his classmates' ski vacations, their piano lessons, and the senior prom, and by the time he graduated from high school, he was universally disliked. But this was just the beginning. The die had been cast, and Howard's image of himself as the perennial Underdog/Martyr Soon-to-Be Hero now took on a life of its own. It served a purpose, and Howard became its primary promoter.

Over the next thirty-odd years, Howard's mythological identity evolved from that of a Nebbish to Spiteful Alley Cat to being an unsung Hero turned Martyr, but one element is invariant: he remains an Outsider and an Underdog plotting his vindication. In its most glorified form, it demands that Howard only tackle giants who are too powerful for any ordinary human being to topple. And as an adult, Howard set out to do just this.

Uniformly, Howard's bosses are destined to be cruelly knocked off their pedestals after a brief honeymoon period, and for what most people would consider minor imperfections of performance or character. His various wives and in-laws suffer similar fates. A mild criticism, an expedient decision—really anything—has been sufficient reason for Howard to begin one of his campaigns, a "holy crusade" that invariably ends with his expulsion and the destruction of the relationship. What could be brief skirmishes with the police or minor altercations with a supervisor or neighbor—his own or his girlfriend's—turn into long-drawn-out melodramas that either end in a stalemate or cost Howard time, money, and position. It was not entirely in jest that the director of the clinic where I saw Howard for psychotherapy advised me to avoid any major confrontations, lest we become the next target of his litigious fervor!

Even in his dreams, Howard insists on challenging the authorities and exposing their blemishes, no matter if it means hurting himself in the process. In one dream, he saw himself driving down a highway, intentionally going out of his way so that he would land his car in an enormous pothole; gleefully he anticipated the suit he would bring against the highway authority. In fantasy and in life, Howard makes a point of not coasting along or appreciating the simple pleasures of the road. Rather, he scans the horizon for flaws and is ready to sacrifice himself for the pleasure of their denunciation.

Howard had provided his feuding parents with an easy scapegoat upon whom to dump their misery, and this is the origin of his mythological identity. But over the years, he transformed the myth of the Little Bastard into the myth of the Underdog Soon-to-Be-Hero, and as David (of David and Goliath), Howard would turn the tables on his parents, at least in fantasy. Having emerged from his childhood with an overarching suspiciousness of *all* authority, Howard arranges his life so that he is continually wrestling with power, poking fun at it, but remaining pure in his perpetual powerlessness. Howard's life mission is to expose the ineptitude and moral failings of "those in charge"—not to become king himself. Like his parents, he is committed to marginality. Were this David to defeat all the Goliaths out there once and for all, he would jeopardize his very identity and be in danger of becoming the next Goliath. Howard prefers that time stand still and that he be forever David preparing his sling and stones, burning with anticipation of Goliath's humiliation. Cut the film here and begin again.

A "SENSITIVE PLANT"

The feeblest and yet the favorite . . .

—Percy Bysshe Shelley, "A Sensitive Plant"

Now it was plain that this must be a real Princess, since she had been able to feel the three little peas through the twenty mattresses and twenty feather-beds. None but a real Princess could have had such a delicate sense of feeling.

—Hans Christian Andersen, "The Real Princess"

Larry's identity as the hypersensitive Mama's Boy, a Sensitive Plant or Hothouse Flower, who by nature *requires* more than the normal amount of love and attention, complements his mother's identity as a veritable Mother Teresa (his name for her, not mine). He demands too much, and she demands nothing; he cannot tolerate the imperfections of this cruel world, and she willingly immerses herself in other people's misery, rescuing her less fortunate neighbors while brusquely dismissing the injustices in her own backyard. One fragile, the other hearty, they are in many ways opposites, but opposites like Maia and her mother, each serving to balance out the other.

The Sensitive Plant is a metaphor borrowed from the poem by Percy Bysshe Shelley. In Shelley's poem, the figure of the sensitive plant feels so deeply and loves so intensely that it cannot endure the vagaries of real life. Paradise is where it rightfully belongs. Other plants are buffeted by the cruel and arbitrary forces of nature but are themselves a part of nature and survive. Straining against Nature, the Sensitive Plant threatens to become extinct.

Most of us have encountered characters such as Larry, who are frustratingly helpless but also compellingly "otherworldly." Sometimes we wish that such a person would just toughen up and not require so much special treatment; at other times, however, we may admire his idealism and wonder whether we ourselves are not too callous; we may even dream of protecting him from the harsh realities of life. Our ambivalence about the Sensitive Plant's vulnerabilities, his refinement, his emotionality, and his insatiability, mirrors his own. As we question whether we want to create a hothouse environment designed expressly for his purposes, he questions the virtuousness of being a mythic character who is beautiful in spirit but who is not a flesh-and-blood person, and therefore cannot survive.

Far from being a Sensitive Plant, Larry's mother raised eleven children of her own, served as her neighborhood soup kitchen, and suffered silently for years, a martyr to her husband's romantic excesses. Whereas Larry screamed and banged his head against the wall, pleading for his mother's exclusive attention, she stoically watched her husband flaunt his affairs with other women right before her eyes. When Larry's father had the audacity to move several of his mistresses onto the family estate, his mother swallowed hard, said her prayers, and proceeded to turn a blind eye! After all, what could she, the mother of eleven, do? Pack up her brood and go where? Her dignity rested upon her proud indifference. Her husband was the Cad, the Don Juan (but, then, she knew that all men were infantile), and she was the Angel; she, not he, would be rewarded in the next world, if not in this one. A pleasing fairy tale, but one that required some other character as an additional anchor point; Larry, her youngest son, was selected to express the feelings that she never would admit were hers. After all, he was her baby—and, what's more, of the weaker sex.

She wasn't clinging or jealous; *she* would never depend on anyone for anything, and *she*, like her husband, was practical, always finding a new "project" in which to invest her energy. But Larry, her little man, was destined to be all the things she was not. He was insatiable, his heart was easily broken, and his head was forever in the clouds, a Romantic, dreaming of the unattainable. What's more, he was so dependent, following her around like a lost puppy dog. Larry would buckle under the weight of reality so that she would not; his frailty was her necessary fiction, because it made her feel strong as she alternately scolded and comforted him when he threatened to crumble.

Larry would regale me with stories of his mother's generosity, pointing out repeatedly how, despite having had a multitude of children of her own, she welcomed into her home still more. She adopted three of Larry's less fortunate cousins when Larry was still in grade school, took in neighborhood strays for evening meals, and even cared for the goats and horses herself, until she was too feeble to get out of bed.

But although Larry was anxious to praise his mother's virtues and characterize her as a veritable Angel of Mercy, I got the sense from his stories that her boundless love was a major source of frustration for him, and that what he had gotten from her personally was so diluted that he was forever hungry for more. Couldn't this be the origin of his presumed "insatiability"? His overdemandingness? His dependent character? Isn't this an alternative explanation for why, according to the family lore, Larry, the perennial baby/Delicate Flower, nursed at his mother's breast until he was six years old! Why else, in the midst of such plenty, was he starving?

We may ask why it was "necessary" for Larry's mother to create the myth of Larry as a Sensitive Plant, and argue that it would have made more sense for her to have invented a superhero for a son, a chivalrous knight who could possibly have rescued her from her unhappy marriage. It seems, however, that her own identity as a Ministering Angel was already too deeply entrenched, and that Larry's role in her mythology was to reinforce this mythic image of herself, not to revise it. As Larry gave expression to all the longings that she forbade herself, she stood by and gently taunted him for his unreasonable feelings. She could have been talking to herself, but this way she retained her dignity. As a Mama's Boy, Larry lost his.

Larry will argue, when and if he is confronted, that he cannot temper his extreme responses to what most people would consider ordinary stress. Seemingly defenseless, he flinches in response to a minor flaw in a musical recording, and painfully ruminates about the plight of the homeless man who approaches him each morning on his way to work. Even though this paralyzes him and makes it impossible for him to enjoy life, Larry maintains that he cannot control himself. "I am my own worst enemy" is a refrain I have heard from him time and again, as well as "I'm programmed."

And, precisely because Larry is resigned to being the victim of his own "constitutional" sensitivity, his claim of helplessness is very convincing. Just as the princess in the Hans Christian Andersen fairy tale cannot help having her sleep disrupted by the pea that she feels through the innumerable comforters and mattresses, Larry, identified with an image of himself as a fragile and hypersensitive Mama's Boy, cannot help feeling distress over his own and the world's imperfections.

As one listens to Larry's stories, it is difficult not to get drawn into commiserating with him, and his perceptions are often remarkably insightful and empathetic. Why, I ask myself during one of our sessions, do I turn my head and move on with my life, automatically screening out all the misery and injustices that bombard me as I walk down the streets of New York City? And am I able to take pleasure in even a flawed musical performance because I am "well balanced" or because I have learned to anesthetize myself? How many peas would I need under my mattress, and how large would they have to be, before I protested and cried "Enough"? These are not easy questions to answer, but because a Sensitive Plant like Larry is in his own way beautiful as well as pathetically impractical, he forces me and other "less sensitive" creatures to reconsider our lives and question the virtues of being so hardy. Larry also vacillates on these questions, uncertain as to what is really the better way to live, and whether he would really prefer to be more robust.

As the Sensitive Plant, Larry is, in his own fashion, in revolt (send the food back—it is not properly cooked) and proud of it, proud to be so sensitive (idealistic), and proud that he does not fit into the mold and toe the line (he's an individualist, not a sheep). And when he says contritely that he is just not "cut out" to (1) make practical plans for the future or (2) be in the military or (3) promote his career as an artist or (4) wait on line for the ballet or (5) make barbecue with the neighbors or (6) live in one home with one woman, his apologies are not to be taken entirely at face value—they do not tell the whole story. The success of his peers is tainted by limitations and compromise. His mother suffered on account of her "strength" (she never voiced a cry of protest), and as her alter-ego he prefers to suffer on account of his fragility.

Larry's career as a Sensitive Plant runs parallel to his career as a Ladies' Man. This is not surprising, since his father seemed to have cultivated an image of himself as a Don Juan of mythic proportions. Like Sherry, the bulimic young woman mentioned earlier, Larry assumed aspects of both parents' projections by becoming a heartbreaker as well as a perennially brokenhearted man. Experiencing himself as that charming but insatiable Mama's Boy—the image that bounced back at him whenever he looked in his mother's direction—Larry applied his talents to transforming that false image into one with more sex appeal. His father's machismo served as a good disguise behind which to hide his shame.

Over the course of a lifetime, Larry amassed numerous relationships with women, and naturally none could satisfy his mythical enormous sexual appetite. But as Larry confirmed his mother's image of him as her spoiled and love-famished little boy, forever in search of a perfect mama, he also managed to match his father's projection: he was a "real man," who could never be loyal to just one woman. He had turned the myth of the Sensitive Plant on its head and became the kind of son that his father could be proud of. He wore the latest fashions, drove expensive cars, and comported himself as if he were a man without a care in the world—*in*sensitively. Of course, this was until he hit a stumbling block and fell on his face, splattering irreparably the handsome image of Don Juan that he had laboriously created.

When I first met Larry, he was fifty-four years old, unemployed, and single, though he had been married four times and had four children, the youngest only five years old. He was living with a woman whom he had met while still married the last time, and she was considerably younger and less educated than he. As he described it, she cooked him sumptuous meals and hovered over him constantly; though it seemed, by his account, that she treated him like a silly little boy who couldn't possibly take care of himself, she was also his greatest admirer. His sophisticated tastes, his artistic inclinations, and his genuine concern for those less fortunate than he were what attracted her to him, and in comparison with Larry most men appeared boorish to her. Slightly built, underweight, but nevertheless rather dashing and sexy, Larry was not at all difficult to imagine as having been a veritable Don Juan at one time.

But the debonair façade had had significant cracks in it since Larry had developed an unusual seizure disorder a year earlier, which interfered significantly with his concentration and ultimately resulted in the loss of his job as a commercial artist. By the time I made his acquaintance, all that remained of Larry's former identity as a Ladies' Man were remnants—a captivating smile, a facility with language, a puppy-dog expression that demanded wordlessly that he be petted and given a good home.

Without a steady job or the prospect of being able to find one, let alone keep it, he experienced mounting financial pressures, compounded by feelings of helplessness, shame, and even guilt. Humiliated by his impairment, Larry had, over the previous year, cut himself off from his usual circle of friends in an effort to hide his mysterious and debilitating symptoms, hoping against hope to avoid the ridicule and pity he "knew" he deserved were the "truth" to be uncovered. For, you see, Larry's real losses (which undeniably were considerable) were magnified tenfold by the symbolic losses associated with them. Now that he was partially disabled and his future was at best uncertain, his "cover" was blown and the myth of the forlorn and helpless Sensitive Plant that Larry had believed in all along but had struggled most of his adult life to deny reasserted its hold on his imagination with a vengeance, claiming victory over his "destiny."

Larry experienced his "flash-outs" (which is how he described his seizures) as a kind of reckoning with himself. To him, they exposed his true, flawed identity, which, as a Ladies' Man, he and he alone "knew" himself really to be—for years craftily disguised as a Charmer, he was convinced that he really was a Mama's Boy.

Indeed, as if he were his own prosecuting attorney, Larry carefully built a case against himself in an effort to persuade me that he was really the mythological figure his family had invented and that he had formed an uneasy alliance with. In a display of self-denigration that I have rarely seen the likes of, Larry laid before me numerous papers (now yellowed with time) documenting his medical discharge from the air force after just six weeks in training. Unable to adjust to military life—the hierarchical relationships and harsh discipline offended him, and he "collapsed" rather than comply—he was diagnosed by the air-force psychiatrist as having a "passive-dependent" personality and retreated home to Mama with his tail between his legs. As his other "mama," I alone was privy to his chronic experience of inevitable defeat.

Yet, as Larry urged me to read carefully the other doctor's damning analysis of his character, he seemed to be freeing himself from a life of subterfuge, and now, as a broken fifty-four-year-old man, he could finally face the "truth." There it was, in black and white, on official United States Air Force stationery. "See, this is who I am," he seemed to be saying to me.

Larry's various romances, his four marriages and divorces, were brought forth as further evidence of his dependency, insatiability, and ultimate inability to function "normally." His attachments to women were intense (he felt as if he couldn't survive without them) but also self-extinguishing, for he found himself easily frustrated and disappointed. Never satisfied with only one woman in his life for very long (just like his "infantile" and "selfish" father), Larry was always looking out of the corner of his eye to see whether someone else would offer him something more. Perhaps then he might be able to construct a self-respecting identity to replace the one he had been handed.

As long as Larry could be attractive to women and could earn a comfortable living doing work that he enjoyed, his living out the myth of the Sensitive Plant was not all that distressing to him or anyone else. In fact, it gave him a sense of uniqueness, and set him apart from the faceless crowd. He surrounded himself with people who appreciated his special qualities, which were many, and moved on when life's frustrations were more than he believed he was able to endure. Eccentric maybe, "high-strung" certainly, he had an "artistic temperament" and was eminently lovable; nobody had to know that he was "programmed" to disintegrate under stress or to die brokenhearted, as he thinks he deserves for wanting too much.

If Larry had not developed the seizure disorder that ultimately led to the loss of his work, his status, his debonair "cover," I doubt that he would have found his way to a psychologist's office or rediscovered the personal mythology he used as his blueprint as he steered his life according to plan. Ironically, Larry had actually to lose his bearings and be forced into a semidependent position in order to realize that unconsciously he had been living his life "as if" this were his fate all along.

THE SIMPLETON OR BLOCKHEAD

"My name is Dorothy," said the girl, "and I am going to the Emerald City to ask the great Oz to send me back to Kansas."

"Where is the Emerald City," he enquired; "and who is Oz?"

"Why, you don't know?" she returned in surprise.

"No, indeed; I don't know anything. You see I am stuffed, so I have no brains at all," he answered sadly.

—L. Frank Baum, *The Wizard of Oz*

The Simpleton or the Fool is a character we encounter in literature and also in some families. He is presumed to be more incompetent and more ineffectual than we would ever dream of being, and because he is so limited we can patronize him, even insult him, confident that he will not take it to heart—"he doesn't understand," "he's easily manipulated," and, what's more, he needs our constant supervision and guidance. He is a child in an adult's body, and so unconsciously we can all identify with him; all of us remember, even if we cannot put it into words, what it feels like to be a child: clumsy, naive, and struck "dumb."

The Schlemiel in Isaac Bashevis Singer's Yiddish folktales, the Blockhead in the Grimms' story of the Golden Goose, and the Dumb Blonde in your typical TV situation comedy are some representative examples of this type of character. As we watch them trip over their feet, we are relieved that their foibles, not ours, have caught the spotlight and are the butt of humor.

The Straw Man in *The Wizard of Oz* is convinced that he is this sort of character—his head is stuffed with straw, and he claims to know nothing. But his tale illustrates the power of the self-fulfilling prophecy, and exposes the potentially *mythic* nature of the character of the Simpleton. The Scarecrow, like his companions the Lion and the Tin Man and even Dorothy herself, is a victim of his own misconceptions, his own debased self-image. As the story unfolds, we see that the Scarecrow can *actually* behave quite intelligently, just as the Cowardly Lion can *actually* behave courageously and the "heartless" Tin Man proves himself to be a loving friend. Dorothy too had the power to get herself back home to Kansas, though she thought she needed the magic of the Wizard of Oz to do it. Once she recognized that his power was illusory and hers was real, then she could accomplish what had only appeared to be impossible.

In real life, however, such revelations are less common, and when we are "born again" it is often in the same form. Simpletons generally continue to live as Simpletons until they die. The role is an important one in some families. In the following case study of an extremely disturbed young man, we will examine the peculiar "benefits" derived from one person in a family playing dumb.

Vincent was thirty-three years old when I saw him for psychotherapy. He was overweight and unkempt; his complexion was pasty and he slouched in his seat; his eyes were defiantly blank; he could have been a model for a study in expressionlessness. Perhaps, I wondered as I looked and tried not to stare, he was playing at being dead, or playing at being a mashed potato; there was no hint that he did not earnestly believe that he was what he appeared to be; he seemed to be his character.

When Vincent spoke, his voice was scarcely audible, and because he forced me to lean over in my seat in order to catch his words as they dribbled out of his mouth, I found myself fighting the urge to feed him the words I presumed he wanted to say. His passivity demanded action, and since Vincent convincingly imitated a lump of dough, dialogue seemed virtually impossible.

I was Vincent's therapist, but the treatment was family therapy, and my job was to see him and his family while he was a patient in the psychiatric hospital where I was working. After his discharge, I was to continue seeing Vincent's family for as long as they were willing to come for follow-up treatment. Unfortunately, in cases such as these, therapy often ends as soon as the patient's condition has "stabilized" and he can manage to walk out of the hospital door.

From the outset, my goals for Vincent and his family were quite modest. Since, upon his admission to the hospital, Vincent's thinking had been confused and his emotions and behavior had been raging out of control, I hoped that, with the help of antipsychotic medication, he would be able once again to speak coherently and become an active participant in his own therapy sessions. Perhaps then we could begin to formulate realistic plans for his immediate future.

Vincent had been doing essentially nothing before coming to the hospital (he was said to remain in his pajamas most days), and I hoped to get him involved in some structured activity outside his home by the time he left. All agreed, staff and family alike, that, given Vincent's history and symptoms, the prognosis was quite poor.

During most of our sessions, Vincent was silent and responded to my questions with a shrug of his shoulders or a faint smile, acknowledging something without identifying what that something was. He could easily have been mistaken for a Dummy, a Simpleton, a Blockhead, but his school records indicated he hadn't always been like this, and even now, on occasion, a wistfully forlorn expression would pass momentarily across his eyes, casting a shadow over his unnaturally white-and-pink face.

Vincent had never had a girlfriend but stated, with barely a glimmer of irony, that alcohol had always been his girlfriend. He used to drink heavily, so I could assume that he had been deeply in love. But three years before, Vincent had tried to kill himself—a disappointment in this form of love, no doubt—and since then he had stopped drinking altogether, which apparently had put an end to his romantic interests. He spent most of his time alone.

Vincent had never supported himself, and had always lived with his family, except for a couple of months when he was nineteen and shared a rented room with a neighborhood friend he had known during high school. At that time, he was still drinking heavily, and when angry words between him and his friend led to blows, Vincent quickly retreated home. Although Vincent officially occupied a separate apartment in his parents' two-family dwelling, his mother cleaned for him, shopped for his food, prepared and served him his meals, and each week collected his laundry. He might have been considered a pampered child if it were not for the fact that his *real* self had been neglected for years and that the substitutes he found for love smothered his potential and left him feeling more hungry than ever.

Vincent's mother maintained, however, that her grown son could not have managed these simple chores on his own. From his demeanor, it would have been difficult to argue with her: there was no visible evidence that he could have, and neither he nor his father waged a protest. But there was more to it than that, as we shall see.

Indeed, for the past several years, Vincent had occupied a very important position within his family. He was indispensable to the family equilibrium. For one thing, he had been sleeping upstairs, on his father's bed, which had been positioned in the hall outside his mother's bedroom, while his father had been relegated to his son's sleeping quarters, down in the basement. His parents told me that this peculiar sleeping arrangement had been devised out of consideration for Vincent, who complained that he felt frightened sleeping by himself downstairs. But I had to question whether anybody in the family *really* believed this, though they all said they did. It did make a coherent story, one that was good for public consumption, with each family member cast in his or her familiar role. There was the Self-Sacrificing and Concerned Mother, the Tight-Lipped and Remote Father, and the Childlike and Dependent Vincent.

Vincent spent his time sleeping, eating, listening to music, and watching television. During the day, he rarely emerged from his gloomy cave, let alone stepped outside the house—he felt sad when he went out, and so he chose not to. His father, I was told, was quite the opposite—the implication being that Vincent certainly did not learn to be slothful from him. However, with some sarcasm in his voice, his father informed me that he wished that *he* could loll around the house all day as his son religiously did. But no, Vincent's father was always on the go (no flabby stomach for him!), and though he had retired two years earlier from his job as a truck driver, he was almost never to be found at home. He left the house early in the morning for his local senior-citizen club, played golf and swam when the weather permitted; he made a point of not returning home until dinnertime.

Father and son existed at opposite ends of a continuum, affording Vincent's mother the opportunity to live with both kinds of men—the one, who asked nothing of her and was hardly ever around, and the other, who demanded everything and hardly ever ventured from her side. Now that her parents had died, she kept busy taking care of Vincent. *She* didn't have time to play golf—"not that Vincent's father would ever have taken me."

Though he was first hospitalized after his suicide attempt three years ago, medicated and diagnosed as psychotically depressed and/or residually schizophrenic, it was not until Vincent "the vegetable" exploded for a second time that his family was urged to join in their son's treatment, and Vincent was strongly encouraged to attend a day program after his discharge from the hospital. (Suddenly and inexplicably, Vincent had announced to the neighborhood that his family home was in imminent danger of burning down; and being a Simpleton, not a Poet, he was clearly unaware that he was speaking metaphorically.) Stabilizing Vincent on his medication so that he could return to what he had been doing before the "conflagration" seemed too limited a goal. I believed that, if somehow Vincent could be induced to leave the house each day and interact with people outside of his immediate family, maybe the person behind the impenetrable mask might finally come back to life. But, then, what was the function of the mask, and how did it fit into the family drama? Could his parents tolerate any deviations from the prescribed life of inaction? And if

Vincent did break out of the spell, what would he become—certainly not a prince, but would he be a monster?

From the outset of therapy, Vincent and his family agreed that they were all miserable, and there was certainly more than enough evidence to substantiate their claim. Nevertheless, Vincent, and particularly Vincent's parents, resisted any suggestions that their life together could be modified, resigned as they were to live out their unhappy "fate."

Vincent's mother lamented her role as caretaker of Vincent, and from time to time threatened to have a heart attack or to die prematurely from worry over her son. Yet she categorically dismissed the possibility that Vincent could be anything other than what he was. Therapy was to serve as a consolation, not as a vehicle for change. Vincent's father expressed sympathy to his wife, but offered nothing in the way of any positive suggestions, eyeing his watch anxiously, eager to be liberated from this unseemly exercise in futility.

Given the nature of the family mythology, the suggestion I made during one of our early sessions together—that Vincent be required to do his own laundry and prepare his own meals—was received as patently absurd. Vincent's mother looked at *me* with a scornful expression as if *I* were crazy, and certainly not the least bit helpful. According to family dogma, *I* was the one who was out of touch with reality. "Oh no, Vincent cannot do anything. . . . He is like a moron," Vincent's mother asserted without hesitating, and when Vincent's father did not argue with this startlingly insulting formulation, I proceeded to address myself to "the moron": "Is that so? Do you think what your mother is saying is true?" Vincent woke up from what appeared to be a semistuporous state and mumbled: "I can do my laundry; I used to do it when I lived alone a few years back." I feigned confusion. Vincent's mother threw me a superior glance, rolled her eyes, and, without having to say another word, silenced her characteristically silent son, who had dared to challenge her definition of the situation, her definition of him.

Whatever minor changes occurred in the family after that extraordinary session were quickly undone and are now lost to history. The treatment ended abruptly shortly thereafter (there were the usual excuses, and then they never returned my phone calls), and I haven't heard from Vincent or his family since. I can only conclude that they had taken flight into the land of their imagination and preferred not to be reached.

Through his behavior, his posture, his dulled expression, Vincent had told us that he did not disagree with his parents' portrait of him; in fact, he proved to us repeatedly that he could not do anything or even hold on to any thought for more than a moment. When, occasionally, he slipped out of role, he quickly retreated to his mythological position on cue. Vincent was his mother's Dummy and his father's Sacrificial Lamb. As a lapdog, he kept her company when her husband fled from her daily, and then glued his eyes to the television set as he gulped down his obligatory evening meal *en famille*.

Vincent allowed his parents to keep a lid on their own feelings of rage and disappointment. During our final session together, his mother and father had hurled insults at each other—she had accused him of being made of ice, an "emotional cripple," and "absent father," and he had accused her of sexual frigidity and had spoken bitterly of how she had turned him out of their bed more than twenty years ago. It had not been surprising that these feelings, which had been smoldering just beneath the surface for decades, had flared up just as Vincent had begun to take some tiny steps toward disengaging from his family. As one myth began to explode, the entire family drama came to a screeching halt.

As the family Moron, Vincent is his compulsive father's alterego and his dependent mother's constant companion. As a Moron, he cannot argue, he does not feel, and therefore he is perfectly suited to be all things to all people: a "fat lazy slob," a "well-worn teddy bear," and a convenient excuse for his parents not to sleep together.

In this family where mother and father live as caricatures themselves, Vincent is essential to the smooth functioning of the household. Without him, there would be no safety valve and, as we saw in the last session, a potentially uncontrollable explosion could ensue. (Vincent's premonition was right; the house could burn down!) So Vincent is consigned to inactivity, and his disgruntled uncooperativeness and vegetablelike existence are carefully orchestrated. He would not have it otherwise, for then where would he be?

If as a child Vincent had lived spontaneously and acknowledged his own intelligence, he would have been forced to see his parents' desperation; he would have been tempted to speak the truth and destroy his family's illusions. Better not to see, better not to speak; better to preserve the fantasy than to destroy it and be left with nothing.

Vincent recites his lines so that his parents can recite theirs, so that his father can feel less guilty as he leaves the house promptly at eight o'clock every morning, and his mother can feel less worthless and less lonely now that her parents are dead and her children are grown. But what was once a family drama has assumed the character of a personal mythology that dictates Vincent's ideas about who he is and what he can do. In this myth he is comatose, he exists outside of space and time, until the ticking of the clock awakens him and sets off another "meaningless" psychotic episode.

When a child is not valued by his parents for being real but, rather, for assuming a mythological character, he learns to devalue reality too (what good did it do him?) and to see his power as residing in his ability to weave a good fantasy, maybe even a better one than his parents did. In the world of the imagination, he can feel omnipotent (he is the master of his own fantasy life), even if his life experience informs him that he is actually painfully limited.

In our personal mythologies, magical transformations can occur, the last can become first, the weak can become powerful, and Love, Truth, and Beauty will triumph in the end. As Max Luthi puts it in his discussion of "Cinderella": "The insignificant thing turns out to be glorious; the dirty child is mere disguise; the clothes of silver and gold finally reveal the true nature of the girl who wears them" (*Once upon a Time*, p. 61). This kind of assurance of redemption is the essence of fairy tales, written and unwritten.

In some families where there is little or no appreciation given to the child for who he really is, the child is forced to choose between being himself and feeling like a worm, and abandoning himself with the hope that in the world of fantasy he can feel like a god or at least an unsung hero. Under such circumstances, being simply a person conjures up images of degradation and nothingness (this is the implicit message his parents are sending him), and so the magical appeal of a personal mythology is bound to be irresistible.

In the realm of "once upon a time," the ordinary laws of probability are no longer operative, and yet nothing is ever left to chance; there, even a Simpleton or a Pandora or a Sensitive Plant can hope to attain glory . . . someday. And if it is not immediately forthcoming, what matters? In that timeless universe, life can be suspended for a hundred years or more, so there is no need to live in the present. When a child sees that his parents refuse to settle for being "just human," he will naturally assume that he wouldn't want to settle for being just who he really is either; with his head spinning with tales from the family mythology, who can blame him?

3

Choreographed Lives: Siblings Growing Up

Once upon a time, a long, long time ago, it was the custom of all the fathers and mothers in China to give their first and honored sons great long names. But second sons were given hardly any name at all.

In a small mountain village there lived a mother who had two little sons. Her second son she called Chang, which meant "little or nothing." But her first and honored son, she called Tikki tikki tembo-no sa rembo-chari bari ruchi-pip peri pembo, which meant "the most wonderful thing in the whole wide world!"

—Arlene Mosel, *Tikki Tikki Tembo*

As we start uncovering the origins of our mythological identities and discover the connecting threads that link our distorted self-images to our parents' "necessary fictions," we become aware of still other disturbing presences. For example, Miranda's image of herself as her mama's girl—small, pretty, inarticulate—exists alongside an image of her sister, Deborah, as her father's brilliant protégée; the two are inextricably linked, frozen together in time. Memories from childhood are formative, even though they may be a reflection more of our interpretation of the past than of what actually transpired. Significantly, some of Miranda's most vivid memories are of her father and Deborah deeply engrossed in conversations that excluded her and her mother. The sounds, the smells, the facial expressions have melded together to create an indefinable but unmistakable family atmosphere that has left a permanent residue coating her sense of self. So Miranda might well wonder whether she would not have become a different sort of a person had she not been witness to her sister's life. Would she have appeared so "feminine," so adorable, and so much like her mother had Deborah not appeared so sophisticated and so unflappable, and so much like her father and his side of the family? And would her tears have earned her the reputation of the Crybaby if Deborah had not already been identified as Mature Beyond Her Years? As they say, hindsight is 20/20 vision, and yet Miranda still has trouble erasing from her mind an image of herself as little and inconsequential. It's all relative (to relatives), after all, and Deborah was bigger, and everyone in the family did take her more seriously.

There is not a person that I know who has not transposed some aspect of an early sibling relationship onto his present-day relationships with his peers. Judith the Wise Stoic (her communist father's loyal comrade in virtue) has little patience for frivolity or for friendship based on sentiment instead of work. She watched with envy and contempt her younger sister, Lisa, indulge herself and be indulged by their father and mother alike—Lisa was the Flirt and the Sexpot, Judith the unadorned Salt of the Earth—and she has little tolerance for such "decadent" characters. And yet the Impetuous Nymph—her mother's kindred spirit, her father's alter-ego—resurfaces in Judith's life, despite her conscious intent. Judith repeatedly finds herself mentor for such personages, who distract her from her purpose and seduce her into a world of sensuous feeling. Her sister lives in a distant city, but there is always someone else in her life to take her place.

And then there is John, the friend whom all friends go to for sound dispassionate advice on any subject; John, whose stern but evenhanded pronouncements have the power to contain even his temperamental and artistic wife's high level of anxiety. John's relationship with his "flaky," mystically inclined younger brother is the forerunner for what we see today. Since early adolescence, John was designated his mother's Knight in Shining Armor, and thus enlisted to help his less favored brother pull himself out of the quicksand he was continually sliding into, kicking aimlessly about.

A thankless task, since the family Schlemiel was as wedded to *his* degraded position as the Knight in Shining Armor was to his more noble one; nevertheless, this prepared John for his future role of Guide and Logician. He assumes this role many an evening, spending hours on the phone meticulously considering first this solution and then that one to somebody else's problems. Weary, and at times frustrated when he sees himself swamped in a never-ending tide of new, often tedious responsibilities, John has difficulty relinquishing control (or is it the illusion of control?), and buries his emotions in the service of pure reason.

Images of our brothers and our sisters, filtered through the prism of the family mythology, linger to haunt us; they challenge us when we attempt to revise our pictures of our parents and of ourselves. They remind us that the family legacy is not ours alone to uphold or to tear down. The family drama gives birth to many different characters, and there are other people to consider before we recklessly decide to cut and paste and rearrange the script. If we dare to tamper with our own mythology, we find that we invariably trample on our brothers' and our sisters' as well. Our siblings' portraits are the backdrop for our own self-portraits; their life narratives are choreographed with ours.

Our appetite for stories about siblings and their relationships with one another appears boundless, and between literature and real life there is always an endless supply of new material. Cain and Abel, Jacob and Esau, Joseph and his brothers, King Lear and his daughters, the Karamazov sons, the March sisters in *Little Women*, Cinderella and her stepsisters are some of the most familiar tales. But as amateur storytellers, each of us adds her own variations based on her "personal experience" as a sibling. And when friends and family unburden themselves over dinner or a coffee, confiding in us their conflicts with an "irresponsible" brother who is perennially getting himself into altercations with his boss, or an "intrusive" sister who is continually offering unsolicited advice, they too are unwitting contributors to our voluminous reference library.

As we accumulate tales of envy and of hero-worship, of favoritism and of camaraderie, of unswerving devotion and of wary alienation, we are forced to conclude that the sibling relationship is a highly charged one, both positively and negatively, one that has been neglected in traditional formulations of the origins of the self.

Yet, despite the fascination with siblings and an eagerness to document evidence of our loyalties and their betrayals, we rarely reflect on how they—and, more specifically, how our images of them—influence our images of ourselves. We are often not aware of how much our interest in the "fate" of a brother or a sister has a great deal to do with our interest in charting our own uncertain destinies.

Our brothers and sisters occupy a unique space within our psyches, one that abuts the very core of our sense of self. Our mental images of *them*, distorted or faithful, lend form and texture to our mental images of ourselves, as through the process of comparison we define who we are and who we must never be. It is not surprising, then, that a recent longitudinal study indicates that closeness to a sibling reported at college age is the single best predictor of mental health later in life (George E. Vaillant and Caroline O. Vaillant, "Natural History of Male Psychological Health, XII, pp. 831–37). One possible explanation for this unanticipated finding is that our feelings about a brother or a sister are intimately associated with our feelings about ourselves, and together these significantly color our feelings about life and people in general.

Most stories about siblings, in books and in conversation, emphasize differences between brothers and sisters in temperament or life-style; indeed, we never seem to tire of pointing out how one set of parents can produce such dissimilar offspring. It is as if this were evidence of our uniqueness—confirmation that we alone are the masters of our destinies. When Laurel, whom we encountered earlier disguised as a Troublemaker, describes her brother, Ethan, as ingratiating, conventional, and pretentious, and complains about how he is constantly dropping names of people, wines, and restaurants, she is, by way of contrast, defining herself as bold, defiant, and forthright, and as someone who would never base *her* self-esteem on such superficialities. Drawing distinctions between herself and her brother seems to make Laurel feel more certain of who *she* is, and more at home within the shambles of her life. *She* surely would not want to be a "conformist" and a "workaholic" like her brother, even if he is invited to elegant dinner parties and his life is in perfect order.

This emphasis on differences between siblings is not limited to one cultural or historical setting; psychologists may have identified and then labeled sibling rivalry, but they surely did not invent it. The Bible suggests that from the very Beginning such tensions existed, and the entire book of Genesis is as convincing an argument as any that, when these differences are highlighted by parental figures who express a clear preference for one child over another, they can lead to fiercely competitive feelings. The failure to resolve these conflicts invariably leads to violence of one form or another. The repressed always seems to return with a vengeance. (Francine Klagsbrun, in her book *Mixed Feelings*, explores these problems and offers examples from the Old Testament of how they can be resolved.)

Cain was a "tiller of the land" and his brother Abel a "keeper of sheep," and this distinguishing feature has far-reaching significance. God (the father) prefers Abel and what he had to offer by way of sacrifice (though in the story we are never really told why), and so, when Cain murders his brother out of jealous rage, and Abel becomes the first casualty of sibling rivalry, it is evident that it had something to do with their being so different.

Jacob and his twin brother, Esau, also could not have been less similar, despite their shared parentage and date of birth. And as we hear tell of their varying character traits and their corresponding positions within their family, we can easily anticipate what is to come. Jacob was smooth and gentle, devout and loyal to family and to home, whereas Esau, his double (as in Dr. Jekyll and Mr. Hyde), was hairy and wild, living on the impulse, free from the cares of domesticity. It is not surprising, then, that Jacob, the younger by only a few seconds, is his mother's favorite though Esau, as the elder son, is favored by the Law. And so, when Jacob deceives his dying father and steals his brother's birthright (all at his mother's bidding), he is actually assuming his "rightful" destiny, and there is no argument when *his* name and not his brother's goes down in history as one of the fathers of the Jews.

Joseph, the son of Jacob, is, like his father, the chosen one from the very start. A Poet and a Dreamer, he is singled out from among his twelve less distinctive brothers, who are simple shepherds. And as his father, Jacob, did in *his* generation, Joseph benefits from a parent's favoritism, though this time it is a father's and not a mother's preference for a particular child that determines his fate. Joseph's magnificent "coat of many colors" is his father's special gift to him, and is a harbinger of great things to come. But when Joseph's brothers can no longer contain their envy and sell him into slavery, he is forced to endure extraordinary hardships before enjoying extraordinary renown. It is all part of the same story, one that relates the consequences of being a Special Child.

But, like people in a fairy tale, these ancient figures are archetypal characters, whose lives assume meaning only within the context of an entire drama that pivots around sibling conflicts. Without siblings, each one of these characters would have looked very different. Perhaps each figure would be scarcely identifiable if he were spirited away from his family and later encountered solely as an individual in his own right.

Consider, for a moment, whether Cain would have been a murderer and an exile had there been no brother Abel for God to have preferred. And if Cain's identity as his brother's killer was just an outgrowth of a transcendental family drama that includes God the father, and not some expression of who he essentially is, what about our identities? Or Esau's? Or any other pair of "opposites"? If Jacob had not been so cuddly and so clearly his mother's favorite, would Esau have been so intemperate, or so shortsighted as to exchange his birthright for a bowl of soup? Did Esau feel doomed from the outset to act out his mythical part in his family saga, once he recognized that brother Jacob had already been cast in the part of the Favorite Son? Each pair of brothers is inseparable, their stories unfold in tandem, their fates are intertwined. But if Joseph had not been the family Poet, the Golden Boy who was destined to do great things, would not some other brother have assumed that elevated position? Perhaps Benjamin or Ephraim or Judah?

Of course, there is no laboratory in which to study "identity" apart from the social context in which it evolves. And we can never know for sure whether our personalities, and hence our lives, would have been significantly different had our siblings been other than what they were. But when we study families in psychotherapy, we can say with a fair amount of certainty that changes in one sibling often trigger changes in another, sometimes in what appears to be a kind of seesaw effect.

So, for example, it often happens that, when the Troublemaker and family Ne'er-Do-Well begins to make good and settle down, his counterpart, the Little Angel, Miss Goody Two-Shoes, picks up where he left off. Perhaps she develops an eating disorder and in her own fashion carries on the legacy of her now "well-adjusted" brother. If he can dabble in being Good, maybe then she can allow herself to be a little bit Bad. Some families cannot stomach too much success, any more than they can weather too many storms all at the same time. Brothers and sisters conspire with their parents to maintain the "perfect" balance.

THE COOL, CALM, AND COLLECTED YOUNG LADY VERSUS THE SMOLDERING VOLCANIC KID

People naturally vary as to how much of their deepest feelings they wish to divulge to others. In the extreme cases, there are those who "wear their hearts on their sleeves" for anyone to see, cradle, or brush up against, and those who are so sealed over that even their most intimate friends know little of their internal experiences. In some families, each parent represents one end of the continuum of emotional expressiveness. This was the arrangement in Sherry's family, and the mythological identities that developed in their three children mirrored those of the parents.

As discussed in the previous chapter, Sherry's mother froze off all of her feelings—be they feelings of anger, tenderness, or despair (a veritable Snow Queen)—and her father was continually leaking, apparently unable to contain anything within his own body (a Sentimental Sap). The one private and frustratingly mysterious, the other intrusive and embarrassingly naked, together they created an atmosphere of unreality which encouraged their children to divide themselves between the two opposing camps.

Sherry and her sister, Lorraine, became opposites, but since they were nourished by the same mythological system, their images of themselves were linked with their images of each other, all unreal images which were fragments of their true selves.

When Sherry was finally hospitalized for bulimia because her compulsive binging and purging was so out of control that even she, an aspiring Snow Queen, was becoming too frightened to continue ignoring her feelings, her entire family was jolted out of their collective trance. For years she had managed to keep her compulsive eating rituals a secret from her parents and her younger sister, whom she had always envied for her naturally slender figure and bold self-assurance. But suddenly the Easygoing child of the family became the Difficult one, and everyone had to adjust.

Since school age, Sherry had functioned as her father's confidante and her mother's faithful helper. Unlike her younger brother and sister, she never spoke back to her parents, and took it upon herself to do the laundry and prepare the meals when her mother was either too busy or too tired or too irritable to take care of the basics. It seems from Sherry's description that she had been unofficially designated as the Woman of the House, with a reputation as Reliable, Levelheaded, and Responsible. Ironically, my eating-disordered patient was the one her family counted on to "feed" and nurture them.

According to the family mythology, Sherry was an unusually undemanding and sympathetic child. She was not like her cold and distant mother, who left her husband and her children feeling ravenous and then ashamed and guilty at their apparent greediness. Nor was she like her father, whose needs for attention and reassurance took precedence over his wife's and children's needs for separateness. And certainly Sherry was not like her younger sister or brother, who were Selfish and Immature and prone to violent outbursts. Only Sherry could fill the void in the others, and nobody cared to know about the void within her, which remained a constant ache. She mislabeled the ache as hunger, and this was at the root of her eating problem.

In stark contrast to herself, Sherry described her sister, Lorraine, as skinny, brassy, and "carefree," and apparently in her mind these are all admirable qualities which go hand in hand. Sherry would frequently find herself acting as a mediator between her sister and her parents, particularly between her sister and her father, who, on account of his good-natured gullibility, was continually being taken advantage of by his younger, seductively savvy daughter, only to then explode in impotent rage. Being a go-between was both gratifying and frustrating to Sherry. It put her right in the center of every altercation, but Lorraine was the star performer, the one with the dramatic monologue, who captured everybody's attention as she swept across the stage.

From Sherry's perspective, her sister Lorraine's rebellious behavior reflected an inner confidence, a steely resoluteness that she herself sorely lacked. Whereas Sherry constantly worried about her appearance and her behavior, monitoring herself lest she make a poor impression on someone or another, it seemed to her that her sister "never gave a hoot" about what other people thought as long as she managed to get her way, which from Sherry's vantage point was what usually happened.

As the Good Girl, the Mature Girl, the supposed Favorite daughter, Sherry could not help feeling jealous of her irrepressible sister's apparent freedom. She wished she could be as sharp-tongued as Lorraine, as tough, as immature, and as selfish.

Sherry's hospitalization—and, what's more, her official psychiatric diagnosis of bulimia—shattered her mythological identity as the Mature, Uncomplicated Peacemaker, and everybody in the family felt the reverberations. Lorraine found herself catapulted into a very new role, the role of family stabilizer. As Sherry's parents and sister discovered that Sherry was not only more vulnerable than she had appeared but also more angry, less generous, and more hungry (literally and figuratively) than she had ever dared reveal to them before, Lorraine was forced to re-evaluate her own strengths and put a lid on her own anger. If she hadn't, the family might not have been able to weather the crisis, since neither mother nor father was prepared to fill the emotional vacuum that Sherry's revelations had created.

From Sherry's reports of her sister's behavior during the months that followed her hospitalization, it sounded as if Lorraine, the family's Pandora, did not know whether to compete with her sister for the title of Problem Child or to relinquish her claim altogether and assume the position of responsibility that her sister had vacated. For a while, Lorraine conscientiously avoided all confrontations with her parents, though, since she was the family Instigator, stirring up conflict had been her modus operandi. And, surprisingly, Lorraine was remarkably successful at maintaining the peace . . . at least until it looked as if everything was back to "normal," and she could safely revert to her former character.

As long as Sherry was openly expressing her negative feelings about herself and her parents, Lorraine took it upon herself to contain hers. There was not room enough in the family for more than two fresh mouths, and their brother's claim to Incorrigibility took precedence over Lorraine's, on account of his sex. Ironically, as the sisters began to reverse roles, Sherry began to express concern that her position in the family as the Good Girl was being usurped and she was in danger of losing whatever advantage she may have had.

As the Responsible daughter and Woman of the House, Sherry had always felt rather stodgy and unattractive and had suspected that, unlike her impulsive sister, she was missing out on life. But now that this was no longer her identity, she wasn't certain whether she had not lost more than she had gained. Her fickle parents seemed to be heaping love and presents on Lorraine, whose problems now paled in significance when compared with her "eating-disordered" sister. Moreover, even Sherry's adoring father accused her, his favored child, of being a "selfish bitch" now that she was no longer a Receptive Ear and was preoccupied with her own problems rather than with his. Indeed, having abandoned her father to his unhappy marriage, Sherry was perceived as a traitor, who threatened to destroy an otherwise harmonious family. It is no wonder, then, that she would look back with a certain amount of nostalgia to the days when the mythological Sherry was all that people knew. Exposed—or, rather, recast—in a new light, she envied Lorraine more than ever, because, as always, no matter what she did, Lorraine seemed to have gotten the better deal.

Lorraine apparently did not agree, and as the months passed

and the drama of Sherry's psychiatric hospitalization began to fade from memory, she resumed her characteristic behavior—she lost her job, she accidentally smashed her father's car, and, to top it off, she became pregnant. Sherry eagerly took the bait, quickly reconstituted her former identity as the Responsible older sister, and with more than a little relief rushed to her "crazy" sister's rescue. As the two secretly conferred and Sherry made arrangements behind their parents' backs for her sister to have an abortion, Lorraine's crisis overshadowed Sherry's and, just as in the old days, the sisters confined themselves to their familiar pattern of relating.

In discussing the origins of identity, sociologists have referred to the "looking-glass self," a self that is reflected back at us from the eyes of others, a self that never exists in isolation but that is, from the outset, constructed in the context of relationships. (Charles Horton Cooley, *Human Nature and the Social Order*, 1902.) Social psychologists suggest, moreover, that, in the absence of clear, unambiguous measures of Right and Wrong, Good and Bad, we are forced to evaluate ourselves not in absolute terms but only in relation to our peers. Through the process of "social comparison," we arrive at some sense of meaning, some approximation of reality—be it the reality of the world or the reality of our self (Leon Festinger, "A Theory of Social Comparison Processes").

Because the experience of the self is so deeply embedded within a social context that, over time, becomes embedded within the individual's psyche, family therapists have argued (with some justification) that it is unreasonable to expect anyone, let alone a child, to sustain changes in his ideas or behavior or self-concept without those changes being mirrored back to him by those with whom he is in intimate contact. Struck by the "invisible loyalties" and unwritten codes that bind families together (see Boszormenyi-Nagy, *Invisible Loyalties*), they speak of the family as a "system" in which the personalities as well as the symptoms of the individual members function at times as part of an "undifferentiated ego mass" (a term coined by Murray Bowen, *Family Therapy in Clinical Practice*). As such, one person's internal experience can only be interpreted in the context of the entire system in which he participates, in person or in absentia.

Although psychoanalytic thinkers have focused primarily on the individual's *internal*, as opposed to interpersonal, world, they too have recognized that, through the process of "projective identification," the characteristics of one person can spill over onto another for the purpose of acting out a particular psychic drama (McDougal, Bollas, Laing, and others). This form of relating is not, by any means, limited to interactions within the family, but the intimacy that normally exists there encourages such "boundary confusion," as mothers and fathers, sisters and brothers exchange and borrow one another's qualities and emotions without even asking, and certainly without formally acknowledging the transaction; it's family, after all, no need to keep accounts! (See, for example, Bank and Kahn.)

But, whatever the terminology, and each discipline has its own, it is generally recognized that the self exists within a social framework and that our relationships with others not only *reflect* our self-image but also *determine* it. Our siblings, as our original peer group, our original standard of comparison, naturally tell us how we measure up and how we fit into the human family; they inform us whether or not the hand we have been dealt is a fair one, or one we can reasonably expect to be able to exchange for another. Insofar as our relations with our brothers and sisters misrepresent reality and distort our images of ourselves, the self-fulfilling prophecy gains momentum as we find ourselves re-enacting our childhood sibling roles in later life.

Mythological identities are the products of a collective imagination, they are an amalgam of an entire family's projections and identifications, so perhaps they, more than any others, bear the mark of the interpersonal context from which they emerge. Each mythic character is but one part of an intricate mythology that includes various other mythic characters as well as implicit rules governing their interactions. Although each family produces its own myths and laws of governance, there is one characteristic that all mythological systems have in common: within the mythological world, Reason does *not* prevail, and magic—white and black—is disguised as natural law. In Miranda's family, for example, it is indisputable that she is too "high-strung" to go to medical school or even to know what is good for her, and on cue she flies off the handle and then bursts into tears. And of course it is obvious that Vincent is too lethargic and impractical to do his own grocery shopping, and, lo and behold, he *is* always lounging around the house in his pajamas!

There are certain dimensions along which siblings are typically placed, and frequently one child is seen as falling at one end of a continuum while a sister or a brother is seen as falling at its opposite pole. ("He's so even-tempered, so reliable"; "she's so emotional, so unpredictable.") Judging from informal descriptions we give of ourselves and of our siblings, it would seem as if there were no midpoints between the two extremes, we so rarely make use of them! Is our vision purposefully clouded (for the purposes of the drama), so that we lose all sense of nuance and only see the whites and the blacks, not the varying shades of gray? Or are the differences that we see an inevitable outgrowth of the self-fulfilling prophecy, whereby we all actually end up conforming to these caricatured images of ourselves? This is as difficult a question to answer as the one about the chicken and the egg.

In Freud's model of the mind, each of us contains within our personality three distinct structures, with the Id representing our instinctual life, the Ego the demands of reality, and the Superego our ideals and moral principles. These are convenient terms by which to organize common personality characteristics. In some families, one child will be selected to embody the Instincts, and this child will presumably live according to the Pleasure Principle. He will be expected to be childishly naïve, carefree, and impulsive, living for the moment, without sufficient regard for the long-term consequences of his actions. Laurel is a good example. Her brother, Ethan, functions as the tempering agent within the family, the pragmatist who always considers all the options before making any decision, in work or in love; *he* never allows himself to be buffeted by his emotions. By embodying the Reality Principle, Ethan effectively contains the impulses that his sister (and mother) wantonly express. A third child may be enlisted to represent the Conscience, in which case she may be cast as a kind of Beauty figure among beasts. Julia's identity as a Ministering Angel and her Wild-Eyed motorcyclist brother overtly express this dualism. Yet another child may give expression to her family ideals, without which there would be no hope of transcendence. As the model person, this embodiment of Freud's Ego Ideal finds herself cast in marble, set upon a pedestal, and from that lofty position she can judge and be judged. Diana seems to have filled that role in her family.

Below, I provide a list of personality characteristics that are commonly used to differentiate people, and I indicate how they might be loosely classified according to this scheme. These characteristics may also be seen as roughly corresponding to transactional analyst Eric Berne's division of the personality into Child, Adult, and Parent states.

ID	EGO	SUPEREGO
Emotional	Rational	Principled
Impulsive	Even-Tempered	Unyielding
Childish	Mature	Patriarchal
Rebellious	Conventional	Loyal
Insatiable	Contented	Ascetic
Whimsical	Ironical	Sober
Simple-Minded	Clever	Wise
Carefree	Measured	Burdened
Naïve	Skeptical	Moralistic
Selfish	Empathic	Selfless

Freud saw elements of each hypothetical structure in all of us, just as Eric Berne maintains that we all alternate between our Child, Adult, and Parent positions. However, ensconced in our mythological identities, we often emphasize one set of characteristics to the exclusion of the others. It is in the nature of myth that there is little "tolerance of ambiguity," little room for nuance. Psychologist Else Frenkel-Brunswik used the term "intolerance of ambiguity" to refer to a tendency to think rigidly, submit to authority, and see the world in black and white, ignoring shades of gray. But this characteristic is not limited to the "authoritarian personality" she was writing about. Most of us are guilty in one form or another of categorizing other people as one of Us or one of Them, and nearly everyone enjoys an opportunity to cheer on the Good guys and hiss at the Bad ("Intolerance of Ambiguity," pp. 58–91).

It wouldn't be a satisfying fairy tale if Snow White's wicked stepmother were a generous and loving wife, or if Snow White was a vain, lazy child or a tattletale among friends.

THE IMPLACABLE SPHINX VERSUS THE SUPPLIANT MAIDEN

One dimension along which siblings are typically compared is that of autonomy. Sometimes one child in a family will be singled out as particularly precocious, which often means he is perceived to be independent and resilient, and responsible beyond his years. He may be treated as if he were not really a child at all but a miniature adult. As a result of the self-fulfilling prophecy, he may actually begin to earn the trust and respect that have been accorded to him. As a counterpoint, a sister or a brother may be identified as unusually timid and vulnerable, dependent on others for guidance and protection. Though there may be cases in which constitutional factors contribute to these personality differences, in some families birth order, sex, or physical appearance is decisive. Moreover, differences in personality may assume mythic proportions, so that one child is perceived as completely self-sufficient, boundlessly wise, and impervious to *all* harm, whereas the other is cast in the role of the helpless waif, gullible and naïve, and forever inexperienced in the ways of the world, whatever actual experience he accrues! The features that distinguish Linda from her sister, Patricia, fall roughly into this category.

Linda, a pediatric surgeon, is five years older than her sister Patricia, an advertising executive. They are forty-seven and forty-two, so five years are not all that significant, but psychologically the difference is immeasurable. As if Linda were seven and Patricia were still only two, Linda remains fixed in her role as Mentor, and as such is presumed to be more experienced, more cultured, and more levelheaded, now and forever after. Consistent with her mental image of Linda, Patricia continues to imagine herself as a fumbling little girl who has managed, for purposes of public consumption, to disguise herself as a competent businesswoman. However successful Patricia might be in maintaining her "cover" on the job, her interactions with her sister, as well as with other intimates in her life, only reinforce her distorted self-image and trap her in a cycle of repetition, regret, and more repetition.

The myth of Linda is that she is impenetrable and that her nerves are made of steel, and since she largely believes the myth, she acts the part so skillfully that few would suspect otherwise. Mythologically speaking, Patricia is an open book; in contrast with her tightly wrapped sister, her feelings spew forth uncontrollably. Living with the image of herself as still a young child, Patricia feels she needs a human container who can offer her protection against emotional leakage.

Understandably, both sisters act in a manner that is consistent with their images of themselves and of each other, though none of this is ever made explicit, since each sister is embarrassed by the glaring inequalities implied. Accordingly, when they are in public places, each goes out of her way to pretend that they have put all of that behind them. They share jokes about their childhood experiences with their "crazy" parents, and emphasize their mutuality rather than the hierarchical nature of their sibling relationship. After all, they are two mature and intelligent women, and there is no need to dredge up old grievances which would only foment resentment and guilt. They like being close, and the past is indeed the past, though neither of them *actually* believes that identities *really* change, and both are still convinced that their mythic selves are more real than real.

I listen to Linda's deep, almost hypnotic monotone, as she responds to one of Patricia's plaintive, higher-pitched queries, and I am reminded of a weary but patient mother who is trying to smooth over her young daughter's ruffled feathers so that both can proceed with the work of living. These impressionistic tableaux that flash across my mind when I see the two sisters together are, I imagine, refractions of past scenes from childhood and prophecies of future dramas.

The sisters agree that their mother was an immature, impulsive, and highly unstable woman whose social charms, flamboyant style, and exhibitionistic qualities made her quite popular among a certain set of wealthy and bored society women, but rendered her highly unsuited for her role as a parent. As often is the case, their father is described as the very antithesis of his wife: strong-willed, temperate, and always in perfect control of his emotions, a responsible gentleman with an impeccable reputation. Their father's reserve, his prestige in the world, and his imperviousness to his wife's periodic "hysterical crises" became the family's model of strength and maturity, and Linda's model of personhood.

According to the family lore, the girls' mother is both the guilty and the "eccentric" parent, and though their father was no more available to them emotionally than his blatantly irresponsible wife, his was the voice of reason, and he was absolved of any blame. As a traditional patriarchal figure of a certain social class, their father was either at the office, at the club, or on the golf course. This remoteness, coupled with their mother's self-involvement, left the two sisters to fend for themselves. As the elder, Linda was prematurely thrust into a position of authority and power. This is the origin of her mythological identity and the basis for the skewed relationship that developed between her and her sister.

Linda became her father's faithful surrogate, the representative of Reason in a household pulsating with confused emotions; she was the stabilizing influence on her volatile mother and her naturally less mature younger sister. But there was one important thing that distinguished Linda from her adored father: unlike him, she was unable to escape from the emotional tumult at home. (Children do not have offices or country clubs to which they can retreat, no questions asked.) She could not simply turn a blind eye to the problems her mother and sister laid at her feet. She had to use her "superior" intelligence and dispassionate attitude in the service of containment; otherwise, she too could be flooded by the unregulated outpouring of emotion.

Linda became the Wise Helper who had no feelings of her own, a kind of Buddha figure who at birth had already attained enlightenment. When, at age six, Patricia developed a serious kidney problem that required hospitalization and years of careful monitoring afterward, this identity of Linda's was further consolidated. Her mother was too scattered and her father was too distant to shoulder such adult responsibility.

In Linda's mind, it was undoubtedly preferable to identify with her father, who was dignified and well respected, than with her foolish and pitiful mother, whose emotions were constantly shifting and whom the relatives spoke of, in hushed tones, with condescension. And so Linda eagerly borrowed certain of her father's qualities in constructing her image of herself. Her authoritative manner, her cool, almost imperious demeanor, and her unflappable self-assurance were all reminiscent of him.

Patricia might also have preferred to cultivate these qualities in herself, but her age, her physical disability, and her normal dependency on her elders, namely her sister, worked against it. At six, she surely couldn't compete for the coveted identity, and after that the pattern was already set. She was needy, Linda was self-sufficient; she was uncertain of herself, Linda was unwavering in her opinions; she was affectionate and cuddly, Linda was concerned but made of marble.

Though it is undeniable that Patricia's adult image of herself as ineffectual, moody, and overly dependent on others for her self-esteem bears some resemblance to her image of her mother, her image of her older sister is, I believe, a mediating influence. Patricia's current distortions of self-image are faithful renditions of the person she was presumed to be in relation to Linda. Indeed, each sister's internal image of herself mirrors her internal image of herself in relation to the other. Patricia sees herself as Linda's clingy, untidy, naïve little sister, whether she is conducting a seminar for businessmen or circulating at an office cocktail party, and Linda feels poised and speaks confidently with everyone, oblivious to issues of status and power.

Today both Linda's and Patricia's relationships with friends and lovers recapitulate elements of their sibling relationship. Linda is single, she works long hours, and among colleagues and friends alike she commands respect, even awe. As a professional, she attracts disciples who are younger and less experienced than she, and hence eager to follow in her footsteps and reach "enlightenment." Linda is receptive to this form of relationship, which borders on idolatry, and treats her protégés in a kindly, almost motherly fashion. She doesn't even have to think about it; the abstracted look on her face suggests that giving advice and offering a shoulder to lean upon come automatically to her.

As long as I have known her, and it is over fifteen years now,

Linda has always had at least one very close friend with whom she spends most of her leisure time. (Typically, she does not have much leisure time, since her professional responsibilities are forever expanding.) And though there have been a number of different people who functioned in this capacity, they resemble one another in their relationship to her. Linda is their confidante, the person they have come to for stability and support, initially in times of crisis. Girlish, effusive, impractical, these women intimates allow Linda to be what she feels most comfortable being: a guide, a support, a stabilizer, Patricia's older sister. Does she divulge her innermost secrets to these special friends? Do they catch a glimpse of *her* vulnerabilities? I wouldn't know. But as with her sister Patricia, Linda can be seen to this day calmly and systematically applying her razor-sharp intelligence to cleaning up someone else's messy emotions, with no evidence that she has actually gotten her hands dirty or her hair mussed in the process.

In a parallel fashion, Patricia has also reproduced her relationship with Linda with her friends and lovers. Lacking in confidence, and desperate to make her own life after finishing college at twenty-two, Patricia married, against her family's wishes, a man ten years older than she, whom she had known for scarcely six months.

From her description of him, Patricia's husband, Jack, was an extremely controlling man, and though this became the basis for a debilitating power struggle that left Patricia alternately trembling with fear and bristling with anger, it was at first part of his appeal. Like Linda, Jack appeared to have transcended his emotions, and though eventually his authoritative air and unwavering stance would infuriate Patricia, at first they were reassuringly familiar. And, then, as long as she was in a constant muddle, as befit her identity, she *needed* a Linda surrogate to lend her a firm hand and deliver her from her various emotional crises.

But after the early infatuation with Jack's implacable manner wore off, and Patricia's desires for herself began to clash with his desires for his mythical "little wife" (she wished to return to school to get an advanced degree in business, and he wanted her to remain at home nights and play hostess to promote his business), Jack became cold and rejecting. By setting goals for herself,

Patricia not only affirmed her independence but also poked holes in his identity as her mentor, and this violated the implicit bond that joined them together. The "little sister" had the audacity to grow up and become a woman!

The marriage lasted only a year, though for nine months Patricia suffered silently, torn between her anger at her frustratingly reserved husband and her overriding guilt at having failed him and ruined their marriage. Ironically, though not surprisingly, it was with Linda's support and encouragement that Patricia finally found the courage to leave Jack and secure a position for herself in a large advertising firm conveniently located in the same city where Linda lived. (Linda had been able to pull some strings and use some of her college connections to oil the way for her sister's entry into the business world.)

Since her marriage disintegrated, Patricia has had a number of minor emotional "crises," amplifying the feelings of childishness and vulnerability that are perpetually incubating just beneath her surface. Usually the crisis had something to do with a man, and Patricia was painfully aware that her moods rose and fell in rhythm with her romantic involvements. And yet she had little confidence that she could have responded otherwise—she was too soft, and her defenses were too flimsy.

But as much as Patricia sought protection and reassurance from the presence of a man in her life, she also resented her dependency. Her idealizations of her lovers led first to slavish devotion but then to feelings of self-denigration. Intellectually she could anticipate the predictable romantic disasters that were, after years, familiar elements in her life, but emotionally she was still subject to her false idols, still the younger sister trailing Linda, hoping to catch a glimpse of the Truth on the horizon of her life.

Not surprisingly, given her mythological identity, Patricia's efforts to live independently, to immerse herself in her career, and to emulate her older, well-collected sister (who *never* had, to anyone's knowledge, an emotional crisis of her own), met with only moderate success. She was not made of the same substance as Linda, she could not fortify herself or even protect herself from impending danger. She could not help wearing her heart on her sleeve, and having it bruised time and again, or so goes the myth.

As adults, the sisters have maintained close ties, though I have been told there were a couple of years when Patricia kept her distance from Linda and her "superior wisdom," and when Linda felt exasperated with her younger sister's apparent inability to assume some of the burden of caring for their aging parents. (Linda once complained that whenever they went home for a visit with their parents Patricia immediately seized the opportunity to sleep the weekend away, offering Linda no relief at all from their mother's constant barrage. Who could expect a helpless, adorable, but fragile two-year-old to pitch in when the going gets rough?)

But now, as each sister continues to bring traces of their early relationship into new relationships, the tension between them is, for the most part, deflected elsewhere. Their conversational pattern may be choreographed, but it is familiar and thus very comfortable and comforting, until one or the other falls out of step for an instant and they are forced to switch from automatic pilot and take a hard look at who they really now are.

Sometimes differences between siblings are emphasized within a particular family so as to *minimize* conflict, which is often most fierce when two or more siblings are competing in the same race and there is only one gold medal to be won. Because parents, not children, invent the rules of the game and evaluate the contestants using their own private measuring rods, it is ultimately the parents who decide whether it is even possible for *both* Jimmy and Cathy to be Brains, or whether a frivolous Airhead is required in order to maintain a proper balance within the family. Does father or mother need a companion in recklessness? Must one person or one sex have a monopoly on intelligence? Are "braininess" and "flightiness" mutually exclusive qualities? And can there be more than one winner in the family, and can he enter more than one race? The judges decree whether the game of life is to be played as if there were only a limited supply of each human quality, and hence whether Jimmy's high honors rob Cathy of her right to be recognized as a brilliant student too. There is no objective standard to refer to when answering these questions, and so each family system operates in accordance with the insights and prejudices of the judges.

In their comprehensive study of the sibling relationship, Bank and Kahn describe families in which each child carves out his or her own particular niche after carefully scanning the field to see what identity has or has not been claimed by someone else (*The Sibling Bond*, 1982). After a brother or a sister has already been designated the Family Genius, a child may decide to withdraw from the intellectual arena altogether, and emphasize instead his social charms, his good looks, his athletic ability, or his pointedly uncultivated "common sense." He finds that, as the family's Mystic or the family's Rebel or even the family's Happy-Go-Lucky, Ordinary Guy, he can take turns sharing some of the spotlight with his intellectual brother and avoid the bloodshed that might result were they to compete for the same corner of the stage. With time, such compromises come so automatically that neither the Intellectual nor his counterpart, the Mystic or the Heavyweight, is aware that an aspect of himself has been shunted to the side, that a part has been sacrificed for the whole.

The straight man always needs a comic. Laurel always looks fatter when he stands next to Hardy, and there would be no Punch without Judy. Unfortunately, if all the "positive" identities have already been meted out, a child may be relegated to the role of the family Black Sheep, the "identified patient," the Pandora, or the Simpleton. Some though not all family systems need to fill these roles; they need a sacrificial lamb to burn, a scapegoat to absolve them of their sins, a fool to laugh at. Being invisible may be the only other alternative a particular child is offered and that may be a far worse fate.

PANDORA AND HER BOX OF TROUBLE VERSUS ALADDIN AND HIS MAGIC LAMP

"You're haunting me, isn't that it? I can't get away from him! I spend half my life with meek-and-mild Ezra and his blasted wooden whistle; I make my escape at last, and now look: here we go again. It's like a conspiracy! Like some kind of plot where someone decided, long before I was born, I would live out my days surrounded by people who were . . . nicer than I am, just naturally nicer without even having to try, people that other people preferred. . . ."

—Anne Tyler, *Dinner at the Homesick Restaurant*

Almost by definition, the identity of a Troublemaker implies the existence of some purer and more upstanding character with whom he is in an antagonistic relationship. After all, the Troublemaker must be making trouble for somebody besides himself (*he* is too perverse to care anyway). He creates havoc where there was order, stirs up controversy where there was harmony, and wantonly tears down what was painstakingly built up. The metaphors we use to describe such figures express our ambivalence toward them—"She opened the can of worms"; "She rocked the boat"; "She's the rotten apple that spoils the barrel"—and then, of course, there's Eve, who eats the forbidden fruit from the tree of knowledge, and Pandora who opens the box; the rest is history.

Sometimes in families the counterpart of the Troublemaker is the Shining Star. He is an Aladdin figure who need only rub his magic lamp and all will be given him and his. Whereas everything the Black Sheep/Troublemaker touches turns to shit, everything the Shining Star touches turns to gold. His mythic power to create and do Good is as magical as her mythic power to spoil. They are perfect complements to each other, both actors in the same mythic drama.

It is not mere coincidence that both Laurel and Maia, each of whom I have seen as a kind of Pandora figure, describe a highly charged relationship with a sibling who is perceived as more temperate, more practical, more successful, and more conventional than she. Indeed, were we to borrow the language of Freud, and in these cases it is tempting, we can say that our Irrepressible Instigators are the embodiment of the Id, and their siblings are the embodiment of the Ego in league with the Superego. These Pandoras never seem to open the box of trouble without glancing over their shoulders at their brothers, who are desperately trying to shut it tight. As much as their characters as siblings seem in opposition to one another, their attraction is mutual and undeniable. Each expresses what the other dares not express. Pandora would like to settle down but cannot; her dutiful brother would like to break loose once in a while but cannot give himself permission.

Anna also occupied the role of Troublemaker in her family, though she was considered more annoying than destructive, as irrepressible as a little baby, and as inconsequential and unproductive as a mosquito who persists in hovering over the family picnic—always in motion but never accomplishing anything besides deflecting the family's attention away from more important matters. How irritating! If only she would go away and leave them all alone!

But Anna's blameworthiness and the effect it has had on her adult friendships cannot be fully appreciated without considering her relationships with her siblings, particularly with her older brother, Mark, whose inviolable reputation as the proud bearer of the family name is a necessary backdrop to Anna's family portrait. But let us first back up a bit and consider Anna's parents and their marriage and what the family looked like before Anna made her appearance on the scene. Only then can we understand how Anna developed her identity as a Troublemaker in tandem with her brother Mark, the family's Prodigy, and why she continues to feel as if she has to apologize for breathing and justify her existence by paying deference to an unending supply of people who live the myth of the Shining Star.

Anna's mother and father had certainly not planned to have another child when her mother became pregnant with Anna at the age of thirty-eight. They had already had their two children: Mark, who was nine, and Susan, who was six. The roles within the family were carefully defined, and the rhythm of life was well regulated.

Anna's mother, Hazel, was a suspicious and solitary type of person, who neither worked outside the home nor much enjoyed the domestic life within. In contrast with his wife, who held a rather dim view of humanity, Anna's father, Joe, was extremely gregarious. An ambitious and well-liked member of the community, Joe was the quintessential optimist and Do-Gooder, who always put a positive gloss on everything, to the supreme irritation of his wife.

As long as the neighbors regarded Hazel as a charming if reclusive kind of woman, and believed that Joe was a model husband and a devoted father (he did chauffeur his wife to the grocery store on Saturdays, since Hazel had stubbornly refused to learn to drive), then all was well, or at least tolerable. With these myths in place, both husband and wife could preserve their self-respect and sustain their individual mythological identities. He was so extraordinarily Patient and Productive; she was so very Cultured and Sensitive.

Mark was the Star of the household, a Brilliant student and a Mature and Responsible son; he promised to be his parents' Pride and Joy, their claim to glory. And Susan, though less extraordinary than her older brother, was always full of good ideas and, more important, "no trouble at all." The family Gadabout, who liked to function as the one and only Organizer, at home and within her circle of friends, Susan filled the vacuum left by her mother's stubborn passivity and hermetic existence.

Given this configuration, where was Anna to fit in? A new baby was bound to disrupt the deceptively peaceful atmosphere within the home, and I gathered from Anna's experience of herself as a Troublemaker that everybody in the family dreaded what might result. One remedy was to pretend that Anna was not a baby, and therefore did not have legitimate needs that should be taken into consideration. She should be able to sit properly at the table just like everyone else! But when this strategy did not work, the family devised another: they labeled her untempered baby energy and natural curiosity as bothersome, if not idiotic, with the implication that she *had* to learn to fit into the family, and that no accommodations would or should be made for her. After all, Anna was the Troublemaker, and neither her parents nor her siblings should dignify her desires by attempting to gratify them.

If Anna was willing to enter into someone else's orbit, that was fine, as long as there was a vacant spot and she was able to keep up the pace and remain sufficiently unobtrusive. However, if she was not able to tailor herself to the needs of others, she would be justifiably condemned to float out into space all by herself. The family drama in a nutshell.

Anna's mother's favorite story about Anna as a baby has been repeated to her innumerable times and is emblematic of their relationship; it sets the stage for her relationships with her older sister and brother. It goes like this: One morning, when Anna was less than one year old, her mother left her sitting on a blanket in the living room while she finished washing the breakfast dishes. Mark and Susan were in school, Anna's father was at work, and the house was the way her mother preferred it—quiet. But when she returned to the room a few minutes later, she found Anna upright and holding on to the glass coffee table with a big grin on her face. Apparently, Anna's mother had not expected this, since it was the very first time Anna had managed to pull herself up without any help. Un-self-consciously, Anna's mother recalls her own reaction of exasperation, which she felt was entirely justified: "I just put you back down, but you just popped right back up, and then I put you down again, but it was no use, you just wouldn't stay still."

Significantly, Anna remembered hearing this story for the first time while keeping her mother company as she played solitaire at the kitchen table, a favorite occupation of this pointedly sedentary woman. Anna had gotten into the habit of sitting *quietly* with her mother and listening to her stories when, each afternoon, she faithfully returned home from school. During her elementary-school days, Anna did her best to resist the temptation to "pop up" after her snack and explore the world outside her mother's narrow horizons. That would come later. For the time being, she was intent on *not* fulfilling the family prophecy (as if that were possible), which meant not being a bothersome kid with boundless energy (just like her father), who disturbed the peace in her parents' home and stirred up trouble by wanting too much and stretching her imagination too far.

Anna acknowledged that she had always stood in awe of her brother, Mark, that Exemplary Individual whom her parents worshiped and her sister, Susan, clearly resented. Moreover, it had never occurred to her to question seriously the family myth of his moral and intellectual superiority. Indeed, rather than resenting his elevated position within the family, Anna had always been very protective of it, defending his right to remain in the limelight to the exclusion of everyone else, including herself.

Over the years, Anna saw through her mother's mythic charm and relabeled her mother's haughtiness as a form of paranoia. She psychoanalyzed her father's jovial, Good Citizen persona and reinterpreted his optimism as a particularly insidious form of denial. And she certainly rejected the myth of Susan's Helpfulness and Creativity, suggesting that she was more accurately described as a controlling and manipulative woman, who combined her mother's contempt for humanity with her father's insatiable desire for social recognition. But Mark's reputation was inviolable. He was forever the Shining Star he was presumed to be, even though this identity of his invariably cast her in the dimmest of lights.

As Mark's baby sister, Anna never dreamed that she could compete with him on his terms but, rather, hoped that, if she avoided all controversy and was sufficiently sensitive to his feelings and tolerant of his idiosyncrasies, she might possibly win his favor. In compensation for subordinating herself, Anna would secure a permanent position within the King's inner circle.

So, in awe of her brother, who seemed to her larger than life, and who was certainly more worthy of her adulation than her all-too-human parents, Anna, a quintessential Pandora figure, painstakingly transformed herself from a rambunctious Troublemaker into a naïve and faithful Disciple, hoping in this fashion to be counted among the "blessed," rather than among the damned. As the Troublemaker, Anna was convinced that she deserved no better than this; indeed, any blessing she received was more than she dared expect. Then again, if she could win Mark's heart (or the heart of brother surrogates she would encounter later in the guise of friends), maybe she would not be so inherently unlovable after all.

A recent incident that occurred after Anna's father's funeral, when Anna was forty years old and Mark was forty-nine, suggested that Anna and Mark still occupied complementary roles within their family—she being the embodiment of Original Sin (titillating, but evil all the same) and he being the embodiment of Pure Virtue.

Anna, her mother, Susan and her husband, and Mark and his wife had gathered together for a solemn family dinner. The room was tense and there was little conversation, since everybody was making an effort to muffle feelings and get the gruesome event over with as painlessly and quickly as possible. From Anna's perspective, it seemed that all of them, herself included, were anxious to pretend that nothing out of the ordinary had occurred, in memory of her father's glibness. They didn't want to have to contemplate what would happen to Hazel now that Joe was gone and she still couldn't drive herself to the supermarket, and they didn't want to have to confront the fact that the obituary in the local newspaper told only part of the story of Joe's life—the nicest part.

But in order to keep the myth going, the myth that everything was and always had been and always would be just peachy keen, they had to push most of their feelings into a closet in their minds where they would not have to see them clearly or test them against reality.

Anna's family had always been uncomfortable with strong emotions, even the happy ones. This is one reason why Anna, the Volatile one, the family Actress, was viewed as such a Troublemaker—she was too damn emotional! Under circumstances such as these, however, the collective anxiety had reached an intensity that made it difficult for the family to pretend any longer, and the atmosphere over the dinner table was so electrified that it seemed as if the smallest spark of life could set off an explosion.

At a certain point, Anna's mother, appearing particularly restless, opened the window wide, though it was wintertime, remarking on the thick cloud of cigarette smoke in the air. She leaned over to ask Anna, who was sitting nearby, if the open window disturbed her, and when Anna replied that it did not it was left as it was. Nearly an hour later, as the family awkwardly lingered over coffee, Mark sneezed, startling everyone and momentarily jolting them out of their individual reveries. Angry and embarrassed at having to look directly in one another's eyes, everyone shifted uneasily in his seat, and Anna's mother jumped in quickly to quell the family's anxiety: "Well, Anna said she liked the window open." In the tradition of ancient peoples, Hazel found a scapegoat and sacrificed her to avert disaster and ensure the group's survival.

Mark sneezed and Anna got blamed! Surely Mark, the Shining Star, the Responsible Citizen, his family's ticket to "glory and a name," could not be held accountable for having so indecorously interrupted the silent vigil around the dinner table. Nasal passages, mucus, infectious diseases were not of his pure realm; the fault must lie elsewhere. Anna wanted the window open, and she must have let the evil spirits in. A perfect story for a modern-day Pandora.

Because Anna believed that if she were not Nothing she would have to be a Troublemaker, she was forever ambivalent about asserting her desires (that is, she was ambivalent about being Something), and when she was successful at what she did the pleasure she experienced was dampened by feelings of shame and guilt. She was convinced that her gain was by definition someone else's loss—her brother was sick because she liked fresh air; her mother was exhausted and frazzled because she had the audacity to learn how to walk; and her sister had to put up with a copycat who not only tried to imitate her but who had her own foolish ideas, which put a crimp on Susan's freedom and encroached on her psychic territory.

The least that Anna could do, if she had to be Pandora, was to subvert her own initiatives, and smother her desires or, if she had to assert her will, to feel properly contrite. She couldn't let anyone know, not even herself, how confident she was and how good she could feel. She had to play the Bumbler, and feel anxious even if, objectively speaking, there was no need to be. Then, within her mythological framework, they could all smugly laugh about her irrepressibility and not feel so badly about their own repressed impulses and constricted lives.

Anna's role as someone else's satellite has not been limited to her relationship with her brother. Ironically, being cast as the family nuisance, the selfish Troublemaker, had inspired Anna to prove herself to be otherwise, and in her friendships she was self-denying and "unselfish" to a fault. Like the bulimic Sherry, Anna hoped to wipe out the effects of one mythic identity by substituting another in its place.

Still somewhat mystified at her own behavior, Anna reflected upon a seven-year friendship with an older woman whom, retrospectively, she perceived as exceedingly self-involved. It was many years before it even registered with Anna that their friendship was predicated on the assumption that Elaine was the more dynamic of the two, and that, consequently, only Elaine should be the focus of their mutual interest. And even then Anna only gradually realized the extent to which she had stifled her feelings in order to preserve the illusion of intimacy between her and her friend—it had come so naturally to her.

But as Anna's own image of herself as Pandora turned Pollyanna began to shift to a more realistic one, Elaine's vivacious personality began to look more like just plain narcissism, and, rather than being fascinated by her friend's sparkle, Anna began to feel bored and angry and even repelled by its artificial glare.

These feelings crystallized when Anna and Elaine were vacationing together one weekend and Anna slipped out of her customary role and began to talk about her life, not just her friend's. Immediately Elaine's eyes glazed over and, without skipping a beat, she countered Anna's modest claim for recognition with one of her own. As she launched into a detailed dramatic narrative about problems *she* was having with her current business partner, Elaine managed to push Anna back out of the spotlight into which she had so briefly and indecorously strayed.

After that maneuver, the weekend went from bad to worse. That evening, when Anna expressed a desire for a light, informal dinner instead of the usual four-course French banquet Elaine traditionally indulged in on vacation, there was no going back. Customarily, Anna would have automatically accommodated herself to Elaine's wishes, dismissing her own preferences before even taking stock of what they might be. This time, however, Anna did not back down the instant she sensed that Elaine was bristling at her suggestions; she did not apologize for her meal preference or make light of her wish to take a bike ride before getting ready for their evening out. Elaine was not interested in a bike ride and was irritated at Anna's idea that they have a more modest dinner; but, more significantly, she seemed *offended* by Anna's sudden claim to personhood—Anna had been essentially a shadow for so long.

Elaine defended her usual position as the Leading Lady by mocking Anna's "health-conscious" attitudes and "ascetic tendencies." Convinced that she, Elaine, was the aggrieved party, she felt justified in hurling insults at her traitorous friend, no doubt certain that she was merely speaking the "truth." How stubbornly and inconsiderately Anna was behaving, and how idiosyncratic were her desires. Why couldn't Anna be less "uptight," less "rigid"? What was the matter with her anyway? Why did she have to spoil the fun? In her friend's attack upon her character, Anna heard echoes of her family's accusations, and anticipated the same reproachful look she used to get from Mark whenever she fulfilled the family prophecy and proved herself to be the Troublemaker. But history would repeat itself only as long as Anna agreed to live as a mythical character, and at that point in her life she was no longer willing.

The women's friendship did not survive the weekend, and after years of regular, if lopsided, contact, Anna failed to return Elaine's infrequent phone calls, which was in itself out of character. As soon as Anna ceased functioning as Elaine's silent admirer, there was no basis for their intimacy. Within the relationship that had evolved between the two women, Anna was either Elaine's diffident disciple (there when needed, invisible when not) or a traitor in exile from her life. (More echoes from the past.)

As Anna attempted to understand how her friendship with Elaine assumed the form that it did, and why Elaine responded with righteous indignation to her fledgling attempts at self-assertion, she realized that she had played a significant part in creating the monster that she found herself in revolt against. Sensitivity to others' needs and unquestioning loyalty were virtues she had worked hard to cultivate. Her relationship with Elaine, whose opinions and desires were always accorded more respect than her own, was the mold in which many of her friendships have been cast. I believe, however, that the origin lies within Anna's relationship with Mark, the mythic Shining Star. His identity fed hers, and hers fed his. This was how the past was repeated without anyone's intending it to be, and how the family prophecy was fulfilled. Anna must deconstruct the myth of Mark if she is to dispense with her own mythic identities once and for all. Only then will she permanently discard those present-day relationships with Mark surrogates in which she recapitulates her unhappy past.

THE SELF-DESTRUCTIVE REBEL VERSUS THE STODGY TRADITIONALIST

In some family dramas, the Troublemaker plays opposite the Responsible Citizen, who proudly carries the family banner, which the Troublemaker tauntingly threatens to drag into the mud. Conscientiously following the straight-and-narrow path, upholding the family's sacred traditions, he hopes to squelch all signs of rebellion and undo the damage the Black Sheep has already done. Whether this character is ultimately considered a dullard and a prude or a paragon of virtue, patronized for his loyalty or commended for his diligence, will depend of course on the values of the parents. In either case, he represents the renunciation of all "animal" impulses, or, in deference to Freud, the embodiment of Civilization, whereas his sibling, the Impulsive Troublemaker, represents the Unconscious and Civilization's "discontents." (The thesis of Freud's *Civilization and Its Discontents* is that, in order to live as civilized creatures, we must sublimate our impulses and renounce a certain amount of gratification. However, as a consequence, we develop neurotic symptoms that express symbolically what we could not express openly. Thus, in order to live in harmony with our fellow man, we must pay in terms of psychic suffering.) Irrepressible but self-destructive Laurel and her stalwart but conventional brother, Ethan, are such a pair.

Laurel's response to her younger, "successful," and infinitely practical brother, Ethan, was completely different from Anna's, but then, his position as the family pragmatist commanded considerably less respect than Mark's. Indeed, it was Laurel, not her "boring" brother, who was originally singled out as her mother's confidante and her father's intriguing favored child. Laurel got the A's in the family, and though they never generated more than a perfunctory nod of approval from her parents, while her brother's A-'s and B+'s were praised to the skies, everyone knew that *she* was the exceptionally brilliant one, though she was also the ornery one who was doomed to go nowhere.

Rather than admiring her brother's worldly success and self-congratulatory attitude, Laurel voiced her mother's unspoken contempt for all things "conventional." He might have status in the eyes of his peers, but in her mind he had sold his soul. At least this is how she talks. Condescendingly, Laurel characterizes Ethan as one would a trained rat running an obstacle course: he tries desperately to reach the goal that has been set for him, agreeing to put blinders on so that he would not stray from the narrow path that has been prescribed; he (not she) is beholden to others, and trapped by his own fear of breaking the rules and losing out on some of the booty.

According to Laurel, Ethan was always highly competitive with her, and by her belittling tone of voice it was obvious that the feelings were reciprocal, if not openly acknowledged. Laurel recalls that in high school, when she got a 98 percent on a statewide examination, he insisted that the following year he would get a 99 percent. When he didn't, and got *only* a score of 96 percent, this fueled his envy, even though his articulate and rebellious teenage sister was still, despite her grades, the prime target of their mother's scathing criticisms. It seems that he was always characterized as an industrious if plodding type of child, and though he was commended for his perseverance and placid disposition, he wondered whether he wasn't actually the less favored child. ("The Tortoise and the Hare" could have been their fable, except that in Laurel's family it is ambiguous whether "slow and steady" *really* wins the contest in the end!)

Though nobody in the family ever seriously questioned Laurel's intelligence, Laurel least of all, it was generally agreed, once she reached adolescence, that her personality was an insurmountable problem, because she was not and would never be a good "team player," which of course Ethan was. As a rule quarrelsome, Laurel did not quarrel about this, and essentially agreed with the family portrait of her as a loose cannon. "I just don't know how to get along with people and end up offending nearly everyone. I guess I'm just too honest and don't know how to make small talk. I never really had many close friends, even in high school, and now there is nobody with whom I can really talk."

Unfortunately, life as a Solitary Genius was not an attractive alternative for Laurel. If it had been, it might have offered her a solution to her "problem personality." But both Laurel and her mother considered Romance and Love as essential ingredients for survival, and, despite her marginality, fears of loneliness and isolation kept Laurel bound to her particular mythological identity, and therefore to her brother's.

Laurel's experience of alienation from others was not, however, really so mysterious as Laurel would have had it appear, and she was by no means a passive onlooker to her unhappy "fate." In various work settings, for example, Laurel was typically convinced that her supervisors and colleagues were incompetent dullards who were uniformly threatened by her innovative ideas and superior intelligence. (In the myth, Laurel's specialness, like her mother's, is her undoing, and there would always be "Ethans" who would resent her "free spirit" and shrink in terror at her boldness.) And although Laurel insisted that she did her very best to be congenial—she smiled a lot and engaged in the usual office chitchat—she always has had the uneasy sensation that her fellow workers sensed that she was not one of them. "Magically," they picked up the vibrations!

The power of the self-fulfilling prophecy was never more evident than in Laurel's case, because, what did you know, the dirty secret of her difference *was* always discovered, and she always would end up the Outsider, who ate lunch alone at her desk and was gradually weeded out, excluded from the most critical company functions, and eventually allowed to drift out to sea. Just as in her relationship with her more conventional brother, Laurel figured as both a victim and a heroine. She was a woman "doomed" to be so daring she would be ejected from her group of peers.

The relationship between Laurel and Ethan mirrored the relationship between their parents, and though their parents got divorced when both children were well into their adolescence, Laurel and Ethan were obliged to remain brother and sister for life, and the sparring continued unabated.

Like Laurel, their mother had always prided herself on her creativity and her passionate feelings, and though she never found an adequate channel through which to express her special talents (the desert flower in the poem, doomed to "blush unseen"), she spoke with contempt for her husband's worldly success, which she attributed to his legalistic mind, prissy disposition, and rigidly disciplined work habits. (Thomas Gray, "Elegy in a Country Churchyard.")

So, although Ethan, like their father, had been able to achieve a modicum of fame and fortune, and Laurel, like their mother, had not, each child had a silent ally and antagonist, each a separate claim to superiority. As a Pandora figure, Laurel may have been perceived as a Troublemaker and an Outcast, but she found consolation in the idea that, like her mother, she was too much her own person, too completely original, to fit in anywhere. Ethan may have been a respected businessman, his father's protégé, and, at least explicitly, his mother's favored child, but he could not help feeling that his sister had the edge, having gotten off free and easy while he religiously reported to his desk at seven-thirty every morning. As Pandora and the Responsible Citizen eyed each other, they wondered who was the real loser and who the real genius in the family, and whether single life as a bohemian or married life as a yuppie was the more gratifying.

A scene that transpired over a recent family dinner is typical of how they continued to relate to each other from their respective positions within the family. On this particular occasion, a few weeks after Ethan announced his plans to marry the following spring, Ethan joined his mother in a full-scale attack on Laurel's "masochistic" character. By accusing Laurel of allowing herself to be once again dragged into the mud by yet another insincere and unscrupulous married man, Ethan assumed the role of the Levelheaded family expert on affairs of the heart. Laurel, convinced that there was some truth in what her brother was saying, and therefore good reason for his contemptuous attitude toward her and her lover, was left speechless, hanging her head like a guilty child in implicit agreement with his damning analysis.

How could she, the family Troublemaker, have defended herself against her virtuous brother's assault? And then, positioned "once again" as the object of her family's scorn and pity, Laurel only confirmed Ethan's theory of her "masochistic" character, limping from the dinner table crushed by her own guilt. The family's interaction was a perfect example of her reputed "masochism," in living color, as Laurel's mother and sister witnessed Ethan push Laurel into her usual corner while the look in her eyes begged them piteously for mercy.

But, disregarding the diagnoses of pop psychologists such as Ethan, Laurel, the self-destructive heroine of *her* mythology, brazenly disregarded her brother's "good advice," which was to "throw the louse out," and added her own twist to the drama. Overtly she deferred to her family's better judgment, to Ethan's Levelheadedness, to her mother's own painful experience, but covertly Laurel insisted that she would not be reined in by reason or by convention. She remained a Free Spirit, even if this meant that, in order to prove herself free, she must self-destruct. From Ethan's vantage point, his sister was as enviable as she was pitiful.

By figuring as the Seductress, the Other Woman, and the Emotional Mess in the lives of her married lovers, Laurel reproduced the feelings of mutual attraction and repulsion that characterized her relationship with Ethan, her "constricted" and insecure younger brother. According to Laurel, when she first met Marty (a married lover of seven years whom she had broken off with immediately before becoming involved with Brian, another married man), he was a graduate student on the verge of failing one of his courses, and Laurel leapt at the chance of rescuing him from catastrophe. As she got to know Marty better, she realized that he also needed to be liberated from a sterile marriage and a pitifully poor self-image. Like her brother, Ethan, Marty was both uncertain of his abilities and painfully embarrassed about his uncertainty. He desperately wanted Laurel to reassure him that he was intelligent and irresistibly attractive, but in order to save face he also needed her to pretend that she, not he, was the fragile one, and that she, not he, was on the verge of collapse and in urgent need of emotional support. This was a familiar routine for Laurel to follow: her brother had always clamored to be recognized as the stronger and smarter of the two. And though Laurel never consciously tried to allay her brother's anxiety or stroke his brittle ego, her role as Pandora did actually serve this purpose, among others. She was the Mess in their family, not he!

As Marty's young, brilliant, and sexy lover, Laurel imagined that she had the power to unleash his tethered spirit, and if in her efforts to boost his self-esteem she allowed him to trample on her own, well, then, that too was quite familiar: Pandora and her wanton desires deserve no better fate. Invisibility was the price she had to pay for her freedom. (Just like Anna.) Her claim to superiority sneaked in through the back door. (Just as with Ethan.)

Laurel's relationship with Brian, her second married lover, was somewhat different, but again she figured as the Bohemian in disarray, whose untempered sexuality had the power to ignite a flame within the heart of an all-too-Responsible Citizen who for years had been allegedly dying a slow death. (His marriage was also devoid of passion, at least according to Laurel's account.) As in her relationship with Marty, Laurel's undomesticated "passion," her self-recriminations, her intellectual arrogance, her failure to adjust at work, and her unwillingness to censor her opinions in order to avoid offending the sensibilities of others, complemented Brian's emotional constriction and were the basis for their mutual attraction and repulsion. Like her brother, Brian envied Laurel her apparent spontaneity (if only he could be as outrageous as she was), while Laurel envied Brian his apparent stability (if only she could be safely married with children).

When, at various points in their relationship, there appeared to be a reversal of roles, with Laurel seeming to be the more stable and successful of the two, immediate action was taken to rectify matters and to restore the original relationship pattern. It made Laurel uneasy to see herself steadily progressing in her career when Brian's was at a stalemate, and he, not she, was feeling at loose ends and panicked.

It was not simply "success" that made Laurel anxious but, rather, the perception that she was slipping out of character, and hence out of her customary way of relating to men. This concern extended well beyond the workplace. She admitted to having felt uncomfortable with Brian during their first weekend of illicit love, when she discovered that she could easily overtake him on a bicycle, he being overweight and out of shape. Wasn't she supposed to be breathless and, literally and figuratively, on the verge of collapse? How could she possibly know what to say to him when he was obviously panting for air and, what's more, embarrassed by it? Paradoxically, the more stable she felt within herself, the less secure she felt in relation to Brian.

So, just when things got cozy and Laurel began to feel grounded, Brian, the Responsible Citizen, the Practical Guy, the Business Sharp, would distance himself from her, and, in near-perfect disharmony, Laurel would orchestrate a crisis and fall apart. Miraculously, they were back on old familiar ground, in the land of mythology: she was Pandora, making trouble and "in trouble" once again, and he was the Responsible Citizen, in control and safely ensconced in domesticity. She shivering on the outside, he in the pressure cooker on the inside—it was just like childhood with Ethan!

THE MINISTERING ANGEL VERSUS THE "SOUL IN PAIN"

Ministering Angels are the embodiment of Unconditional and Transformative Love. They exist in order to prove that love has the magical power to uplift even the most fallen of souls, and they need fallen souls to make this point. An Upstanding Citizen such as Ethan is symbiotically tied to a Pandora such as Laurel, whom he can reproach for brazenly violating the accepted rules of decorum; a Shining Star such as Mark finds his counterpart in a Guilty Troublemaker such as Anna, who agrees to enter his orbit so that his radiant light may purge her of her sins. But a Ministering Angel, such as Julia aspires to be, needs a previously unidentified Buried Talent and Lost Soul to fulfill her mission. Her dead brother, Brendan, was the prototype of the Undomesticated Mystery Man, the Prince disguised as a Beast. And though Julia was unable to rescue him, she was able to re-create their relationship and affirm her mythological identity time and again, if only some Soul in Pain would cooperate.

Julia came to me explicitly denying that she had any need for psychotherapy. She was, as mentioned earlier, seeking couples counseling for her and her latest boyfriend, Peter, to whom she had devoted the last year or more of her life.

Peter was a recovering alcoholic who, with Julia's strenuous encouragement and round-the-clock support, had recently become sober. A disheartened musician, barely able to make ends meet by occasionally writing jingles for television commercials, Peter was a virtual recluse before Julia insinuated herself into his life and identified him as a Buried Talent. They had known each other by face for years before they finally got together, living in the same neighborhood and frequenting the same local health-food store. Both were vegetarians, and once there was even some vague mention of having tea together, but this was not followed up at the time.

After Julia's marriage broke up, however, her chance encounters with Peter at an all-night grocery, or on her way home from work in the evening, assumed new meaning. His forlorn look, his remote smile, and his pale, almost translucent skin must have touched something within her, because she found herself plotting to bump into him "coincidentally" at their favorite haunts, and in no time concluded that she had fallen deeply in love. With a resoluteness that Peter himself was unable to muster, Julia applied herself to his recovery. Even if nobody else cared to look beneath the surface, *she* had done so, had penetrated the icy façade (at least in her imagination); she became intent on freeing the anguished soul within, which was systematically being drowned by drink.

Success did not come easily for Julia (nor had it with her brother), but after a number of relapses that brought Julia rushing out in the middle of the night on a moment's notice, Peter began to emerge from his glacial cave. Leading him out of the lower depths in which he had dwelt for more than ten years, holding his hand every step of the way, Julia rejoiced at his transformation, naturally expecting to continue to help him "reclaim his life" and find his soul (and hers) forever after.

Life, however, does not ordinarily conform to fairy tales, and things did not go as Julia had imagined they would. Peter no longer needed her to cajole him out of his apartment once he began to attend AA meetings every evening, and since he was seeing an AA counselor for individual and group sessions at least twice a week, Julia's central role as his spiritual guide was rapidly being usurped. Having been "saved," Peter no longer needed Julia to save him; moreover, since it was no Prince that she had unearthed but, rather, a wounded, angry, and mistrustful little boy who had been frozen in time, he had no intention of playing the part of Prince and completing *her* myth. He had his own drama that he needed to play out.

So, while Julia was openly fantasizing about having Peter's baby someday, in the not-too-distant future (this was her "pound of flesh"), now that the Beast (alcohol addiction) had been defeated, Peter was becoming increasingly remote, even hostile. Ironically, Julia would fail with Peter just as she failed with her brother, Brendan—both men would forever be inaccessible to her, leaving her to be a perennial Beauty figure in search of another bewitched prince.

"LADY" AND THE TRAMPS

When a family consists of Ne'er-Do-Wells of all varieties—Prodigal Sons, Victims of Abuse, Parasites, and Sorry Saps—it is in dire need of a saintly figure who, not afraid of dirtying her hands as she descends into the bowels of hell, nevertheless remains miraculously uncontaminated by what she encounters on her mission.

Only such a figure is capable of sustaining a glimmer of hope in everyone. Helen became such a character—an Idealist among Cynics, a Tower of Strength among Cowards—though her psychiatric problems are testimony to the fact that, in the long run, such an identity is untenable and despair is indeed contagious.

Helen, whose family nicknamed her Lady, lived a very different life from Julia, and outward appearances gave no reason to suspect that their unconscious images of themselves would be similar. Julia, who was white, middle-class, and well educated, projected an image of innocent delicacy; in contrast, Helen, who was black, poor, and the only member of her family to have earned a high-school diploma, initially impressed me as dignified, stoical, and just plain good. Nevertheless, since both of these women functioned as Ministering Angels in relation to distinctly un-Angelic siblings, their adult friendships as well as their love relationships bear a similar stamp.

Helen was one of nine children, all born out of wedlock, all with different fathers, and all fated to spend the first years of their lives scrambling for recognition and affection in a home where both were in scarce supply. From the stories that Helen would tell me, I was able to see how each of her brothers and sisters had, over the years, devised a different strategy by which to achieve that end; all had carved out distinctive roles for themselves, and these roles psychically connected them to one another while simultaneously providing them with the illusion that they were each unique and indispensable. There was the Baby, the Drone, the Gigolo, the Bitch, and the Wise Guy, among others. And then, of course, there was Lady.

Helen's mother, Eunice, was only fifteen when she had her first child, with Helen coming next, when she was seventeen. Whether Helen, as the oldest girl, was unofficially selected by her young mother for her role as the Lady (whom I see as very similar to Julia's Beauty), or whether Helen gravitated to it herself in response to the family's urgent need for such a figure, is unclear; probably both factors were operative. In any case, the myth evolved over the years, and nobody in the family argued with it or competed with Helen for her special position as the Spiritual Guide. Indeed, as long as everyone could believe that Helen was uncomplicatedly good and yet undaunted by the evil around her, there would always be a faint glimmer of hope that the future had better things in store: Helen would take it upon herself to transform things magically, and nobody else had to take responsibility for change. All the others had to do was allow Lady to do her work.

As Helen described it, her mother's home was a caldron of seething emotions that always seemed on the verge of bubbling over but never actually did. Indeed, retrospectively, Helen felt that it would have been a tremendous relief had some of the feelings gushed out and the family forced to confront the mess that was brewing. Instead, the atmosphere remained unrelentingly thick with discord of a sort that was never clearly identifiable, let alone articulated. The chronic state of disorder that Helen's mother seemed to thrive on functioned as a smoke screen, keeping the inhabitants of the household in a perpetual fog. Blinded to what was actually going on in front of them, they spent their time imagining this or plotting that, never sure of what they were seeing or where they were headed.

Everyone was kept in a state of unrelieved suspense because, for one thing, the composition of Helen's family was in constant flux. New men were always entering and then exiting precipitously from the picture. New babies were being born, and others suddenly were sent off to live with relatives for indefinite periods of time. Chaos bred suspiciousness and envy, and relations between mother and children, brothers and sisters were as in a mythic jungle: one child's loss was another child's gain, and survival at any cost was paramount in everyone's mind. Amid this horror, the stage was being set for the appearance of a Beauty figure, a Ministering Angel to deliver them all from this earthly hell. Only a saint could possibly sustain the faith in a family like that.

In the family myth, Helen was such a character. She was good, sensible, and self-sacrificing, and though her mother was eminently unreliable, a greedy, undisciplined child herself, Helen could always be depended upon to lend a sympathetic ear (or her last dollar) and to pull the others out of the muck they were constantly sinking into.

In contrast to her siblings, who were street smart, ruthless, and parasitic, Helen was simple, pure, and gullible. Moreover, she has conducted her life as if these qualities existed independently of her volition, now and forever. Real people change in response to varying circumstances, but Helen had locked herself into her mythological identity and could not.

Despite her bad experiences as the family's Ministering Angel, Helen stubbornly continued to bend over backward to help her sisters and brothers as well as her mother, her girlfriends, her children, and the various men who came in and out of her life. It was as if she did not know better and could not do otherwise. Surrounded as she was by siblings who figured as Drones, Gigolos, Babies, and Bitches (mythical figures in their own right), Helen had become an object of reverence as well as an easy prey in relationships outside her family.

Helen complained that her girlfriends called her on the telephone in the evenings expecting that they could speak to her for hours on end of their problems and intrigues. Whether they were embroiled in a financial or a romantic crisis, or whether they were simply bored and had gotten into the habit of using Helen to fill in some empty time, they rarely called to ask her how she was, and failed to notice (or, if they did notice, seemed not to care) that Helen spoke scarcely a word about her life or her troubles and rarely voiced an opinion of her own that could have been considered in the least bit controversial. But, perhaps more significantly, Helen hardly noticed it herself. If her friends never thought that she might have been exhausted after a long day on the job, it was not surprising, since Helen ignored her aching limbs and growling stomach. She imagined herself as a Ministering Angel, and an angel is pure spirit and lives on hope alone.

Helen's grown children treated her similarly, assuming that she could baby-sit for her grandchildren at a moment's notice. And why shouldn't they? She always did. When they came to visit her, at their convenience, they sat passively while their toddlers wreaked havoc in her immaculate house. It never occurred to her sons or her daughters-in-law to offer to help Helen clean up the children's mess afterward or replace the broken knickknacks that Helen deposited in the garbage without a word of reproach.

And even as an adult woman, divorced, with two adult sons and two grandchildren of her own, when there were holidays, birthdays, family barbecues, and family crises (and there were always crises), Helen continued her rescue mission in relation to her numerous siblings. With each visit back to her mother's house, where various brothers and sisters and grandchildren continued to live as transients, Helen hoped finally to break the evil spell that still had the power to cast a pall over her life. She wanted desperately to transform the ugliness she saw into something beautiful.

So Helen listened, advised, and gave what little money she had. She cooked and served and then washed the dishes, and never expected anyone to listen to her or to lend a hand. Predictably, none of her siblings volunteered, and Helen retreated to her home utterly depleted, a saint and a martyr. Her only escape from the mythological identity she had sustained over the years was her "depression"; it was her only opportunity to abdicate responsibility for other people's salvation.

Perhaps like Julia, Helen was terrified to discard her mythological identity, afraid that, if she stopped being so unworldly and so virtuous, stopped playing the Lady, she would discover the "beast" within her own personality. Were she to be angry, or demanding, or simply unavailable or indifferent to other people's suffering, how could she or anyone she knew ever manage to preserve hope? And without hope, however delusive, she felt as if she would go crazy. In her experience, growing up as she did amid a collection of pathetic and unsavory characters, life outside her myth did not appear to be worth living.

Of course, differences between brothers and sisters in disposition and abilities are not merely figments of parents' imaginations, though parents may misinterpret their significance and magnify their extent. Indeed, mythological identities may just as soon arise when real differences are ignored rather than exaggerated, when parents expect all their children to conform to one particular mold of humanness without regard for their individual strengths or weaknesses, interests or aversions.

The "deviant" child, the child who does not readily conform to his parents' expectations of what *their* child should be like, may come to believe that just being different from his brother or sister is tantamount to being not fully human. He may eventually conclude, based on his observations of those around him, that *he* is abnormal; after all, within his family culture he *is* outside the norm. Look at how easily his brother (or sister) has picked up the mother tongue, while he still stumbles over his words and speaks to his family as if in translation! Larry's "sensitivity," for example, might have stigmatized him just as much had it been denied altogether instead of magnified. Either way, his being "emotional" separates him unduly from his tough-skinned and practical-minded siblings, who are indubitably the way people are supposed to be and who are therefore presumably "normal."

Despite the deviant's attempt to blend in, to pretend that he is one of the guys (and Larry did try), he remains convinced that he is really an alien creature. His parents' inability to understand him can mean only this. As he watches his "well-adjusted" brother or sister make friends, find jobs, accumulate all kinds of medals, his identity is confirmed, and he feels fated to remain forever a stranger in a strange land, where he can be either an impostor or a freak.

THE DELICATE FLOWER VERSUS THE SALT OF THE EARTH

To dream is to be human, but some people, whom we call Dreamers, seem more suited to life in the ideal world of the imagination than life on this planet, with all its ups and downs, its pleasures and misfortunes. The Levelheaded Pragmatists, the Robust Sensualists seem to be able to endure (or is it deny?) the painful realities that are an invariable part of life on earth. But the Sensitive Plants (and in big families there is usually one) threaten to crumble, because they are so finely attuned to their feelings and keyed into ours. They give voice to their sturdier sisters' and brothers' pain, defend their ideals, and create the art and music their siblings enjoy but have no time to create for themselves as they busily navigate in the world of dollars and cents. These caricatured figures are Seers but also Sacrificial Lambs, embodying Beauty but also Weakness, in families that have lost touch with their spirit and ignored their vulnerabilities.

Larry, the Sensitive Plant, the Mama's Boy, the youngest in a family of eleven, was, in his experience, surrounded by brothers and sisters who, unlike him, were hearty souls, robust, unsentimental, and extremely practical. *They* never seemed to depend on anyone (certainly they never cried for Mama), priding themselves on their ability to laugh off life's disappointments. Born with thick skins and nerves of steel, Larry's brothers and sisters did not seem to feel the pain that Larry felt so intensely, and thus they could endure what he could not. Indeed, from Larry's admittedly distorted perspective, nothing ever seemed to faze them, neither a heart attack at forty-five, nor a child's death by an overdose of alcohol, nor their father's murder. (After a long history of philandering with the daughters and wives of his neighbors, Larry's father was finally gunned down when he was sixty-six years old!)

Since Larry's siblings set the standard of normality within the family, he was considered, by comparison, endearingly fragile, foolishly idealistic, and unreasonably oversensitive. Whereas five-year-old Larry moped miserably in the corner of his bedroom while his mother calmly went about her daily chores without him, he remembered his brothers airily doing what boys were *supposed* to do: they wrestled, they got into scrapes, they chased girls, they sneaked cigarettes, and they set up cockfights in the neighboring backyard. If their father caught them and gave them a beating, they didn't seem to mind the bruises, nor did anyone else really take it all that seriously; it was part of growing up and becoming a man.

Of course, as Larry grew older, he tagged along and even tried to mimic his older brothers' brazen self-assurance, but he was never convinced of his own prowess. How could he really be one of the guys when he was always weaker, always more sensitive, and when he really preferred to mind the goats on the family estate or carve little animals out of scraps of wood rather than to torment the neighborhood roosters or play practical jokes on the grade-school nerds? No wonder he ended up a "failure," a divorcé four times over, suffering from a "mysterious" seizure disorder, while they were all wealthy professionals who drank too much and didn't think twice about routinely cheating on their wives. In Larry's mind, it all made perfect sense: "We're programmed."

If as the Sensitive Plant Larry was the object of his brothers' gentle teasing, as he claims to have been, he was also the recipient of his older sisters' near constant fawning. Before his sisters married, they were all eager to rehearse being mothers, and Larry, as the family baby, was the perfect guinea pig. They would feed him, protect him from harm, and fondle him as his own mother rarely had time to do. If he was reluctant to join his brothers in their adventures, he found that one sister or another would happily play with him as long as she was able to dictate the rules of their game. He complied, with misgivings, soaking up their adulation as well as their subtle condescension.

Larry reported that a couple of his sisters and brothers still continued to flood him with unsolicited advice. His sisters advised him about food and women, instructing him as to how much he should indulge himself and what types (of food or women) he should stay clear of altogether. His brothers did the equivalent, though their lectures revolved around his "attitude" toward life: he took things too much to heart, he wasted his time on frivolous hobbies that went nowhere, he allowed himself to get unreasonably discouraged over minor setbacks, he needed to be shrewder in his business dealings, and he had to begin to understand the harsh realities of life and stop being so thin-skinned! He listened to the advice, agreed with the wisdom his siblings offered free of charge, and proceeded as always, as if he'd never heard a word.

Larry was tremendously ambivalent about his siblings' "concern" for his welfare, particularly once he became financially dependent upon them because of his seizure disorder. He was grateful for the presents of clothes, chocolates, and gourmet coffees that regularly arrived at his doorstep without his ever having to ask, and adamantly insisted that, without the monthly checks one sister punctually sent him, he would have had to dip into his meager savings to cover his rent. Nevertheless, feeling humiliated and also feeling incapable of extricating himself from this all-too-familiar humiliating position, Larry complained bitterly, but only to me, his therapist, about his sisters' nagging and his brothers' "homespun" philosophy lectures, which he felt were patronizingly pious. He had not rallied the courage to voice these opinions directly to his siblings but, rather, oscillated between feeling smothered and angry, and anxious and guilty. "They mean well. And who am I to say anything to them? What have I done with my life? I'd be out on the street if it weren't for their support."

Larry's ambivalent relationships with women over the years mirrored the ambivalent relationship he has had throughout his life with his seductively nurturing but highly controlling older sisters. Larry has been married four times, and, according to his own account, all of his wives were good and loving women who were highly intelligent and exceptionally capable, and eager to devote themselves to nurturing the artist in him. Larry's image of himself as hypersensitive, dependent, and unworldly made him gravitate toward women who enjoyed treating him as if he were the Sensitive Plant and Cuddly Puppy he presumed to be. Larry described a couple of his wives as "professional" women—one was his former college teacher, and another was a highly successful lawyer. (Significantly, this is the identical term he used to describe his brothers.) Both had already established themselves in their careers before marrying Larry. None of his wives were Sensitive Plants. At least initially, each of Larry's wives was willing to negotiate the harsh realities of the market place for him as well as herself, and, at least superficially, their needs complemented one another's.

Yet, as romance settled into domesticity, and Larry settled into his boyhood pattern in relation to his older and wiser sisters, who had loved him as they would love an adorably rambunctious little puppy, he would invariably begin to feel confined and restless. Secretly he planned his escape. What puppy wouldn't look for adventure, and then afterward search for another cozy pillow to curl up on when, hungry and tired, he found that he had strayed far from home?

If we try to see the world from Larry's perspective, from the perspective of the mythological family Baby and Sensitive Plant, the repeated dissolution of his marriages becomes intelligible. In each relationship, Larry expected to remain forever his adoring wife's favorite child—indulged, pampered, excused from assuming adult responsibility—for that was the implicit contract they had struck at the altar. But as the Baby/Sensitive Plant, Larry naturally became anxious and resentful. He objected to having to step aside and share the stage, even with his own children (he was Insatiable), but he also objected to being in the position of a child himself, more dependent on others than they were on him. Whether he was gratified or frustrated in his desires, Larry, as the mythic character, was destined to feel unfulfilled and to search futilely for paradise.

Rather than competing for his wife's attention or settling for just one piece of the maternal pie, Larry looked elsewhere, though never within himself, for emotional sustenance. Conveniently, another woman would appear on the scene (he had many sisters in his youth), and if she was unattached and free to devote herself exclusively to nurturing him, Larry would put himself and his life in her hands and fall passionately in love.

Under the guise of being an incorrigible Ladies' Man (a face-saving device he must have learned from his father), Larry the Insatiable Mama's Boy re-created his dependent relationship with his older sisters. With shame but also a sense of relief, Larry would flee from the older sister who had turned into a scolding mother and run into the arms of another adoring older sister, and history repeated itself again and again.

But the mythological identity that Larry was wedded to was not so easily exploded, despite his sexual bravado and fickle behavior in affairs of the heart. His conscience plagued him for his escapades, whereas his father's and brothers' consciences apparently did not. Sensitive and therefore empathetic, Larry saw his inconstancy as further evidence of his basic flaw, his guilt as proof that he was just a sniveling baby.

As a guilt-ridden divorcé, Larry regretted that he was the type of person who was tormented by regrets, but he was understandably uncertain whether he wished to be as hard-boiled as his brothers and his father appeared to be. His father was dead as a result of his cavalier attitude, and his brothers all had drinking problems and lives steeped in deception.

The myth of Larry's brothers' machismo was part of the myth of his fragility (a person was either one or the other, there was nothing in between), and this was the same myth that had seduced Larry into living a sheltered and diminished life, protected by various mythic older and wiser sisters who mediated between him and the world outside the nursery. If Larry gave up *his* identity, his entire sibling connection would be fractured.

Whether differences between siblings are unrealistically amplified or stubbornly ignored, the result will be the same. Mythological identities will develop at the expense of the real self, which, for protection, burrows itself deep underground. (It seems to serve no purpose here on earth.) But by locking ourselves into a fixed position in relation to our siblings, whatever that position is, we narrow our horizons in relation to the world at large. Thus positioned, we live and breathe our sibling stories every day of our lives, with sister and brother surrogates substituting for the originals when they are no longer physically present themselves. Friends, bosses, husbands and wives, even our own children bear the burden of history, as we try to rectify now the sibling relationships we lived long ago.

THE GODDESS VERSUS THE PIPSQUEAK

When one child is selected to play the role of family god or goddess, the other children are bound to feel diminished, inconsequential, and flawed by comparison. Unlike their exalted brother or sister, who appears to have transcended human limitation, they are fated to be merely mortal, and by some standards, albeit unrealistic ones, this constitutes a major blow to their self-esteem. Once one mythological identity has been created, it gives birth to another, as the child growing up under the shadow of the "perfect" sister or brother invariably develops a distorted image of the self. The myth of the Ideal child nourishes the myth of the Inadequate child, and vice versa, as each imaginary character depends on the other to sustain their shared experience of unreality.

Diana, the imperious Goddess, and her sister, the impotent if vocal Pipsqueak, eyed each other uneasily from their respective places on the family totem pole. But despite their mutual antipathy for hierarchical relationships, as long as Diana was perceived to be on top it was impossible for the Pipsqueak to get out from under, and as long as the Pipsqueak was firmly planted down below, Diana was obliged to dangle uneasily aloft.

If Diana, the Marble Statue, had had a sister or a brother, a mother or a father who had also been placed upon a pedestal and treated as a god or goddess, then perhaps as an adult she would not have felt so terribly lonely looking down at the world from her elevated position. But she didn't have a brother like Apollo or a father like Zeus, nor was she surrounded by such prepossessing female figures as Athena and Venus, who, being goddesses in their own right, could be companions of sorts.

Within the mythological world of her family, Diana's father was a physical and emotional Wreck, her mother was a simplehearted Peasant, and her younger sister was a Pipsqueak, whose hypersensitivity made her "cute," and whose frequent outbursts of temper only proved that she was impotent and locked her into a subordinate position in relation to her older sister.

Nobody within the family was Diana's equal—that was a given—and so, according to the family mythology, Diana was literally without a match. Although Diana envied her little sister's spontaneity and was fascinated by her emotional intensity, she could not take her seriously (nobody did), and she would certainly never consider changing places with her or even joining her for more than a very brief excursion into her inner world. For who in her right mind would choose to live on earth when she had already secured for herself a home on Mount Olympus?

Diana was only slightly above average in size, but she was an imposing woman whose presence seemed to dominate whatever space she entered. From my observations of her in group settings, I would have to conclude that people tended to feel dwarfed by her erudition, and as a consequence stumbled awkwardly for words, even if they were otherwise quite articulate. It was as if they felt, for some inexplicable reason, that they could not possibly measure up or know as much as she appeared to know. Perhaps it was Diana's abstracted way of looking through people that made them feel inconsequential; she rarely made sustained eye contact or seemed to feel the need to negotiate a mutual understanding.

Of course, Diana did not realize that her overconfident air set off feelings of inadequacy in other people; she only saw the result and mistakenly concluded that the world was largely populated by insecure bumblers whose egos had to be stroked and who could not rival her in intelligence or poise. Wasn't that what she had learned at her father's knee, and wasn't theirs the kind of idolatry she had come to expect from her little sister?

Although as a child Diana had complained that her sister was a crybaby and a copycat who always wanted to tag along after her, only to become frustrated and resentful because she just couldn't keep up, as an adolescent and an adult Diana cultivated just this sort of a following. Like Diana's sister, Diana's friends and even her lovers were more her admirers than her true companions; they reinforced her mythological identity rather than challenging it, frustrating her and demeaning themselves in the process.

A sister who is no rival is not threatening, but she is also a disappointment; like their father the Wreck, Diana's sister, the Pipsqueak, left a vacuum that Diana the Goddess felt compelled to fill. It was no wonder that Diana was so expansive and had to puff herself up to look so big—if she hadn't, there would have been too much empty space, and then everyone would have been miserable, awkwardly floating around in limbo.

Although Diana claimed to despise the imbalance in power that had characterized her relationships with her peers, saying that it reminded her of her "loudmouthed" father's unfair subjugation of her sweet but "passive" mother, as a mythological figure—by definition bigger than life—Diana behaved in a manner that encouraged this inequality. Because she automatically assumed that her opinions about politics, art, sexuality, or diets were the correct ones, she inadvertently engendered doubt in those who were less confident than she. There was no room for controversy, and eventually her friends submitted or else moved on. As a consequence of Diana's mythological image of herself, she was the natural object of adulation and enmity. Like that of any heroic figure, real or imaginary, her popularity ebbed and flowed in what appeared to be an endlessly repetitive cycle of infatuation and resentment.

Diana's relationship with her sister, the Pipsqueak, was the model for what was to come under the aegis of friendship, and the mold that Diana would eventually have to shatter violently. Although the Pipsqueak was in awe of Diana, she was also known to attack her, and on occasion even tried to scratch the Goddess's eyes out. The game of Monopoly was the unlikely precipitant of these outbursts. Diana repeatedly beat her sister at this game, which thus became a metaphor for their entire relationship. The perpetual Loser could not endure the pity and contempt she saw in the eyes of her sister, the perpetual Winner, and Diana's "Monopoly smile," full of pity and contempt, became a symbol of the tension between the sisters.

That the Pipsqueak could not tolerate always being the low man on the totem pole was obvious throughout the girls' childhood. Less apparent was that Diana was also tormented by her lofty position vis-à-vis her sister. However, years later, when the social climate presented a convenient vehicle through which to express her personal conflicts, Diana joined the "revolution," took up arms to defend society's underdogs, and committed herself to the leveling of all differences and the destruction of all hierarchies. By shedding the outward trappings of status and power, Diana attempted to cleanse herself of her experience as a sister, an experience that evolved out of both their mythological identities.

CINDERELLA AND HER STEPSISTERS

If it is now quite obvious that the expectations we bring to our relationships with friends and lovers bear traces of our early experiences as siblings, it should not be surprising to find that our experiences as somebody's brother or sister are bound to color our feelings about our own children as well. The Black Sheep may place unreasonable demands on his offspring to be the Shining Stars he never was, or may instead experience it as a betrayal whenever they resemble his successful and conventional siblings more than they resemble him. The Airhead may cringe every time her daughter gets less than an A on her report card, because it reminds her that her sister was the family Genius and that she was "just a pretty face." Her unacademically oriented daughter, whose grades are less than perfect, is damning evidence of the truth of her own mythological identity, an identity she now wishes to distance herself from. Each generation bears the burden of the previous one, so the Bible tells us, and conflicts between parent and child often bear the mark of conflicts that began years earlier between siblings.

Sonia is a young woman who sought help for her two-and-a-half-year-old daughter, Ariana, whose "wild," uncontrollable behavior and fits of temper frightened and enraged her. As the story unfolds, however, it is evident that Ariana's willful behavior took Sonia back to her own childhood, and specifically to her subservient position in relation to her elder sisters. Because she experienced herself as a kind of Cinderella figure whose spirit was crushed and whose desires were frustrated, Sonia had refused to set any limits whatsoever on her own high-spirited daughter, with whom she strongly identified. Yet—and this is the irony—in her desire to be compensated for past grievances as a child under the thumb of her two older half-sisters, Sonia created a situation in which she once again found herself catering to someone else, though this time it was a daughter. Although she loved Ariana and chose to dress her like a princess in a storybook, she also found herself having to struggle to contain those old familiar ugly feelings of impotent rage at being "forced" to admire someone else's pretty clothes, and "forced" to watch someone else get her way.

Sonia's responses to her daughter—her admiration, her fear of her temper tantrums, her angry resentment—had less to do with Ariana, who was only two years old and, like any normal two-year-old, was both egocentric and charming, and more to do with the sisters she made a point of never seeing again. They were also narcissistic and demanding, and they, unlike her little daughter, actually did have tremendous power over her, when she was a child herself.

Sonia lived with her two elder sisters from the time she was ten years old until the time she ran away to marry at eighteen. Her mother had left her family in Puerto Rico, hoping to build a better life for all of her children in New York City. Although she promised to retrieve Sonia, her youngest daughter, as soon as she had established herself in a home and a job, she never did. Instead, Sonia's younger brother was summoned, while Sonia's care was permanently if unofficially relegated to her two older sisters.

From her description of her two sisters, one of whom was married with two daughters of her own, it is apparent that Sonia has perceived herself since earliest childhood as a victim, a modern-day Cinderella with a rebellious streak. According to Sonia, there was never any affection between her and her sisters, who after all shared only a mother and not a father with her. So, when they reluctantly agreed to take care of her as a favor to their aging mother, who was desperate to make a new life for herself in New York, they felt that they had license to use her as they would a servant. And just in case Sonia mistook her brother-in-law for a potential ally, she was told at the outset that he had enough to contend with without yet another mouth to feed, and that she should be grateful to have any home at all.

Although Sonia was not much older than her nieces, they were pampered and fawned over, while Sonia was held responsible for most of the domestic chores. And, perhaps because she was pretty and popular with her classmates and her nieces were purportedly fat and terribly spoiled (just like the mean stepsisters in all of the fairy tales), Sonia was never permitted to spend time with any of the boys or girls in the neighborhood (lest *she* win the prince's heart while her nieces languished), but was expected to return promptly each day after school.

When, eventually, Sonia rebelled, dropped out of school, got pregnant, and ran off to America, not with Prince Charming, but with Ariana's poor but devoted father, her sisters told her that she was an ingrate and, what's more, that she had always been hysterical and crazy. Hadn't she failed all of her classes in the eleventh grade and gotten herself into "trouble," just as they had predicted?

And yet, despite Sonia's scathing indictment of her sisters and her sacred vow not to see them ever again, she did not challenge their portrait of her. She was, in her mind, what they said she was—an aggressive and selfish child—and, after providing detailed descriptions of her humiliation and her sisters' emotional abuse, she reproached herself for her moodiness and fierce temper. Even as an adult, Sonia seriously questioned her own sanity, and I adduced that this was the deeper reason why she came to me with questions about her daughter's.

Immediately before Sonia came to see me, Ariana had bitten an older cousin who had refused to give her a toy. This is not all that shocking, given that she was two and a half years old at the time. But Sonia felt so embarrassed by the incident that she was reluctant to allow Ariana to play with anyone at all, for fear that there might be another "shameful" episode.

However, despite her reproaches and her anxiety, Sonia's feelings about Ariana were by no means entirely negative, and as soon as she saw that I, the "expert," was not alarmed by her daughter's "aggressive," "crazy" behavior, she relaxed, and spoke glowingly of Ariana's strong character and intelligence. There was no question in my mind that, on some deep level, Sonia worshiped her devilish little girl, and that Ariana was slated to be her mother's revenge for her own mistreatment at the hands of her sisters.

Sonia had brought Ariana to our initial session, and from Ariana's carefully combed and fancifully ornamented hair to her colorful and frilly attire, it was immediately obvious that Sonia took tremendous care with her grooming and prided herself on having a beautifully coiffed little girl. Without a doubt, considerably more attention and money were spent on Ariana's appearance than on her own.

Ambivalent as Sonia was about her mythic identity as a Cinderella-like figure, she comported herself in a manner consistent with that image. Her clothes were drab and shapeless, and though she could not hide the fact that she was an extremely pretty woman, she seemed largely uninterested in trying to look attractive. All of her thwarted narcissism was invested in Ariana. It was not in the least bit surprising, therefore, that Ariana was becoming more, not less, tyrannical each day.

Inasmuch as Sonia identified with Ariana and burned at the memory of her own subjugation as a sibling, she had a secret investment in her daughter's "wildness," her rebelliousness, even her aggressiveness, but she also had more reason than most mothers to feel oppressed and enraged by her two-year-old's insensitivity to *her* desires.

The drudgery and the degradation that Sonia experienced as an adolescent at the hands of her older sisters inspired her dreams for her only daughter. But her pleasure in revenge evaporated when she found herself once again playing the part of the obsequious maidservant, this time in relation to her own child! One moment Ariana appeared before her as herself transformed into a beautiful Princess, and the next as a haughty and controlling Stepsister who ordered her around as if she were a veritable scullery maid. (Mythological identities in collision!) It is not unusual for a parent to try to balance the scales that were unbalanced in her childhood relationships with her siblings, and in the process to find that she has reproduced the very experience she hoped to reverse. Vicariously living through her daughter, Sonia could not bring herself to temper her daughter's narcissism, though ultimately she became its victim rather than its benefactor.

It is in our relations with our brothers and sisters that we first learn about freedom, justice, and equality. This is because, as siblings, we discover where we stand among our peers and begin to formulate answers to the question "Why?" Life may be disappointing and frustrating at times, but if everyone appears to share more or less equally in the disappointments and the frustrations, it is easier to tolerate, for it is not a reflection on our particular character per se but just a part of the human condition. As siblings, we come to the realization either that we are all in this together or that it is every man for himself and that we are all essentially alone and therefore somehow blameworthy.

In the process of comparing ourselves and our lots with those of our brothers and sisters, we begin to create a picture of the world as fundamentally just or fundamentally unjust, and a picture of ourselves as basically worthwhile or basically not good enough. In the matrix of our sibling relationships, we formulate an image of ourselves as one of the Lucky or one of the Unlucky, as one of the Oppressed or one of the Nobility, as an object of others' desires or as the subject of our own lives with the power to shape and then revise our identities as we see fit.

Finally, as siblings we learn about free will and determinism, about being different and being similar; we figure out whether to be optimists or pessimists, True Believers or Skeptics, Fighters or Peacemakers, Rebels or Upholders of Tradition.

Each day, over family dinner or over a game of Monopoly, or baseball, or paper dolls, we receive and send messages to one another about who we are and about who we expect one another to be. Because, as children, we tend not to be critical of what we see and hear, we often swallow these messages whole, without fully evaluating their merit or thoroughly digesting the implications they have for our future lives. Then, leaping from concrete experience to abstract formulations of character, we use the information we have gained to construct our personal identities, real and mythological.

In families where mythmaking is not the favorite pastime and where there is a high tolerance for ambiguity, we have the chance to discover what it means to be a real person rather than a mythological character as we get to know our brothers and sisters and see close up that they are made of flesh and blood, not cardboard. When, in the process of growing up alongside a sibling, we come to understand that he has as many sides to his personality as we have to ours, we will have laid the foundation for true intimacy later on in life.

Juxtaposed against our images of ourselves are our images of our siblings, giggling uncontrollably or sulking miserably, in play, in bed, in the bathroom, in the park, on vacation. Whether, as we grow up, we commit ourselves to carrying on the proud banner of the past or make every effort to unravel the skein and create for ourselves a new order, these images from childhood weave themselves seamlessly into our adult lives. In the world of the imagination, we cannot *not* be our brothers' and sisters' keepers, because they are always with us.

4

Falling in Love: Posthypnotic Suggestion and Finding Your "Other Half"

> What children have experienced at age two and have not understood need never be remembered by them except in dreams . . . but at some later time it will break into their life with obsessional impulses, it will govern their actions, it will decide their sympathies and antipathies, and will quite often determine their choice of a love object for which it is so frequently impossible to find a rational basis.
>
> —Sigmund Freud, "Moses and Monotheism"

The Greeks invented the god Eros, whom the Romans named Cupid, to explain the seemingly arbitrary and irrational nature of sexual love. By this poetic device, they solved the great mystery of why we love the ones we do by not solving it at all but, rather, by declaring that there is no logic, no predictable pattern, and that even gods and goddesses fall victim to the whims of an impulsive and mischievous little boy whose motives are rarely pure. Once we are struck by Cupid's golden arrow, there is no choice but to surrender to the mysterious force that propels us toward our fated lover. And, once afflicted, we surely cannot pause to consider questions of pain and pleasure, let alone evaluate whether the rewards of love are worth the risks.

Today nobody believes in Cupid, and perhaps nobody ever really did, but even more than a half-century after Freud "discovered" the Unconscious, the language of love is still shrouded in mystery; perhaps we too, as much as the Greeks and Romans, prefer not to delve too deeply into our motivations for choosing one "love object" over another. We refer to "chemical reactions," "electrical sparks," and other intangible happenings to explain why we "fall" in or out of love, or why we find one person irresistibly attractive and another not at all. Or, in reaction against such "romanticism," we rationalize our feelings, and speak of "common interests," "shared values," and other necessary but not sufficient causes for our attachments.

For the psychologically curious, none of these explanations satisfy, and though at times we wonder about the role of chance in all of this, if we are honest with ourselves we can sense that there is indeed a method to our madness, though it may be hidden from us and we do not wish to be held responsible.

When we "fall in love," whose arms do we imagine we are falling into? And when we repeatedly fail to find these arms and end up splattering messily on the ground instead, who do we imagine will be there for us, to bear witness to our injuries and maybe even nurse our wounds?

Freud, among others, has suggested that our experiences in love at very early ages are stored away for later use, and, without being fully aware of it, we learn how to love, whom to love, and how to be lovable by living and breathing the atmosphere within our families (see Jules Henry, *Pathways to Madness*, p. 37). Psychoanalyst Christopher Bollas speaks of an "idiom of care" that we imbibe in our early relationship with our mothers. He maintains that as adults we care for ourselves in the very same manner in which our mothers cared for us when we were infants (*The Shadow of the Object*). Accordingly, we treat ourselves tenderly or coldly, sympathetically or critically, lovingly or sadistically, as if we were following some posthypnotic suggestion given before we even had the capacity to say, "Yes, this is good," or "No, this is not."

But internalizing our parents "idiom of care" is not the only way we manage to perpetuate the past. We construct our lives and choose our relationships so that we continue to breathe the old familiar atmosphere (poisonous as it may be), convinced that we would not survive under different atmospheric conditions. And in a way this is true: our *mythic* identities would begin to disintegrate if we weren't able to enlist other characters in support of our drama.

As mythological characters, we do not exist outside of the myth or fairy tale. We have not learned that we can live and breathe on our own. Our very existence seems to depend on others, who, by loving or tormenting us, allow us to play out our destinies as they are prophesied. This symbiotic dependency is all very well for characters in storybooks, but it raises problems for real life. Real people are unpredictable and beyond our control, and in this world miracles cannot be counted upon.

To the extent that we are wedded to our personal mythologies, we must seek out companions who will confirm our fantasied images of ourselves. Only fellow conspirators can aid us in our self-deceptions and fill up the vacuum that our self-betrayals have left us with. We develop special antennae that pick up signals that may be invisible to the untrained eye as we go in search of our "other halves," and find husbands, wives, and lovers who seem to embody what has been forbidden us.

> Was she first a ghost before she constructed her own world of ghosts?
>
> —Christopher Bollas, *Forces of Destiny*

Before Laurel assumed the identity of the Troublemaker, the Outcast, and the family Mess, she had the distinction of being a "Speck of Dust" (scarcely visible), floating luminously at the edge of her mother's dreamlike existence. Indeed, Laurel boasted that she was so adept at remaining inconspicuous that during her earliest years both her parents seemed largely unaware she had any independent needs of her own. Since she was seen but rarely heard from except to echo a needy parent's sentiments (and Laurel claims that even as a small child she had a vague sense that her parents *were* very needy), nobody could accuse Laurel of stirring up trouble.

During Laurel's childhood, before her parents got divorced, Laurel's father figured as the Troublemaker in the house while her mother was the Tragic Heroine. *His* explosive outbursts of temper, *his* stubborn refusals to give in were identified as the source of the family's misery, as he repeatedly trampled on his wife's romantic dreams and she quietly harbored her grudges and systematically plotted strategies of revenge.

Initially, Laurel played a peripheral role in the drama her parents were embroiled in; however, as their marriage began visibly to disintegrate, after years of not-so-covert sexual infidelities on the part of Laurel's "passionate" mother, this began to change. Laurel became her mother's necessary comfort, someone who would presumably understand her and never criticize; it was to her Unassuming daughter, Laurel, that she entrusted her darkest secrets about her emotionally sterile husband, her "elusive" married lover, and her own singularly deep capacity for sensual love. Ironically, Laurel's *faceless* role as the family Security Blanket became her individualized stamp, her personal mythological identity, which she would re-create and then violently repudiate in her own love relationships.

As her mother's loyal subject, the mirror on the wall that flattered rather than told, Laurel became a master at emptying herself of her own feelings, and applied her considerable talents to boosting her proud mother's faltering self-esteem. Laurel's ability to make herself disappear complemented her mother's need to take up space (perhaps for fear of disappearing herself). And if Laurel felt dowdy and insubstantial, then maybe her mother's forced radiance might not appear so artificial; if Laurel felt unhappy with herself, then maybe her mother's bitter self-hatred would not seep through to spoil her veneer of arrogant self-assurance.

Even today that image of her own weightlessness, a necessary element in her relationship to her mother, threatens Laurel whenever she is unattached and out of love. Because she has no substance of her own, being alone is tantamount to disintegration. In her fantasy, Laurel could easily be blown away without anybody's ever noticing. Of course, the Speck of Dust is only a myth, but it is the original myth that continues to lie buried beneath the myth of Laurel as Pandora, the brazen Troublemaker, who, in studied contrast to the Speck of Dust, is dangerously seductive and impossible to ignore.

Ironically, as long as Laurel was willing to agree that she was Nothing more than a "ghost" in someone else's imagination, she was able to stake a claim on being Special. After all, her very nothingness made her indispensable to her mother, and distinguished her from her "hateful" father and conventionally successful siblings. If that wasn't love, it would have to serve as a substitute.

Over time, however, being needed was not compensation enough for being invisible, and though Laurel lost her mother's favor by materializing during adolescence, she hoped at last to create some semblance of a life of her own. What emerges from the alchemist's laboratory is Pandora; by assuming that mythological identity, Laurel repudiates the fate of slavish nonexistence while still securing herself a place within the family. As long as Laurel agrees to absorb all the blame for everything that happens to go wrong, she preserves her connection. (Her father was banished because he refused to assume the guilt.) Feeling Bad but perennially guilty is the price Laurel is willing to pay for an illusion of "freedom," and an identity she can call her own.

To be loved in her family, Laurel had to either be a Speck of Dust or else a Wild-Eyed Rebel who invariably falls into disgrace. Because neither of these mythological identities poses a threat to her inclusion in the family drama, Laurel can feel *relatively* secure as long as she is assuming one of these identities or another. When she looks for love outside the family, she wants that security, and so finds men whose needs mesh with hers—men who appreciate her special talents.

"When I was fifteen years old, my mother told me that I had terrible judgment, and that unless I relied on her I would bounce from one disastrous situation to another." Justifiably aggrieved, Laurel claimed that even at age fifteen she was aware that it was very destructive of her mother to make such a dire prediction. Nevertheless, Laurel has lived her life so as to fulfill the prophecy.

One way she has managed to do precisely what her mother warned her she would do is by gravitating toward men who, like her mother, thrive on feeling superior to her. Laurel has a knack for projecting the image of one who is in dire need of being rescued (after all, as a Fallen Angel/Ne'er-Do-Well, she is, isn't she?). And there are always certain kinds of men who will leap at the chance to take control of her mess and in the process ignore their own. With relief, they smugly observe that, in contrast to hers, *their* "houses" seem in good order!

It was *Marty's* poorly concealed vulnerability that first attracted Laurel to him, though, as we shall see, the myth that evolved within their relationship was that Laurel was the dependent and distraught partner whose life was always on the brink of unraveling. Marty was black and, unlike Laurel, who came from a background of privilege, Marty came from a poor and uneducated family. Marty was proud to be the first among his brothers and sisters to graduate from college and establish himself in a prestigious and lucrative field of work. But, according to Laurel—and, ironically, this was the basis for her attraction to him—Marty's ego was fragile and his psychic equilibrium rested tenuously on his ability to deny deep-seated feelings of insecurity. He worried that his colleagues secretly patronized him and were ready to finger him as an impostor were he to falter for an instant.

After marrying a woman whose background and ambitions were similar to his own, Marty had doubled his efforts to advance his career, consolidate his successes, and suppress any lingering impulses he had to defy the established system that he had been excluded from for much of his life. But the nagging sensation that something was missing from his life would not go away. And if Marty was expressly *not* interested in thumbing his nose at mainstream society, he was apparently tickled when he found Laurel, who was more than willing to thumb her nose for him! She dared when he could not; he compromised when she could not.

Laurel met Marty shortly after he had decided to pursue a master's degree in business by attending classes four evenings a week after work hours. He was stressed and nearly failing one of his courses, and Laurel guiltily confided that Marty (not she) looked as if he were on the verge of collapse. For all his flirtatiousness and bravado, Laurel realized almost instantly that Marty was a man in desperate need of a boost to his self-esteem. In fulfillment of her mother's prophecy, she was drawn to him like a magnet, pretending for both their benefits that she did not see what she saw. Neediness masked as arrogance was comfortingly familiar to

Laurel, and what started out as pity for a wounded giant developed into an irresistible attraction that kept Laurel dangling on the edge of Marty's life for more than seven years.

Meekly, Laurel offered Marty her humble services as a tutor and then as a lover, and quickly she became an essential, if insufficiently acknowledged, presence in his life (a Speck of Dust, but one that could not be blown away). As if by magic, she transformed herself into *his* slave, barely remembering that this was *her* strategy, and that when they met she was the one who had been confident of her abilities and it had been *his* life, not hers, that was careening out of control. But, after all, as long as Laurel felt so weightless, she needed to find a place to land, and even a life in bondage was preferable to floating aimlessly in space.

Just like Laurel's mother, Marty demanded that Laurel surrender up herself to him so that he could have the "illusion of control," if not over his life over hers. ("Illusion of control" is a phrase I first heard used by social psychologist Ellen Langer.) Marty expected Laurel to be available for him whenever he wanted her, whenever he could grab an evening away from his presumably unsuspecting wife, but, according to the rules of their game, a game they constructed together, he was free to come and go as he pleased, no questions asked. In return for Laurel's naïve devotion, Marty promised to keep her forever hanging on the periphery of his world, which was a familiar, if precarious, position for her to take.

If Laurel questioned Marty's commitment or asked for something above and beyond what was allotted her, he balked—she was not playing fairly by the rules! Laurel was supposed to be his Flattering Mirror, his Free Spirit, his love potion, not a Nag, or a Confessor, or a dose of truth serum. So, as soon as Laurel overstepped the boundaries that kept her just where Marty wanted her and where she had agreed to dwell—within the frame of his life but on its very edge—she was instantly transformed. His delectable piece of forbidden fruit had turned out to be poisonous, and his involvement with her threatened him with expulsion from the purer realm of marriage and family, a realm he was not willing to give up. His Bohemian mistress was a Troublemaker, and as such deserved to suffer for her transgressions.

• • •

Marty would accuse Laurel of not understanding the myriad pressures and obligations that he, a Virtuous Married Man and Father, was subject to (she had never had to shoulder the responsibilities of married life, and she wasn't black); moreover, she was unduly suspicious of his intentions, which were pure even if his behavior was wanting. How selfish and how destructive could Laurel be!

But before we see Laurel as a victim of abuse, we must point out that this situation enabled her to reconstitute her identity as a Troublemaker, a myth she was wedded to and would have been loath to surrender. With Laurel's collusion, Marty always succeeded in turning her arguments around, so that the fault lay within her and she was obliged to apologize and make amends. *She* was being provocative by making such unreasonable demands upon him, and in doing so *she* was spoiling their otherwise passionate lovemaking. If Marty could not always maintain an erection, she must be to blame, not he.

After heated protests and angry tears, Laurel would finally "come to her senses" and agree with Marty's judgment of her, remembering that, according to her mother, her own ability to judge was permanently impaired. And after agreeing that her desires for more time and greater commitment were at the root of all their troubles, Laurel would guiltily submit to Marty's superior will.

This tendency of hers to flip-flop from Pandora to that Speck of Dust and then back again repeated itself in Laurel's relationship with Brian, Marty's successor. He too demanded that she function as his faithfully unfaithful mirror, reflecting back to him just what he wished to see. He too expected his Bohemian mistress to devote herself slavishly to him, so that he could vicariously partake in her brashness at no risk to himself. And though Brian, like Marty, indulged in the myth of Laurel's Specialness, and reveled in her untamed passions and associated catastrophes, his admiration for her spirit went only so far. Just like Marty and just like Laurel's mother, Brian could not tolerate sharing the spotlight even with his own lover.

Brian needed to play the hero and to have a woman who would reflect that image back to him. Laurel sensed this, of course, and since his mythology fit neatly with hers she complied. She was his

Maiden in Distress, who felt guilty when periodically she rebelled against her identity and broke out of the castle in which she was supposed to be helplessly imprisoned, making much commotion and considerable damage.

Heroes need maidens who need to be rescued, and who in ogling them affirm their heroic identity. Such "heroes" were the men Laurel found best suited to play a role in her romantic fantasies. At her mother's prompting, Laurel had learned the art of idolatry, and in the process of learning the rituals she must perform and the penances she must pay, she came to realize that her idol depended upon her as much as she depended upon her idol.

Since in Laurel's mind love was fused with mutual idolatry, she believed that her power as a lover lay in her presumed powerlessness. As a consequence of her definitions of what it means to love and to be loved, Laurel has looked for men who are convinced that they themselves are really Nothing and who therefore need to see her as really Nothing too. "Falling in love," Laurel rediscovers her twin identities as a Speck of Dust and the embodiment of Original Sin. Her chaotic—or, as her brother would say, "masochistic"—love life is the natural outcome of these opposing images.

> Thus she had achieved a remarkable feat in discovering a husband able to express and carry into action all the aspects of her own needs and wishes that she had had to disown. . . . All that was forbidden to her she enjoyed vicariously, rather like a preacher engaged in the passionate pursuit of sinners whom he hopes to redeem for the many sins he is unable to commit.
>
> —Joyce McDougall, *Theaters of the Mind*

Howard needs to see himself as fearless, defiant, and uncompromising, consumed by some transcendental mission that glorifies his position as an inveterate Social Outcast and a Soon-to-Be-Heroic Underdog. Having developed special antennae designed specifically to pick out any potential allies or antagonists, Howard is continually reaffirming his mythological identity as he wages battle against the Powerful and their followers, the Impotent

Conformists, and falls in and out of love with them both.

Being the ultimate hybrid of a cynic and an idealist rolled into one (he trusts nobody and yet dreams of utopia), Howard finds himself attracted and repelled by both cynics and idealists, who together express his own ambivalent relationship to himself and the world. He revels in the defense of the defenseless innocents (whom he both loves and scorns), and though it infuriates him that their trusting "good nature" makes them vulnerable to exploitation (as did his), they provide him with the opportunity to vent his spleen. (He needs one of these "pure" souls in his life in order to cleanse himself of his own suspiciousness and sweeten his own bitter vision of human relations.)

But although Howard claims that he would love to rid the world of all the cynics, who embody the darker aspect of his own personality, they are as essential for the enactment of his epic drama as the misguided idealists, and his life would not be worth living without them. As we shall see, Howard's wives and lovers fall into both of these categories, sometimes alternating between them, depending upon what Howard needs to see at any given moment.

Since Howard is perennially fighting a battle against imperfect reality (Solitary Idealist that he is), anyone who has agreed to bargain with the "enemy" may be considered a traitor, and Howard is never happier than when he can locate the traitor's vulnerable spots and puncture holes in his (or her) seemingly impenetrable armor. It is as if in the spilling of blood he pumps new life and new hope into his own clotted veins.

But if Howard despises the "worldly," and insists that he wants neither their fame nor their fortune, he also envies them their power and their complacency. Attracted *and* repulsed by women who succeed in this world because they are willing to strike a compromise, Howard cannot rest easy as long as they are resting comfortably on their laurels. Thus for Howard love and anger are inextricably linked, and sexuality is contaminated by the overriding desire for conquest.

Rarely missing a chance to prove that he is indeed his mythological character, Howard enlists his counterparts, the "innocent" and the "corrupt," to play their complementary roles. Various women have been selected, and their characters have been interpreted so as to inspire Howard the dramatist to reinvent his drama. These women must cooperate if he is to distinguish himself as the Solitary Idealist, who is a unique combination of pure spirit *and* shrewd intellect, and who, consequently, is relegated to a life of isolation and martyrdom. If his relationships fall apart and he ends up alone, it is because the pragmatic cynics of the world envy him his goodness, and the gullible idealists tremble before his power—or so goes the myth.

As Howard launches his self-defeating attacks against the less-than-perfect Powers That Be *and* their female followers, he means to proclaim that he is no weakling, in body, mind, or spirit, and that, despite all appearances, *he* is exalted, not they. This is his message, though his audience may not be able to decipher its meaning, seeing only that he flails his arms in impotent rage and is burned by his own fiery invectives.

Howard's protestations inadvertently express the distinctly *ignoble* identity that he believes is actually his. Weak and inadequate, the Black Sheep of the family, his father's "little bastard"—this was the identity that his parents foisted upon him, and the one Howard has vowed to purge himself of. Since this spoiled image of himself has become a part of his mythology as well as theirs, he feels compelled to defend and justify it by giving birth to a new transformative myth (the myth of the Underdog Soon-to-Be-Hero). But the old myth lives on, and Howard needs help if the transformation is to be at all convincing. His wives and lovers are chosen as his helpers, and they unwittingly validate the truth of his mythological revisions. They are not so much people as grist for his mill.

So, for example, sometimes Howard imagines that a woman is the embodiment of his heroic ideal—she is graceful and unflappable, gliding smoothly through life—in which case he feels envy and admiration for what he is not. He cannot rest easy until he has conquered her heart and with it incorporated her nobler identity. At other times, however, a woman will come to represent Howard's puny and ineffectual childhood self—she is awkward and insecure, tripping over her feet as she attempts to impress other people—and he is consumed by pity and contempt for that which he has shamefully denied in himself. Alternating between mothering his women as he would have liked to be mothered (tenderly) and mothering them as he actually was mothered (bitterly), he lives out the myth of the victim and the myth of the powerful hero, finding completion in both.

Howard's debased image of himself has its origins in his earliest experiences as a child loving his particular parents. But, as we shall see, he rediscovers this hoped-to-be-forgotten identity in his later experiences in love, as Howard the Alleycat/Underdog turned Knight in Shining Armor/Martyr uneasily embraces and then discards his lost "other halves."

The portraits Howard paints of his parents and his relationships with them are critical in understanding the origins of his personal mythology as well as his basic mistrust of women and of love itself. For this reason, we will postpone our discussion of his current love affairs until we have analyzed more extensively his early childhood misadventures, which set the tone for all later affairs of the heart.

Howard inveighs against his alcoholic father, whom he describes as both cowardly and sadistic, not unlike psychologist Theodor Adorno's now classic description of the "authoritarian personality," in which extreme arrogance and extreme diffidence go hand in hand (*The Authoritarian Personality*). According to Howard, his father ingratiated himself with his superiors, groveling for their benefit, quavering under their authority, only to turn around and abuse those less powerful than he. His wife and two young sons were the regular recipients of his blows and insulting remarks, and thus Howard's father managed to transfer his own feelings of degradation onto them. Howard has very little good to say about his father, who neither fit in with the surrounding culture nor openly rebelled against it. Indeed, he casts him as the prototype of corrupt power—duplicitous, lazy, and cruel—and appears surprisingly comfortable in his naked hatred of him.

When Howard speaks of his mother, however, he betrays feelings of sympathy, admiration, and even gratitude, and this although he describes her as a bitter woman whose endless demands on everybody, including herself, made her a master of humiliation and a slave to her own perfectionism. He appears more uncomfortable when he speaks of his mother than of his father, because it is his *love* that is a deep dark secret, not his hate. Love is what he associates with shame and weakness, and he does not trust himself to feel it. He imagines that if he had not loved he would have been free; ironically, there is some truth to this.

When Czech novelist Milan Kundera asserts in one of his philosophical asides that "He is free who is spat out from the sky and touches the earth without a pang of gratitude," he is proclaiming what Freud and many psychologists have intimated, albeit in less poetic terms, which is that *nobody* is entirely free, because nobody can possibly meet these conditions! (*Life Is Elsewhere*, p. 121.) Love and gratitude for simply being born connect us (sometimes against our will) to other people, namely our parents. In Howard's case, the connection is experienced as a ball and chain around his neck, but it is a connection nonetheless, and one he has come to recognize as love.

There is no doubt in Howard's mind that he was a great disappointment to both his parents, particularly his mother. Try as he might, he just couldn't measure up to her high standards, and his failure to be loved by one whom he loved so much is at the very root of his ambivalence about love itself. Whether it was his writing, or his drawing, or his gardening, or the way he kept his room, Caroline made it clear that Howard could never satisfy her, that he would always fall short of the ideal.

Of course, Caroline's picture of her son Howard as a Ne'er-Do-Well and a Drone had more to do with her feelings about herself, her husband, and her own life than with Howard. He was simply a convenient vehicle through which she expressed *her* frustration and despair. (*She* was déclasée; *she* was married to a man who refused to hold down a job; and *her* life surely did not measure up to her romantic dreams of the "aristocratic" household.)

Years later, Howard would follow in his parents' footsteps and use women as both his parents had used him—as a sponge to absorb their own self-loathing, and as a scapegoat by which they were able to postpone the inevitable dissolution of their marriage. Like his parents, Howard would abdicate responsibility for his own internal experience and deprecate one wife for being simpy and dependent, another for being cunning and manipulative, and would speak contemptuously (in his mother's tone of voice) of a lover's "pathetic" aspirations to rise in her career and be a "success." The biting critiques he offered of the women he had presumably loved at one time, only mirrored his self-criticism, which in turn mirrored his parents' irrational condemnation of him.

But as a child how was Howard to know that his mother's picture of him served the purpose of maintaining *her* psychic equilibrium? Or that it was based more upon her fantasy than on reality? He loved her and trusted her perceptions. Besides, he had to believe in her. As long as he agreed to take the blame for his mother's disappointment with him and thereby judge *himself* as sorely lacking, he could continue to love and to have faith in his mother's benevolence, and this was crucial. Having one malevolent parent was frightening enough, two would have been intolerable! There was safety in "identifying with the aggressor," and so Howard did. This meant, however, that he had to learn to disparage himself and to adopt the spoiled identity she handed to him—no backsies! (See Anna Freud, *The Ego and the Mechanisms of Defense.*)

If a readiness to assume blame in the service of "love" is "weakness," it is one that is universal to all children. But as an adult who still felt himself a child, Howard could not forgive himself that "weakness." His natural desire to love and to surrender in order to be loved is what troubled him most as an adult, and what he religiously defended against by living as if he were a mythological character with other mythological characters.

Howard stammered and his eyes flashed angrily when he spoke of how he "allowed" himself to be subjected to his parents' taunting criticisms (as if he could have prevented it). But to this day, they echo through the chambers of his mind, as Howard hypnotically joins in the ghostly chorus, drowning out the voices of his parents so that they are scarcely distinguishable from his own.

In what may at first appear to be tangential but turned out to be psychologically quite relevant, Howard spoke heatedly during one of our sessions of the Jews of Europe, who had, according to him, submitted passively to their own victimization during the Nazi era. "How could they have blinded themselves to their impending doom?" he wondered aloud with noticeable frustration. And why hadn't they realized that, by accommodating to the oppressor and assimilating into the dominant culture, they had set themselves up for their own destruction? Howard was not himself Jewish, but he clearly identified with the Jews as a marginal people who throughout history have been persecuted for being different. Like Howard, they have been a convenient scapegoat. But his identification went one step further, reflecting his own idiosyncratic interpretation of his childhood victimization. He has described himself as a childhood nebbish, the Jewish word for a pathetic, distinctly unvirile character. And just as he blamed the Jews for having "allowed" themselves to be gassed to death at Auschwitz, he held himself in contempt for having tried ever so hard to curry favor with his powerful and unsympathetic parents. It was as if he *should* have been able to disarm his oppressors, as the Jews *should* have been able to disarm theirs. His failure to rise above his circumstances was taken, moreover, as evidence of his real inadequacy, and, what's more, justification for his parents' contempt and abuse.

Ironically, by condemning himself for having been once a helpless child, Howard buttressed the family mythology, casting yet another black shadow across his face, and the mythical Black Sheep of the family appeared even blacker. Unreasonably, Howard reasoned that, in failing to defend himself against his parents' slanderous vision, he has proved himself unworthy of defense! Circular thinking at its best.

Writhing under the curse of childhood "weakness," dependency, and submission, Howard invented the myth of the fierce and unrelenting antihero as an antidote to the myth of the contemptible little wimp. His mother Caroline's stories of Howard's violent journey through the birth canal spawned fantasies about Howard's primal destructiveness, which were the earliest seeds from which sprang this alternative identity. When we recall how, according to Caroline, Howard "ripped her apart" when he made his entry into the world, it becomes apparent that—in his mother's eyes, at least—Howard's *only* power lay in his destructiveness (just like his father). And since, moreover, *his* auspicious beginning put an end to *her* sexual desire (a symbol for her ability to love and to have pleasure), Howard was conceived as nothing other than a curse, the harbinger of ill-times, a demonic form of Hercules. Indeed, Howard distinguished himself by his power to wrench his parents apart, not by his power to bring them closer together.

Constructing an identity around such images, Howard did not consciously wish to secure any positive recognition for his capabilities or achievements. This was an impossible dream that maybe his women could foolishly pursue as he watched from the sidelines. *He* preferred to be the radical, who undermined the "system" (whatever it was), who tried to "get away with murder" in pursuit of some noble cause and then was caught red-handed. In this manner, he declared a secret victory over his detractors. *This* was his special identity and his special achievement, the gift that nobody could take back. Fated to be "no good," Howard had embraced his fate wholeheartedly and unilaterally declared himself the winner.

This leitmotif has followed Howard throughout his life and set the tone for his relations with women. For, though Howard saw himself as a Solitary Idealist, a Knight in Shining Armor, his idealism only manifested itself through destruction. He smashed the false idols his women uncritically worshiped, analyzing their waking dreams and heartfelt ambitions until they appeared quite pitiful. But as he tore down the elaborate edifices they have used to inspire and protect them, he offered them little in the way of a substitute. (In the myth, he had the power to destroy his parents' corrupted love life, and yet was incapable of providing his mother with an adequate substitute.) As an adult, Howard never imagined that he could build something worthwhile with a woman, nor would he risk trying to create something beautiful. Once he had rescued her from the dragon (her parents, her boss, her parasitic friends, her shallow idols), he was at a loss for what to do next and could only wield his sword against her.

In order to cultivate his own personal mythological identity, Howard has found that relationships with other people must be carefully regulated. Living within a mythic frame, Howard has had to cordon off large portions of his personality and suppress many of the feelings that were central to his experience as a young child. Fear, envy, shame, admiration, and even love were among the various emotions he forbade himself to feel; they clashed with the idealized portrait of a heroic underdog, such as David in the

Bible, who, *despite* his unprepossessing figure and humble origins, slew Goliath and became a king. Nor are such feelings consistent with the image of Prometheus, another mythological figure who in my mind embodied Howard's ideal for himself. Like David, that bold and rebellious Titan risked his life to benefit mankind. *He* never faltered or compromised or tried to bargain with Zeus, the oppressively jealous father; Prometheus never regretted his deeds, though as punishment for stealing fire he was chained to a rock to have his liver eaten by vultures for millennia.

These were the images Howard valued; theirs were the virtues he extolled. Howard's own, less glorious feelings were by comparison debased, and since they were only proof that he was not what he dreamed he should be, they would have to be denied.

But the despised image of the Wimp lived on, and he wrestled with it perpetually. Howard's "unacceptable" feelings were not magically dispelled at will, but were cunningly disguised as *someone else's* experience, and thus continued to figure prominently in his life. Feelings of vulnerability and dependency, of inadequacy and subjection, his voracious hunger for recognition, and even his desire to conform and reap the benefits of belonging, found expression in his relationships with women. Not that he allowed himself these experiences as a husband and lover. Instead, Howard gravitated toward women who felt what he used to feel but would not allow himself to admit into consciousness; as these women acted out his impulses for him, Howard would watch, fascinated, offering advice, help, and scathing criticism.

Usually Howard was drawn to women who were as innocent and naïve as he was skeptical; as conventional as he was iconoclastic; as naked in their desire to excel as he was defended against his. A confirmed skeptic in love as elsewhere, Howard sought a woman so childlike in her trust and so dependent that he never needed to acknowledge that he still felt like the dependent, hopeful, and disappointed child he had been. As Howard alternated between supporting and bullying the women who embodied his secret unheroic self, he held on to this self, refusing to abandon it entirely in his "quest for glory" (Karen Horney, *Neurosis and Human Growth*).

In therapy, Howard spoke little of his two marriages, and his portraits of his former wives were remarkably one-dimensional. The gaps in his autobiographical account reflected his tendency to minimize the importance of other people in his life and deny any feelings of affection, loss, or sadness. His women were only supporting actors in his drama; once they had left the stage of his life, their individual features faded from memory.

After a brief infatuation with first the one and then the other, Howard was programmed (to borrow the language of another patient, Larry) to be bitterly disillusioned with both of his wives, and by his disillusionment justified his misanthropy and reclusive tendencies. Repelled by the very qualities that had attracted him to them in the first place, Howard vomited up the women he had hungrily incorporated into his life, just as he disowned large portions of his inner experience. By possessing them and then distancing himself from them, he reasserted the myth of who he was.

Howard met his first wife, Alice, during college, when he was "the poor kid on scholarship," brilliant, hardworking, and with a promising future. On the surface, she could not have been more different from him. Born with a silver spoon in her mouth, Alice was, according to Howard, a sweet but highly conventional Midwestern debutante, who appeared to him as a virtual princess. Entranced by her un-self-conscious gracefulness, Howard was determined to become her "frog-prince." In the fairy tale "The Frog Prince" by the Brothers Grimm, a hideous frog insinuates himself into the bed of a beautiful princess, who, after benefiting from his services, is repulsed by his desire for intimacy. Of course the frog turns out to be really a prince, who is ultimately embraced by the beautiful princess, who breaks the evil spell under which he has been cast.

But if settling down and raising a family in the suburbs of Michigan were consistent with Alice's image of herself and her future, it was not long after their marriage that Howard began to feel irritated by his wife's "sunny disposition," and uncomfortable in floating "blissfully" alongside her on top of the world. Where was the battle? And if there was none, what was he to do with all his heavy armor and sophisticated weaponry? They could stay in cold storage for only so long.

Howard's image of himself as the baby who, simply by being

born, ruined his parents' sex life and permanently extinguished his mother's sexual appetites demanded that his marriage suffer a similar fate. The light of the Shining Star was extinguished, as a sultry Howard cast a permanent cloud over his life.

Christina was the most recent woman to gain admission into the dark shadows of Howard's life, and he was living with her when I was seeing him in therapy. Unlike Alice, Christina was a kind of renegade in her well-to-do Southern family. Having abandoned the life of material comfort that was offered her, a life that included a "good" position in the family tobacco business and an array of eligible men who were offered up as suitable mates, Christina chose instead to live on the edge of society, slavishly devoting herself to "making it" in the big city as an artist and photographer. Howard thought he saw in Christina a fellow traveler, a kindred spirit in an alien world. I detected the ghost of Howard's mother, Caroline, hidden within the image he painted.

But their mutual attraction was not simply an attraction between like-minded individuals, though on the surface they seemed to share certain ideals and values. As much as they both led an unconventional kind of existence, and both conscientiously avoided making references to marriage or commitment or to the accumulation or sharing of wealth, they had very different relationships with the mainstream culture, and this, I suspected, was as much a factor in their "love" as anything else.

Whereas Howard was immediately suspicious of any person who had *any* sort of control over him—a traffic officer, a librarian, let alone his supervisors at work—and he proudly resisted complying with even the most trivial rules of decorum, Christina was diffident and self-effacing, ever anxious to remain in the good graces of those in charge, hoping that if she avoided all confrontations she too might one day share in their glory. Or so Howard reported, with more than a hint of exasperation in his voice. Could Howard have possibly forgotten that he had had similar expectations during college, and that his dreams of soaring to stardom were not so unlike Christina's?

Whether or not Howard recognized himself as he watched Christina arduously try to make her way in the New York art world, smiling bravely as agents condescendingly agreed to review her portfolio, he knew that he wanted to protect her from the ugly realities of the market place, and lay exclusive claim to her unstinting adulation and devotion. In her rebelliousness against her family he saw an ally; in her submission to the powerful he saw a victim. In either case, his mythic identity was confirmed by hers.

Christina was Howard by proxy—not Howard as we know him today, but Howard the innocent little boy, who was still gullible enough to believe in the future and dependent enough to want desperately to please and to succeed. And because Howard loved and hated that image of himself, an image of vulnerability that of necessity he plucked from his own mind's eye, he also loved and hated Christina, whom he wanted to control but could only control when her need to be defended complemented his need to defend.

Although Howard depended on Christina to be his timid maiden, exploited, insecure, and in urgent need of rescue, he found himself repelled by her dependency ("She's too insecure, too wishy-washy") and was continually fantasizing about some bolder, prouder, tougher woman whom he thought he caught glimpses of far away on the horizon. It was not an accident, however, that this fantasy woman never really entered into the reality of his daily life. (His first wife was the closest facsimile, and look what disgrace he had heaped upon her!)

Each time Christina actually approached success, by signing a contract or winning some praise for a job well done, Howard experienced her achievement as a betrayal of their secret pact. He may have complained when Christina allowed herself to be taken advantage of, but he vilified her ruthlessly when she managed to reap some tangible benefits from her efforts to "make it." Then her worldly aspirations were not merely pathetic; they became evidence of her capitulation to their common enemy, and her unwillingness to live his myth.

I suspected that, unless Howard relinquished his mythological identity, his relationship with Christina would last only as long as she remained his misguided but well-meaning little girl. If she ever rejected this identity and became the boldly independent woman of Howard's dreams, she would assume the position of his adversary, and Howard would once again have lost touch with his "forgotten" but needed other half.

> Choices made in favor of safety leave a bitter memory of pleasure lost and a hope of pleasure to be found "someday"—in the sky, perhaps.
>
> —Jules Henry, *Pathways to Madness*

Fascination with the Forbidden is a recurrent theme throughout literature, beginning with the Adam and Eve story. For some people, however, this becomes an obsession that dominates their relationship to love, so that they invariably gravitate toward whoever appears most dangerous and most inaccessible; it is as if the very qualities of Danger and Inaccessibility had value in and of themselves. From a psychoanalytic perspective, the attraction to that which is alien and hence mysterious actually represents a desire to reconnect with aspects of ourselves that we have repressed. It should not come as a surprise, then, that those spotless, "wrinkle-free" characters who lead tame and ultrasanitized lives are often most intrigued by the Daredevils, the Sinners, the Wretched of the Earth, whose psyches are as murky as their own are presumably crystal-clear. As Freud warned us, the repressed returns (often in the guise of our children).

When a person has compromised too much, buckled under too deep for the sake of "security," be it social, emotional, or financial, he hungers for adventure, even pain—anything that can make him feel alive again. The Mystery Man or Woman promises to give him what he deprived himself of years earlier. Julia, her mother's virtuous and dutiful daughter, acts out in her sordid love affairs with various Souls in Pain what her mother imagines she has missed in her sugar-coated life.

Julia's mother must have panicked upon hearing the news of her soldier-husband's death. The world was at war, food was being rationed, and the sound of air-raid sirens was a constant reminder that life was tenuous and victory for the Allies was as yet uncertain. What's more, Katherine was pregnant with her second child (Julia was only three years old at the time), and was already feeling saddled by the responsibilities of motherhood. Completely on her own, and yet in no position to look for steady work for several years, Katherine felt her future was grim. How could a single mother, struggling to make ends meet, ever expect to attract a man, let alone find another husband? Once the war was over, the "eligible" men would find an ample supply of women more "eligible" than she (a widow at twenty-five, with two children), and Katherine, renowned for her exceptional "good looks" and sweet disposition, would be destined to live out her days poor and alone. This was her bleak vision for herself, reconstructed secondhand from her daughter Julia's narrative.

And so Katherine's marriage to Julia's stepfather two years later, a "decent" American man with a family business and solicitous parents, a man whom she admittedly never loved, was a reasonable compromise designed to make the best out of a bad situation. As Katherine packed her bags and turned her back upon England, her "mother country," determined to begin a "new life" for herself and her children in America, romance and passion were hastily relegated to the realm of fantasy, and considerations of security superseded all others.

Although Julia did not fault her mother for having chosen the life she did, she was convinced that her choice in favor of safety left her feeling disappointed, empty, and aching for something more. But Katherine was committed to denying herself her own feelings, convinced that this was the only practical course to take if she wanted to make her way in the world. Desire had to be pushed underground and could only gain readmittance through some back door; her children were destined to serve this purpose.

Once she succeeded in deadening herself with the tedium of extraneous housework and the goal of "perfect" motherhood, it would take violent jolts to bring Katherine out of her self-induced stupor. Her Wild son, Brendan's impulsive behavior throughout childhood and his eventual death in a motorcycle accident periodically woke her up and assured her she was still alive; but her sweet daughter, Julia, lulled her back to sleep again—Julia's forays into the netherworld being less obvious than her brother's.

Katherine never hid from Julia the fact that she experienced her new husband as embarrassingly dull, and that her feelings for him were undeniably shallow. Indeed, from Julia's perspective, her mother's life as she was living it was a repetitive exercise in dissimulation. Beauty without any substance, with a hideously dreary emptiness lurking just beneath the surface.

"Never tell a man what you really feel; it will only upset him, and then you'll never get him to agree to what you want. Only if you let him think what he wants to think will he ever be willing to do anything for you," was Katherine's response when recently Julia confided in her that she was having problems getting her boyfriend, Peter, to make a commitment. And as Julia tells her story, this Machiavellian approach to "love" was not uncharacteristic of her "beautiful" mother.

But as Katherine modeled these techniques of "love" for Julia in her own marriage, and played it safe in order that *she* could discreetly get her way, she lived a life devoid of any genuine excitement and sent a double message to her student-daughter: "Be like me and you will be beautiful and safe; be like me and you will dry up and lose your soul."

Though Julia resisted seeing any connection between her sexual promiscuity in college and her mother's old-fashioned homilies about male-female relationships, I could not help thinking that these "opposites" expressed a similar world-view. Within the framework of her mother's homespun philosophy of love, sex was a powerful means to an end, and abnegation of the self, which included the body, was the ultimate "sacrifice" that Julia could make in her quest to transform the Beasts in her life into handsome Princes. Though on one level indiscriminate sex was Julia's antidote to her mother's self-imposed sterility, on another level it was an expression of it, since it reflected Julia's own dissociated relationship to her body and her feelings. Having followed her mother's pious example and emptied herself of her own unpurified emotions, Julia the Ministering Angel doubling as a topless go-go dancer depended on men (bestial or chivalrous) to fill her up with their feelings and thereby restore to her her spirit. By becoming either man's spiritual guide or his sexual liberator, she hoped to infuse her life with spirit and passion.

From all appearances, Katherine was a paragon of wifely virtue, whose interests rarely extended beyond her household. Her home was a model of suburban living, modest but fashionably modern, comfortable but impeccably clean; there was always good nutritious food in the refrigerator, and dinner was served each evening promptly at six o'clock. But, if you recall, behind closed doors her frustrated desires occasionally burst forth, disguised as memory, as she continued to sing praises in honor of her children's dead father years after her second marriage and his disappearance from her life. In the myth she wove, he was a war hero, who, unlike her present, undistinguished, and mild-mannered husband, had dared to court danger on the battlefield and in the bedroom. This shadowy and elusive figure who could never *really* satisfy her (now that he was dead) was the one that deserved her love and her undying loyalty. Her real husband paled in significance; their life together was not her real life.

Julia, her mother's Hope and Beauty incarnate, dreamed her mother's dreams alongside her, dreams of absence, sorrow, and immeasurable passion. But, also like her mother, Julia proceeded to construct a bloodless identity founded on the creed of self-denial in the service of the self. Together mother and daughter cultivated a secret fascination with the darker underside of life, while publicly they posed for a joint portrait of Virtue and Temperance.

As long as Julia was protected by the aura of her mythological identity she felt free to resuscitate her mother's smothered impulses. As long as she was a Ministering Angel, a fairy-tale Beauty figure, nobody would ever recognize them as her own, and she could be safe as well as daring, her mother's replica and her mother's alter-ego. But as long as Julia was confined within the myth of Beauty, she required a Beast, just as her mother lived for her memories. And this was how "love" became a lifeline to the self, and the "beloved" became more an addictive substance than a separate person. Julia's addiction to Peter mirrored his addiction to alcohol. She felt as if she needed him (or someone like him) to quell the gnawing emptiness which itself was but an illusion designed to hide her "ugly" feelings.

Julia hoped that love could shatter her false identity and liberate both her as Beauty and Peter as the Beast from the evil spells under which they unhappily lived muffled lives. Julia loved the Beast in Peter so that she might love those aspects of herself she (and her mother) had betrayed. She saw beyond his surface appearance (or so she thought) so that he might see beyond hers.

Angry and forlorn and sick to death of self-denial, Julia had always been horrified to discover that she, presumably a sweet, innocent, and selfless creature, could have any "mean," ungenerous feelings—if anyone found out, she'd surely perish alone and unloved. So Peter expressed these feelings for her. She could commiserate and secretly identify with him, and deny herself so that *he* (her proxy) never had to know of self-denial. With a Beast-Prince, she could integrate the Bad with the Good and thus feel more real than her paper-doll mother.

Without Peter's sullen presence and knotted feelings, Julia experienced herself as insignificant, her cheerfulness as insubstantial, and her life as vacuous. This was her mother's legacy, but was now the product of her own mythology.

Once abandoned by Peter, her "other half," whose vivid feelings lent bright colors to her washed-out pastel life, Julia was left floating like a bubble in midair. Up there in the clouds, she encountered an image of her mother, whose picture-perfect household dissolved upon touch. With nothing substantive to hold on to, she was "destined" to pop noiselessly or rematerialize as a person, not an angel, to crash messily to the ground; then how could she reconstitute that comfortingly beautiful image of herself amid the blood and guts and howls? Another Beast would have to be unearthed to save her from her "ugly" feelings and resurrect the myth. Her ex-husband reappeared, just in the nick of time!

> I wandered lonely as a cloud
> That floats on high o'er vales and hills,
> When all at once I saw a crowd,
> A host of golden daffodils;
> Beside the lake, beneath the trees,
> Fluttering and dancing in the breeze.
>
> —William Wordsworth, "I Wandered Lonely as a Cloud"

Unlike the "golden daffodil" of Wordsworth's poem, a person who experiences himself as a kind of Sensitive Plant is inevitably at odds with nature—what he presumes to be his own and what he presumes to be everyone else's—and this perhaps is the root of a melancholic relationship toward love, the proverbial "he can't live with her or without her." Such a person feels incapable of surrendering to the beauty of the moment (though he hungers for

Beauty in the abstract) and cannot join with another person in an unreflective celebration of life. The Sensitive Plant is so delicate and so precariously balanced that even the breeze is too distracting, the sun's light reflected on the lake is too dazzling, and the trees that are supposed to protect him from the harsher elements are themselves too overpowering, diminishing his already too-diminished self.

By definition, the Sensitive Plant's feelings are easily hurt, his sensibility is easily offended, and his enthusiasms are easily dampened. He is uncomfortable in his body, uncomfortable in a world inhabited by other bodies, and uncomfortable perceiving his own level of discomfort, which he "knows" exceeds all others'. Even in the privacy of his own bedroom, this insubstantial image of himself hovers over him and casts a pall upon his life and loves.

Larry's experience in the realm of love is emblematic of the Sensitive Plant's dilemma, as he oscillates between the image of himself as an Insatiable Mama's Boy and a charmingly incorrigible Ladies' Man—a related but more dignified version of the original. Larry's puppy-dog dependency on women, coupled with his compulsive sexuality and never-ending quest for "something better," explains why he "falls in love" repeatedly, infuses his lover with extraordinary powers, and for a time worships her as one would worship a redeemer—after all, in his mind she promises to restore to him his virility and with it a modicum of self-respect.

With every new relationship there is at first the dream that the feeble, hypersensitive hothouse flower whom he recognizes as himself will disappear, and in its place there will be a dashing and robust young man, the person Larry really is but has never really been, if that makes any sense. Then, when it becomes apparent that this transformation is not so easily accomplished, there is Larry's hope that wife or lover can at least protect him from his self-loathing; she will bathe him in her unconditional motherly love and then gently rock him until he's fallen into an untroubled sleep.

But then, as might be expected, when love is mixed with wishful fantasy born out of need, Larry develops a repulsion for the "love" he was addicted to, for he finds that it is tainted with contempt for all involved. He was a fool to think she could transform him or, when that failed, comfortably envelop him without the risk of suffocation, and she was a fool to think that she could too.

Once again Larry finds that he has demanded the impossible (as his mother always said he did), asking for someone who would love and cater to his "special needs," and yet someone who would also help dispel the myth that he is a Mama's Boy and Sensitive Plant with "special needs" that need catering to. His love affairs and their inevitable demise prove just what Larry sets out to disprove: that he is Insatiable and not constituted to live in this imperfect world.

Larry's medical discharge from the air force at age twenty followed two suicide attempts related to the breakup of a romantic relationship. Having been abandoned by the girlfriend of his dreams, whose love had inspired him to leave the safety of his home and become an air-force hero, Larry was left feeling distinctly unheroic, once again a Mama's Boy, more suited to the comforts of his mother's kitchen than to the daily drills of military life. His commanding officers had little tolerance for Larry's "sensitivity," and he was quite ambivalent about their program to toughen him up and turn him into a "regular guy."

Twenty-five years later, Larry's defiled image of himself as an air-force "reject"—nervous, frail, and overly idealistic—continued to prevail. With a curious mixture of relief at having given up the pretense, and shame at having recognized who he really was, Larry related to me the semitragic, semicomic story of how he abandoned his dream of becoming a pilot to resume his mythological identity as a Mama's Boy or, if you will, a Sensitive Plant in need of an atmospherically controlled hothouse, not a military barracks.

As the Sensitive Plant, Larry was in desperate search for an uncomplicated and undemanding soul who would appreciate his sensibility and agree to negotiate reality for him, gratify his needs, and at the same time place realistic limits on his "unreasonable" demands for always more. But who would play that role for someone else except a parent? (Or someone committed to the myth that she is a parent of a small dependent child?) And how could Larry live with that myth for long without rebelling or throwing a temper tantrum, which would only serve to confirm the myth (he *behaves* like a demanding little baby, so he must *be* one), and prevent any actual and enduring change from occurring?

Despite, or perhaps because of, his presumed "failings" of character, romantic love has always played a prominent role in Larry's life. He, as much as any mythological figure, felt incomplete without his mirror image, with whom he could act out his mythological part. As a Sensitive Plant, he needed to be carefully cultivated (he could not survive in common soil). As a Mama's Boy and Ladies' Man, he needed to be fed, both literally and metaphorically, and tucked into bed at night, even if he had played all day with the older boys in the mud or caroused till all hours with the other men at the bar. Larry found women who provided him with just this kind of insulation from the world, only to choke frantically for air upon recognizing the price he had to pay for such confinement.

If we look at the history of Larry's love relationships, it is clear that he was caught within a vicious cycle. As the illusion of finding a transformative lover faded against the stark reality of marriage and parenthood, Larry's identity as the captivating but ungrateful Mama's Boy proved to be humiliating, and home became as much a source of claustrophobia as of comfort. Love had promised to be his panacea, to infuse him with a sense of pride, not shame, but the very form of love he sought was fated to betray its promise to him: it reinforced his feelings of impotency and increased his envy of what he did not have within himself.

As much as Larry wanted a woman to serve as his protector, and feared that without one he would fall apart, such a relationship demeaned him, and the mother or big-sister surrogates who fed and sheltered him inevitably failed to give him what he really hungered for.

How long could he suffer the indignity of such "love"? That depended upon how deeply convinced he was, at any given point in time, of his fragility, and how receptive he was to consider an alternate version of himself and his life. Married four times and each time unhappily, Larry has repeatedly discovered that the pleasure of being taken care of, one that he has actively sought, is inevitably very partial. So Larry predictably recoils from his wives and lovers, whose maternal hardiness he had originally gravitated toward. These motherly women, who over time appear to him more like Amazon warriors than Patrons of the Arts, lose their appeal. Their resilience and practical know-how becomes evidence of their "insensitivity," and therefore just as good a reason to fall out of love as it was a reason to fall in love in the first place.

Ironically, Larry's wives and lovers are doomed to disappoint him as his actual parents did before. They collude with him in his own infantilization, and mythologize him as he has mythologized himself.

The garden of Eden turns out to be disappointing once we have accrued enough worldly experience to recognize that we are no longer innocent children and that there is a whole other world beyond. But since Larry was not certain if he was *really* a sensitive little boy in need of a mother or a man in search of a lover and a companion, when the world beyond beckoned him to venture forth, he answered its call, only to retreat in a futile attempt to recapture his childhood.

Unfortunately, in his search to find a better surrogate parent to replace the one he is now eager to leave behind, Larry merely reasserted his mythological identity. His Don Juan was but the flip side of his Sensitive Plant. Both characters were restlessly in search of the "perfect" woman, and neither could be satisfied with what he was or what any woman, real or imaginary, had to offer him.

When Larry briefly settled down with yet another woman, hoping that maybe *she* could supply the tools he needed to repair his damaged self-image, the cycle only recommenced: he hoped, he dreamed, he woke up, he was disappointed, and eventually he took flight.

Although Larry always managed to leave his women before they left him, he had not managed to divest himself of his shameful identity, and spoke contemptuously of his own duplicity in love. His infidelities have only the appearance of power. His pride in conquest was short-lived, as he redisovered time and again that he had no machismo once you scratched the surface. (Nor did he really want to be macho.) A Don Juan who was the victim of his own voracious appetites, Larry saw himself as weak, guilty, and destined to be forever his mother's ravenous little boy.

• • •

Nicole's love stories bore more than some resemblance to Larry's romantic tales. Because she was a woman, however, her delicacy and emotionality were less noticeable, and less readily attributable to some peculiarity of hers, or some distorted self-image. Indeed, these characteristics correspond closely with our cultural mythology of what a woman is. Nicole's wide-eyed innocence, her kittenish appearance, her hesitancy at voicing any controversial opinions, and her wistfully sad demeanor exemplify the romantic feminine ideal. Refined but flirtatious, deferential but nonetheless cultivated, Nicole was the embodiment of many men's dream of a waiflike princess in dire need of being rescued from the dragons. Particularly a man who has denied his own "gentler" emotions finds Nicole a captivating spirit with whom he can surreptitiously identify.

But the various men in Nicole's life did not realize that they had been seduced by a myth and that, once rescued, Nicole *the person* was not content to live out her days as the ornamental china doll she appeared to be. Like Nora in the Ibsen play *The Doll's House,* Nicole was gradually sickened by their "baby-talk" language of "love," even though she induced her lovers to address her in this manner and join with her in her mythological image of herself as a beautiful foundling—childlike and too pure for this world.

Nicole's actual life circumstances complicated matters further and have, throughout her adult life, lent credibility to the image of vulnerability that she projected. Her personal history as a political refugee and a victim of racism was certainly significant in the development of her sense of self. Unfortunately, the "facts" of her life allowed her to justify her posture, and to pass off her mythic identity as real. After what she had experienced, who would have had the audacity to argue with her that the world isn't full of cruelty and that she hadn't suffered more than your average American woman as a result? She called out to be cuddled, and people usually responded.

Nicole is a woman of mixed racial background who spent her childhood years in Haiti, a country that is rigidly stratified along color lines. Her parents were highly ambitious people whose own parents had consciously chosen to identify themselves exclusively with the upper-class European society that had traditionally held power. The family's social and financial success (and they were undeniably included among the country's elite) hinged upon their blending themselves into that culture. Light-skinned and well educated, Nicole's parents "passed"—if not entirely, close enough. So, although Nicole was adored by her parents, who invested heavily not only their money but also their self-esteem in their children's future, she internalized an image of herself as "slightly damaged goods," an "honorary" member of white society whose real identity had to be tactfully understated.

But Nicole could not hide herself entirely, and she adduced that this made her all the more vulnerable to rejection. Her facial features were identifiably black, more so than her parents' or her younger sisters', and she was acutely aware that this was potentially a serious liability in the world she and her family were fated to inhabit.

As far back as Nicole could remember her mother, Marie-Claire, was anxious about Nicole's appearance, stressing the importance of making a good impression, and implying by her worried glances that there was a considerable risk that she would not. (In her mother's mind, that meant not looking or acting sufficiently white.) From the time Nicole's hair was long enough to be put in the traditional braids that many of the neighborhood children wore, Marie-Claire conscientiously straightened Nicole's hair, and emphasized the importance of speaking as her *white* classmates spoke—French, of course. She warned her against inadvertently mimicking the dialect of their servants, even though they were considered "almost family" and deserving of the children's love and respect. It was not difficult to imagine the picture that Nicole developed of herself and the world—a picture of Precious Fragility barely staving off cruel Nature.

Indeed, when, during college, Nicole did let her hair grow naturally, her mother was horrified and repelled. Each time she saw Nicole, she could not desist from telling her how hideous she looked, and how pretty she could be if only she'd take the proper precautions. It was her daughter's boldness that terrified and disgusted Marie-Claire, not her timidity. And Nicole's desire to identify herself as a proud black woman represented a betrayal of their shared identity as Sensitive Plants, apolitical, floating outside of space and time. Thus Nicole's parents communicated their own sense of shame and helplessness to her, and she learned through example to equate being true to her real self with being vulnerable to injury.

Although, in contrast to Larry's mother, Marie-Claire needed Nicole to mirror back to her her own self-image, not its antithesis, in order to feel strong, the result was the same. Nicole developed a picture of herself as a Delicate Flower, perennially on the verge of being crushed, who only through her "weakness" could hope to disarm her enemy. By living in disguise as a beautifully Delicate Flower, Nicole secured her relationship with her mother, who, according to myth, was similarly constituted, and her father, who enjoyed acting as a buffer between his little women and the cruel world outside their home. Just as important, however, by this subterfuge, Nicole protected her real self from potential harm.

Despite having lived for years under the threat of exposure, Nicole identified herself as having been a "pampered" child. These contradictions in her early childhood experience explain the odd combination of fragility and resilience evident in her adult personality. Under the strict tutelage of her mother and her parochial-school teachers, Nicole was cultivated to assume the role of a "lady." As part of her training, she was segregated from children whose families were not well educated or cultured and whose manners were not sufficiently refined. Nicole was advised, bluntly as well as by way of innuendo, of the dangers of straying outside the borders of her beautiful but circumscribed garden. And if *her* life was, by design, even more cloistered than her friends' or her sisters' lives, and she believed that it was, that was because she "needed" that extra protection, on account of who she was presumed to be. (She looked more "black," so she was more vulnerable; therefore, she had to act more "white," and wear thicker armor.)

And then what was perhaps inevitable happened, and the house of cards within which Nicole and her family had lived luxuriously, but ever-watchfully, collapsed around them. Political upheavals in her country that threatened the livelihood if not the lives of her family, forced Nicole and her sisters and mother to flee to the

United States, only months after her seemingly invincible father died suddenly of a heart attack. Though not impoverished, the family was forced to give up their insular life-style and their claim to special treatment (as honorary whites), and to mingle, like other people, in the larger, cruder world.

Significantly, even though like her mother, Nicole seemed to have retained an image of herself as a hothouse flower who, by definition, could never survive the vagaries of life outside the hothouse, Nicole *did* manage to adapt to her new environment, and very successfully too. In high school and later in college, Nicole proved herself to be a conscientious student whose modesty and unprepossessing attitude created an aura around her that set her apart from her peers. Indeed, her "sensitivity," her refinement, was her mark of distinction, and a source of strength, not of weakness. Although campus life was rife with racial tensions, Nicole did *not* crumble, nor was she frightened into withdrawing from the fray, whereas her mother (who was more deeply wedded to the myth) literally cloistered herself and chose to live permanently among nuns in a special residence, even though this meant that she could not have her children with her or have an overnight visitor without first asking someone's permission. Yet—and this was the paradox—to see Nicole and to hear her speak, it was evident that her experience of herself had remained fixed, relatively invulnerable to assimilating new, disconfirming information. She was still shaking tremulously and still on the lookout for Guardian Angels just in case she needed one.

Although her family's exile from their native country was undeniably traumatic, I suspect that Nicole's experience of herself as a kind of Sensitive Plant doubling as the Princess and the Pea had been well entrenched years before. This personal mythology has shaped her life and her choices in love perhaps as much as her very real identity as a displaced person and a member of a minority group.

Because she lived within the mythology, Nicole felt obliged to rush into marriage (to a man who she admitted never inspired passion in her) before she even graduated from college. "Love" seemed to be what Nicole required, though she was not "in love" and objectively speaking there *were* viable alternatives. She had been encouraged by her professors at the university to pursue a graduate degree in the field of her choice, but, just as she accepted Frank's proposal of marriage only eight months after they had met, she declined a scholarship that would have enabled her to live on her own, with support from the university until she was ready to live on her own without it.

As a Fragile Lady, Nicole *needed* a Guardian Angel more than another diploma. Her mother, her model of a maladjusted Sensitive Plant, applauded her decision, though she intimated that Frank was a bit "dull," and that they really had nothing in common.

I met Nicole's husband shortly before they separated, three years after their precipitous marriage, and I was struck by the incongruities between their physical and emotional makeups. Frank's blond hair, his ruddy complexion, and the awkward manner in which he carried his bulky frame contrasted sharply with Nicole's delicate mixture of Mediterranean and African features, and her girlishly slender figure. If she was the embodiment of a Bodiless Spirit, he was the Salt of the Earth.

Frank would gaze tenderly at Nicole, almost as a father, and would hover over her as if he feared that she might otherwise evaporate and he would lose his most treasured jewel. In awe of her beauty, and patient with her timidity, Frank had a towering presence that made Nicole appear even frailer than she did when she was alone. When she was with him, Nicole spoke barely above a whisper, and her tentativeness encouraged Frank to jump in and lend her his support, as if without it there was a danger that she would falter or perhaps even fade away altogether. He was her all-American clean-cut guy, her chaperon in white America. She was his exotic flower, his aching soul, whose tears he loved to wipe away, and whose worries he loved to magically dissolve.

Frank was the son of a blue-collar family, the first among his seven brothers and sisters to have made it to college, and the only one to have expressed any interest in the finer things of life—books, poetry, good wine. He was built like a farmer in the storybooks, and he behaved like a jock among friends. But in college he had majored in classics, and when he and Nicole married he was just beginning a doctoral program, planning to bury himself in the library for the next six years. His contradictions were the mirror images of Nicole's, but on the surface he was Uncomplicated, Unruffled, and Stoical, whereas she was entangled in a web of emotions and appeared to be continually on the verge of tears.

Their myths complemented each other, and for a time it seemed only natural that they would be happy together. He could tuck her safely away in a secure suburban home, and while he negotiated the crasser world outside their nest, she could forget her troubles and make babies. She need never worry about practical reality, about racism, about money, about graduate degrees (he would take care of all that), and he need never worry that he was only a rough-hewn "hick," a farmer boy disguised as an intellectual, as one of the elite; a Delicate Princess was depending upon him—she listened with rapt attention to his musings, she made him his favorite homemade pies—and that confirmed his refurbished identity.

Retrospectively, however, Nicole's marriage was doomed from the start. Nicole confided in me that she never felt that Frank could really understand her, and I don't doubt the truth of this. After all, their relationship was founded upon pretense, and she had made sure that he would see only the myth. She pretended not to hate it when he touched her under the blankets, and pretended to succumb to his clumsily passionate embrace. She pretended to be interested in the work that he did, and pretended to enjoy the company of his good-natured mother, who was distinctly not a Sensitive Plant.

So, of course, Frank never understood her; it was set up that way from the beginning: Frank was chosen as her lover precisely because he was "too thick" to participate in her pain. She was the Sensitive Plant and he was a mound of common clay upon which she safely anchored herself—if only temporarily.

Like Larry, Nicole grew to despise her protector, sickened by the diet of pablum she had lobbied to be fed. Contemptuous of Frank's naïveté in thinking that she was as insecure and dependent as she appeared to be, and that she was perfectly content to make quiche and be his captive audience each evening when he returned home from the library full of ideas about Greek philosophy, Nicole set out to prove herself the stronger and more pragmatic of the two.

After reassuring herself that her college mentor had not forgotten her, and that there was still a place for her in the graduate program of her choice, Nicole secured herself a job as a live-in nanny (while Frank, unsuspecting, was in the library studying) and then abandoned her stolid husband to his books and his own sad confusion. Who was the Innocent, the Idealist, the Sensitive Plant, now? When mythic characters fall in love, such role reversals are not so difficult to accomplish. After all, illusory identities are by their very nature unstable.

Yet, despite her steely determination and successful negotiation in the "real world," Nicole's little-girl image of herself was not so easily shed. It was resurrected immediately after her separation from Frank. Over the next few years, one hothouse would always substitute for another, and though there were periods when Nicole supported herself and lived more or less on her own resources, she was always ready to exchange her independence for the security of someone to depend upon, and "love" was never a necessary condition. Nicole did not expect to be loved for who she was, and had always believed that she was destined to lead a melancholic life. Deep down a confirmed cynic, she could only hope for shelter, not for a genuine home.

Nicole's wide-eyed innocence and timid expression continued to be her identifying features well after she was thirty and had acquired the social and intellectual skills necessary for navigating in the adult world. After the breakup of her marriage, Nicole had resumed her studies, had completed her graduate education, and, with the solicitous support of various male mentors, had carved herself a comfortable niche within the walls of academia. There, at that stage of her life, Nicole's characteristic wounded-doe look was out of place, an expression from a former time that no longer reflected anything real. And yet, to Nicole, no other look felt more essentially her own.

When confronted with the incongruities of thinking like an adult but feeling like a glass figurine, Nicole would plead ignorance, and I would have hesitated to accuse her of mere dissimulation, though I have heard others who have known her say that she was an artist of manipulation. When a person believes in the truth of a mythological identity, a very thin line separates insincerity from genuine misunderstanding. For Nicole, her real life was as much the sham as the fantasy image—the academic achievements, the money that she had earned through her own hard work, even her friendships she found difficult to believe in. Why else would she repeatedly endure the strain of living incognito, with men she didn't respect, let alone love? Why else would she continue to compromise her own dignity and ingratiate herself with professors she didn't really admire? And why else would she feel so offended when, on one occasion, frustrated by what I sensed to be her duplicity, I challenged her childlike posture?

Long after there was any true basis for her claims, Nicole insisted on being the Misunderstood Easily Wounded Princess, cloistered but still uneasy within the walls of her magical garden. That was the image in which she had been cast, and she has reproduced the feelings associated with that image and transferred them to every new terrain.

Nicole has been reluctant to surrender the identity she had assumed, though it stood in the way of her ever really falling in love. Through this identity, she fulfilled her parents' prophecy that their gentle and imperfect daughter was destined to be wounded by the harsh realities of the world. I believe that Nicole has held on to these melancholic images because in her mind her fragility has been her greatest strength and her most attractive quality. That being the case, wouldn't she be a fool to readjust the lens and get herself back into focus? Or, then again, would she?

> . . . a female figure more exquisite than
> a woman that was born could ever match . . .
> the statue yields beneath the sculptor's touch,
> just as Hymettian wax beneath the sun
> grows soft and, molded by the thumb, takes on
> so many varied shapes—in fact, becomes
> more pliant as one plies it. . . .
>
> —Ovid, Metamorphoses (Pygmalion)

It is an interesting contradiction to contemplate that a child who has been idolized as if he were a god will grow up feeling more *and* less than human, "entitled" to the best and yet profoundly uncertain as to what is truly best for *him*.

Idols, whether they are made of marble or of flesh and blood, are more a reflection of the idolater's wishful fantasies than of anything else. So, when a parent projects a beautiful image onto a child whom he claims to love more than anything in the world, he is worshipping *his* creation, is enthralled by *his* creativity, and in the process denies that child the right to an identity of his own. As a product of a parent's imagination, a child grows accustomed to seeing himself as but an object and not a subject in his life; even granted that he is an object of reverence, what can be more dehumanizing than that? Never having had the occasion to initiate her own actions, a person who has been revered as if she were a work of art has no confidence in *her* creative powers, but only in her ability to calculate her effect on other people; she devotes her energy to figuring out what they want or think of her.

If we turn to myth, we find that such was the fate of Galatea, the marble statue that Pygmalion the sculptor molded to suit his tastes. Although in the story the statue comes to life, it is in answer to Pygmalion's prayers, not hers; it is *his* pain that the goddess Venus hopes to assuage, not Galatea's. Indebted to her creator for her very existence, Galatea is "pliant" and yields to the very man who worships at her feet. How could she resist the pressure of his touch? He gave her life, and she is too deeply sunk in debt to him to be able to make use of the gift. Hence, when I draw the analogy between the idolized child and a Museum Piece, it is by no stretch of the imagination a flattering one!

In fulfillment of his parents' dreamlike image of him, the idolized child may be put on display just like any other work of art, and superficially he may appear quite self-possessed. But although his glassy eyes may convey an air of self-absorption, the person raised as a Museum Piece never learns to distinguish clearly between the self he *actually* possesses and the reflection of himself that he sees in his parents' love-blind eyes. It is this reflection that absorbs him and that he grabs on to for dear life, terrified that without it he is nothing more than worthless. Paralyzed by his stonelike image of himself, what could he do if he woke up to discover that he had been replaced, put into cold storage, traded in for a newer model that commanded a higher price as a commodity among commodities!

Grown-up, but still a child of myth, the idolized child goes forth into the world in search of someone special who can justify her claim for specialness (it is her mysterious legacy, and yet she cannot draw on it as long as she's alone). The ramifications for her experiences in love are manifold. In order to confirm her mythological identity, she will need to find someone who will worship her, and who is also deserving of her worship. (If he's not "special," then she's not, and in her experience that would mean that she is nothing.) But can one person serve both these functions, or are they mutually exclusive outside the realm of fantasy? Is she doomed, like Narcissus in the Greek myth, to reject all lovers who follow her in hot pursuit, only to love an elusive image that can never love her back?

It has been years since I saw Jessica in psychotherapy, but what I recall most vividly when I think back over the more than two years of weekly sessions is her constant vacillation. First as to whether or not to get married, and then, once that was decided, as to which photographer to use during the ceremony, and which place setting to rent for the reception. Indeed, Jessica and her mother, who since early childhood was her companion in ambivalence, conspired to infuse the preparations for the wedding with familiar feelings of anxiety and doubt. Her mother accompanied her to numerous stores, always encouraging her to go to yet one more, until in a frenzied state of exasperation Jessica resigned herself to the limits of just one wedding gown. Just like old times! And this was only the prelude to the anxious ruminations that came with buying a house and furnishing it.

After a while, it dawned on me that the specific contents of Jessica's dilemmas were to some extent irrelevant, and that Jessica's tendency to ruminate was pervasive; it consumed her energy and made it difficult for her to enjoy even the simple pleasures of life and love. To marry Michael or not to marry Michael was the immediate question to address, but the larger issue for us to tackle in our work together was her generalized resistance to settling on any one line of action rather than another. Jessica had difficulty living comfortably with the consequences of her choices, whatever they happened to be, and this put a crimp on her spontaneity, leading to endless "mystifications" and postponements within the treatment as well as outside of it. (R. D. Laing uses the term "mystification" in reference to communication patterns within families whereby confusion is created for the purpose of denying the implications of a message. The recipient of the message that is being sent, albeit denied, is mystified precisely because he cannot understand whence his feelings arise, nor can he be certain how to proceed, not being certain what has already transpired. See *Sanity, Madness and the Family* for illustrations of this process.)

At the core of Jessica's vacillation was her seeming inability to have what in colloquial terms is called a gut response to anything. Most likely, when she did have such an unmediated response she censored it, not allowing herself the freedom to know for sure just what it was. Rather than seeing the world in black and white, as many mythological figures tend to do, Jessica saw *only* shades of gray, and lived, as it were, in a blur of muted feelings and stymied actions. Living in this kind of an atmosphere meant living with what psychologists characterize as "free-floating anxiety," for Jessica's lack of conviction—whether it had to do with how she wanted to spend her winter vacation, what job she would prefer to take, or whom she wanted to marry—reflected a more fundamental lack of conviction about who she really was and who she really wanted to be.

Although Jessica frequently complained of the murkiness of her emotions and of her apparent difficulty making even the simplest of choices, we discovered during the course of therapy that the muddle Jessica described was a natural outgrowth of an image of herself as perfect, an image that she could not possibly match but was reluctant to revise, for fear of the alternative.

Jessica's explicit reason for coming to therapy was that she could not make up her mind whether to marry her boyfriend Michael, or to break off the relationship entirely. During our first session, she promptly assured me, lest I think the worse of her for wasting her time with some sort of schlemiel, that Michael was on all accounts a "model" person, just as she was supposed to be—honest, ambitious, and unusually affectionate, someone who she was sure would make an excellent husband. But as she proceeded with her legalistic arguments in favor of the marriage, drowning me in verbiage, rationalizations heaped upon rationalizations, it all seemed too "perfect," too theoretical, too unreal. As it turned out, Jessica was not accustomed to making decisions based on real feelings, being too distracted by the images of how she was *supposed* to feel, which, being images, invariably eluded her grasp.

Jessica and Michael had been going with each other for more than a year when she came to me with her dilemma, and had from the outset spent most of their weekends and evenings together, enjoying the usual movies, skiing, and eating in restaurants. But when it came to "love," well, Jessica was vague about what that really meant, now that she was over thirty.

Aware that her "biological clock" was steadily ticking away, and that, unlike Sleeping Beauty, who remained a teenager despite her hundred-year sleep, she would not find time standing still for her, Jessica realized that if she wanted to have children she had better start thinking seriously of finding a suitable mate and settling down. But this was not so simple a proposition as the fairy tales made it seem, though, according to her family fairy tale, she was *supposed* to be a Princess. This presented a problem, since she could see, try as she might to deny it, that Michael was *not* Prince Charming. Moreover, although he professed to love her as befit a princess, his promises to protect her from potential dragons were unconvincing—he didn't even realize that she was not who she appeared to be, and that what threatened her the most was what he was most enthralled by: her mythological identity as the Perfect Child.

In the myth that her family had woven, and that she then embellished upon, Jessica was supposed to be Perfect, which was an indirect way of saying that she was actually not good enough. Because Jessica had as a child been forced up onto a pedestal by her parents, who needed to believe that *their* daughter could do no wrong, she had assumed a mythological identity which included diametrically opposing images of herself: she was a Perfect Statue and at the same time a rather poor specimen of humanity. Since she was treated as if she were a figment of her parents' imagination, she lacked a heart, a mind, and a backbone of her own.

As Jessica's therapist, confronted each week with her paralyzing ambivalence about nearly everything—including me and psychotherapy generally—I frequently felt as confused and frustrated as she, inadvertently reproducing my patient's internal experience (a well-documented professional hazard). In my efforts to formulate a coherent explanation for the stalemate in Jessica's life and her subjective experience of unhappiness, I found myself swinging on the same pendulum she had fastened herself to.

Sometimes I was convinced that her expectations in love were indeed "fated" to be unrealistically high, as Jessica herself feared they might be, and I concluded that this was the reason for her reluctance to tie the knot with such an exemplary young man as Michael. Wouldn't she feel similarly ambivalent with anyone short of an Olympian god? From the stories Jessica told, this seemed to be a real possibility, since, when she was a child, it was only a distorted image of her that had been loved, not the person she really was. Once she had been loved as an image, how could she love anything other than images, and mightn't she be predisposed to reject real men and women, who are by definition too substantial not to be flawed? The myth of Narcissus was her myth, so perhaps his fate would be her fate as well.

But, then again, Jessica had good reason to resist the pressure she was experiencing to settle down and marry Michael, the epitome of the "good catch." Couldn't her ambivalence be seen as a healthy expression of her desire—*finally*—to interact with real people and not images? Jessica admitted that she felt little passion for Michael, even though he worshiped her and looked "wonderful on paper." Perhaps for the first time in her life, she did not want to ignore her "instincts," to do just what was expected of her. So what if she was now over thirty and he came highly recommended; if her heart wasn't in it, but only his, could this be called love? Did Jessica want too much from a marriage partner, or not enough? That was the question that plagued her (and me), until I came to realize that, paradoxically, both propositions were true.

When the image of her presumed perfection was in the forefront and in focus, Jessica could never be satisfied (she wanted too much, and nobody could ever hope to meet her lofty standards), but when she fell down off her pedestal, she saw only the image of a little girl, inordinately dependent on other people's admiring gazes, and from this perspective Jessica felt so unsteady standing on her own two feet that she was ready to lean on almost anyone willing to prop her back up; in this state of mind, she was not particular enough about her choice of mate, and one of the many voices within her told her so. Each of Jessica's mythological identities clamored to be heard, and each gave her different advice as to how to live her life; in the commotion, it was impossible for her to know which voice to listen to, if any.

So, whereas Michael was eager to make a formal commitment (*he* knew what *he* felt, even if she didn't), the idea of making a decision filled Jessica with anxiety and doubt. Intoxicated by the myth of who she should be (a statue) and tormented by the myth of who she is (a sniveling little girl), Jessica the person was immobilized, for fear of breaking the spell, and for fear of living complacently within it only to discover, too late, that she had built her life on top of a bubble that was sooner or later going to burst. As Jessica oscillated between her contradictory images of herself—some accurate, others highly exaggerated—she remained caught in a state of limbo. But this was a familiar place for her to be.

Of course, there were also specific reasons for Jessica's feelings of ambivalence about Michael, who was after all her opposite in many respects, and as such was her forbidden and therefore needed "other half." Jessica worked within the field of education and enjoyed interacting with all sorts of people, children as well as adults, whereas Michael was in business and preferred to wrestle only with the "facts." In politics, Jessica was a liberal and Michael a conservative; he teased her mercilessly about her "bleeding heart," and she rebuked him for his bloodless hardheadedness.

Michael lived in a world of certainty and knew exactly whom he liked and whom he didn't, where he wished to be twenty years from now, and in what restaurant he wanted to dine on any given occasion. For him, there were few gray areas in politics or in the realm of love, and he saw no reason to temper his "politically incorrect" opinions. Jessica, on the other hand, was a master of diplomacy, and introspection was her favorite pastime as well as her private obsession.

Thus it was understandable that Jessica was both attracted and repelled by her lover, he being the very antithesis of all she thought she was or should be. And though sometimes it was a tremendous relief that at least one of them knew what to do about the situation in the Middle East or the homeless man on the corner, it was exasperating that Michael's solutions were one-sided and unnuanced, and that her more subtle and more tentative formulations were often dismissed good-naturedly as the overly complicated and impractical musings of a naïve child.

It seems that, although Michael was Jessica's faithful subject, he also set himself up as the Authority in their relationship, patronizing her as he urged her to let him hoist her up onto the pedestal. Consequently, Michael simultaneously confirmed and disconfirmed Jessica's identity as a goddess and fit right into her own psychic meanderings and family drama. No wonder she couldn't make up her mind whether to embrace him or abandon him for being a kindred spirit. Michael's "love" reminded Jessica that her exalted image of herself existed only as long as there was someone there to reflect it back to her, and yet even then there were transparencies. Beneath the image of the Perfect Child, Jessica could not help seeing the image of the perennially Dependent Child, and as long as she looked into Michael's eyes, she could not see one without seeing the other.

As the nature of their relationship came into sharper focus, new questions arose. Was Jessica content to be Michael's lovable baby who could do no wrong, in exchange for also being the perfect woman whom he idolized? Was it worth it to be propped up by Michael's blind adoration when the same blindness resulted in a failure on his part to be sufficiently reflective, about her feelings or about his own, and so ultimately served to knock her down? Was this inflating-deflating cycle "love"? Her parents seemed to think it was, and who was she to disagree?

But there was yet another piece to the puzzle, and perhaps one of the most important ones of all for getting to the root of Jessica's tangled feelings. According to Jessica, Michael bore more than a slight resemblance to her father, whom she described as frustratingly dogmatic and uncompromising but also comfortingly reliable and unswerving in his devotion to her mother, whom he explicitly adored. Therefore, by implication, any decision Jessica made about marrying Michael could be seen as a kind of evaluation of her father, and by extension an evaluation of her mother's decision to marry him despite his obvious shortcomings. Apparently, after having weighed the alternatives, her mother had "given in," settled, and married her "other half." Did Jessica want to repeat the past and marry hers too? And if she didn't continue the family drama, could she ever hope to be *whole* all by herself?

Growing up, Jessica had become accustomed to the discourse of phantom images, so when she saw Michael worshipping her she also recognized that he was looking through her and thus holding *her* in contempt (he loved his adorably impractical Airhead). This was a familiar scenario, and, according to her family, what love was all about. Uneasy about a mutual love of images, but a foreigner in the land of flesh and blood, Jessica could neither blindly rush to repeat her past nor let it go entirely; she didn't fully believe in her family's myth, but was unprepared to face a world without it.

As long as Jessica agreed to live with Michael in their mythological world steeped in illusions about each other, Michael could protect her as her father protected her mother. He was decisive, certain of his ideas, and, unlike her, ready to act forcefully on his convictions—a regular storybook hero. Outside the boundaries of this world of blacks and whites, however, Michael was as much of a novice as she, if not more of one.

Although Jessica presumably came for therapy to clarify *her* feelings, so that she could cease floundering and proceed along *her* chosen path, there was actually another, hidden agenda. As much as she wanted me to help her disentangle what she felt from what other people told her she should feel, Jessica also wanted me to help her squelch her feelings. Only then would she be able to embrace her fairy-tale lover and agree to let him build a home for them in the land of "forever after." There, with Michael's help (and maybe mine), she hoped never to have to admit that deep inside she felt like Silly Putty, in desperate search of a form. If Jessica the person wanted to stop spinning, the mythologically spineless little girl who had been placed upon a pedestal was afraid of what she would see if she stood still.

As the Perfect Child, her parents' Precious Treasure, Jessica felt certain of one thing, however: that the little girl crouching beneath the pedestal could not endure being unattached—that is, single—all of her life. The mere thought of her parents' dying one day and leaving her "completely" on her own was dizzying. As a mythological figure, Jessica *needed* to have a substitute, her "other half" when her parents were no longer there to buttress her up with their adoring gaze. She *needed* a Prince.

Significantly, when, after having made her decision to marry, Jessica spoke to me with anxious anticipation about her wedding, she acknowledged being terrified of fainting as she walked down the aisle or took the marriage vows. It was as if in her mind the very act of marriage to Michael confirmed her image of herself as insubstantial. Just at the moment when she was to capture the spotlight in her carefully chosen wedding gown, and have all eyes expectantly fixed upon her, she felt destined to lose her footing, even lose her consciousness.

And so, for months, the questions continued, though they usually seemed to go in circles and lead us nowhere. "Do I only think I'm too good for him, and will I end up being punished for my arrogance? Will I regret it forever if I let Michael go and find myself single and childless at forty? Or will I regret it even more if I marry Michael, whose shameless adoration I can neither reciprocate nor fully enjoy? Am I fatally flawed"—like Narcissus—"or am I just more sensitive than most to his flaws?" All good questions, but as she asked them it became difficult not to be seduced into Jessica's nebulous world of doubt, and then, once there, go spinning round and round with her, considering one hypothesis after another, unable to settle, to compromise, or to take action.

Jessica did finally decide to marry Michael, and with this decision I gather she felt that she had accomplished what *she* had originally set out to do by coming for therapy. But, ironically, her decision came after she began to lean in the opposite direction, and it may have been fear of losing her bearings, were she to give up her lover, more than any solid conviction that prompted her to make the choice she ultimately did.

At the time of her decision, Jessica was in the process of identifying characteristics within Michael that reminded her of her loving but exasperatingly opinionated and controlling father. Then, rather unexpectedly, she put the lid on any further analysis. Fleeing from the specter of a life alone, a life without mother or father or love as they knew it and she had learned it, Jessica set a date, six months away. With what seemed to be genuine relief, she sheepishly informed me that she had made up her mind. After months and months of oscillation, I hesitated to question her self-definition now, not when she was determined to go full steam ahead.

Jessica's feelings of complacency were short-lived, and, as I mentioned at the beginning of this analysis, her doubting quickly found a new arena. Planning a wedding and setting up a home provided her with fertile ground in which to cultivate new forms of old anxieties. Jessica's mythological quest for the intangible Perfect solution that was always beyond her reach, and her discomfort at settling for anything less was transferred onto smaller stages, where it was more easily contained. She had managed to make the "big decision" and continued to torment herself with minor ones.

Marriage did not free Jessica from the stranglehold of her mythological identity as the Perfect Statue doubling as the Quavering Little Girl, and Jessica the imperfect woman could only continue to be confused about her feelings and then confused about the legitimacy of her confusion. But at least she had her "other half" firmly positioned by her side, and, as much as she questioned the depth of his insight into her real but elusive self, he said he "loved" her and confirmed her dual mythological identities if nothing more. He would never force her to dismantle the myth or threaten to push her over the edge of the storybook cover, where she might fall into an endless abyss.

Months after her marriage, Jessica complained that she often felt lonely and irritable, and was ashamed of these feelings—the honeymoon was scarcely over—but she never expressed any regrets about her decision to marry, even though Michael was clearly not a Perfect match. She had come too close to choosing a life alone, and as Galatea she could not imagine life without a Pygmalion who loved her and molded her to his image.

Two years of tampering with her mythological identity in therapy, and Jessica had had enough, though clearly all was not resolved. She admitted that she had chronic problems reaching orgasm when she had sexual relations with Michael (though he never seemed to realize it, blissfully ignorant of what was *really* going on inside of her), and she wondered whether this was not related to a two-year clandestine lesbian relationship she had had after college. Was she a homosexual? she wondered. But why open up that can of worms? When Jessica terminated her treatment, she thanked me for all my help, and I do believe she did catch glimpses of her unadulterated self behind the pretty mask. But, not fully certain that she liked the self she saw enough to live with it on a daily basis, Jessica gratefully slipped from sight. What she lost in spontaneity and sense-certainty she gained in security—or, rather, the illusion of security.

In assuming a mythological identity, we cut ourselves off from large portions of our personality. Love promises to make us complete, just as we promised out of love to complete our parents' lives for them by becoming their mythological children. Both promises must be broken, however, even if we may like to pretend otherwise. As long as we continue to live the mythic identity, we must betray our own and others' real selves, and in that betrayal there is no possibility of sustaining a feeling of wholeness, and no possibility of genuine love.

PART TWO

IN PURSUIT OF THE "REAL SELF"

5

Thesis and Antithesis: Exchanging New Myths for Old

A puppet is no less a puppet when the strings are crossed.

—René Girard, *Deceit, Desire and the Novel*

If as children we are cast in a form that is not our own and handed a script that requires us to deform our natural speaking voices, as adults we search for ways to regain control, or at least to persuade ourselves that, despite these psychic insults, we really are free—shapers of our own destinies. Even an attractive mask is tiresome after a while. It pinches our faces as we try to conform to its contours, it cuts off our air supply so that we can only breathe shallowly, and it restricts our vision, confining us to a world of two dimensions. Most important, however, as long as we hide behind the mask, it robs us of our dignity even as it offers us refuge from assaults to our self-esteem.

If Rapunzel is confined within a tower, Sleeping Beauty is alive without consciousness, Snow White is dead but only in appearance, lying prone within her glass coffin, seen but not seeing, and Beauty's Beast is forced to live within a grotesque body that does not accurately reflect his inner spirit, it is because we too feel as if we have been leading constricted lives, simulated lives, even lives of degradation. Our true identities, no less than theirs, have been concealed, so that our outer forms have been mistaken for our essences. We have not been cast under a spell by an evil witch, like characters from fairy tales, but often we find that we are living under the spell of the self-fulfilling prophecy, like characters in our own lives.

The stories that I hear in my psychotherapy practice (and among my friends) echo the antique stories that I read to my six-year-old daughter many an evening at bedtime. Feeling frozen in time is a recurrent theme, so I can only conclude that it reflects a universal experience. Anyone who has felt this way hopes, moreover, that someday a dramatic reversal will occur, at which point "real life" will begin again and we will be restored to our proper form.

Of course, we play all sorts of games with our minds, and some people manage to preserve their sense of control over their lives by convincing themselves that their mythological identities are not mythological identities at all but, rather, true, if unflattering, renderings of their real selves. So, for example, on some days Larry insisted that he *was* (which means he could not be anything but) a hypersensitive Mama's Boy, a pathetic weakling, a prophetic seer. Or Lisa resigned herself to being the epitome of the Babydoll she was supposed to be, arguing that she might as well stop "pretending" to be the Dignified Woman she aspired to become.

Then there are people who acknowledge that they are living on automatic pilot, semicomatose, as if they were entranced, and yet, like many characters in fairy tales, imagine that they must wait patiently (or is it passively?) to be rescued from their ghostlike existence. Or, dreaming that renewal lies just around the corner, they look outside themselves for the magical cure for the ailment they cannot name. Perhaps that new job, another diploma, a husband, a baby, or a winter vacation will be transformative, and they will emerge unscathed from the cave in which they have been hibernating for too long. Perhaps, but perhaps not! Julia, for example, believed that by rescuing Peter, her remote, artistic lover, from his addiction to alcohol, she would resuscitate not only him but herself as well. She was disappointed on both counts—the magic did not take—but as long as magic is all she has to believe in, she'll try again.

Ingeniously, we invent yet another "cure" for the despair that comes from being swept along by the momentum of the self-fulfilling prophecy. We revolt and noisily make an about-face. Howard, for one, has staged a number of violent revolutions in his life, and each time, out of the debris, has attempted to create a new order. (The first became last, and the last became first, and the weak, he being one of them, inherited the earth.) By dramatically turning his back on the past, he explicitly refused to embrace his fate, which was to be a Nebbish and a Ne'er-Do-Well, as it had been prophesied. He set out to "prove" to anyone who was gullible enough to take him at face value that he was an Idealistic Young Man with a Promising Future. More important, however, he set out to prove to himself that he was a "free spirit" (though he had been an indentured servant), the sole director of his own life drama (though he had memorized someone else's lines for years up until then).

The story of Pinocchio, the wooden puppet who struggles restlessly to become a real boy, illustrates how hollow a victory such a bloody rebellion can bring. Dreaming of self-fulfillment and freedom from constraint, Pinocchio embarks on his various misadventures. He rebels against his constricting identity, defying his father and his own conscience in a futile effort to establish himself as a person, not just a puppet. Yet, when Pinocchio rebels and does just what he is *not* supposed to do, we see that he is no closer to becoming a real child than when he was but a wooden toy. His freedom is illusory, and though on Pleasure Island he thinks he is pursuing his own pleasure, he grows donkey ears (he literally turns into an ass), and when he lies his nose becomes unmanageably long, making him appear more ridiculous than ever. What's more, by abandoning his father in his quest to cut the "strings," Pinocchio has denied, but not eliminated, his deepest feelings of attachment, and these are the very feelings that are essential to being human.

Nobody wants to feel like someone else's puppet; all of us struggle to create our own unique identities, and though our efforts sometimes prove to be misguided, nobody should quarrel with the earnestness of our motives. Diana, her family's Goddess and Shining Star, was on the fast track to success when without warning she slammed on the brakes, became a "populist" and a defendant of the Common Man, and took a nose dive off the pedestal, splattering her ogling fans with mud. Patricia, on the other hand, was her family's Dummy/Airhead, so she had to go to graduate school and accumulate all manner of honors to prove that she was master of her fate. Lisa, the sexpot, vowed celibacy and became involved in feminist politics, and Sherry, the Cool, Calm, and Collected Young Lady, binged on cake and potato chips and regularly vomited three times a day. Iris, a Dedicated Scientist known for her competitiveness, has flirted with Zen Buddhism, and Howard, the Scruffy Alley Cat and family Bastard, became a regular Horatio Alger and temporarily flirted with Success. All are on a mission in search of their "true selves," and as they violently regurgitate the myths they have swallowed, the pendulum swings furiously back and forth, and back and forth again.

But, as with Pinocchio, flamboyant self-assertion can be more illusory than real, and when we have purged ourselves of worn-out images of the self, it is not enough simply to exchange them for other images, even if these are our own creations. When Rebecca the Self-Sufficient Rationalist toyed with the idea of becoming Rebecca the Touchy-Feely Mother and Pampered Housewife, she may have succeeded in shedding one false identity only to have assumed another.

In Freud's paper "On Negation" he identifies a psychic mechanism by which we disguise our feelings by asserting their opposites, suggesting that in the Unconscious "we never discover a 'no.' " Thus a statement such as "I would never wish to hurt you" may be psychically equivalent to the statement "I do wish to hurt you," the only difference being that the former statement can be admitted into consciousness whereas the latter cannot. Other psychoanalysts have extended this notion of negation to the development of identity. Erik Erikson argues that, when an adolescent is, for whatever reason, unable to consolidate a positive sense of himself in relation to others, he will fill the vacuum by constructing a "negative identity" based upon what he is not, rather than what he is (*Identity, Youth and Crisis*). But what he presumably is *not* continues to figure prominently in his life and indirectly determines much of his behavior. What we see, then, when we meet such a person is but a slave disguised as a rebel, whose very act of protest feeds on that which is being protested. (Psychoanalytic theorist Nancy Chodorow suggests that, in the process of developing a separate identity, little boys more than little girls define themselves in terms of what they are *not*, because their primary caretaker and love object is in most cases not of the same gender as they. As a consequence, boys feel obliged to exaggerate qualities of difference, rather than qualities of sameness, in their effort to assert their autonomy. See *The Reproduction of Mothering*.)

But psychological theory only confirms what we intuitively know to be so. When a little child in a Superman cape announces that he is afraid of nothing, or another child proclaims furiously that he cares not one little bit for anyone, we need no psychoanalyst to interpret the not-so-hidden meaning of the message that lies just beneath the surface. Feelings of impotence and dependency are commonplace in children, whether they make a point of "whistling in the dark" or scream for Mama to come turn on the light or for Daddy to scare away the monsters lurking in the shadows. So too the bluster of the class bully and the tears of the "crybaby," one two-year-old's willful temper tantrums and another's clingy separation-anxiety are flip sides of the same coin, alternate expressions of identical conflicts having to do with autonomy and control, power and powerlessness.

Psychically speaking, then, opposites are the same—idealists are close cousins of cynics, and the most abject and self-effacing of people often turn out to be as self-righteous and insidiously demanding as their narcissistic counterparts. Haven't we all been manipulated, at one point or another, by a presumably "helpless" martyr whose power lies in his capacity to convince us that he is powerless, and that we will have his blood on our hands if we do not do precisely what he wishes us to do?

Sometimes, however, we are fooled by apparent transformations in behavior (our own and others'), and trick ourselves into believing that we have made a radical change in our lives when actually the change is just cosmetic (a new image, the psychic equivalent of a complete "makeover"). We hope that by some magic we can succeed in instantly wiping out history and be reborn, eliminating all traces of our former selves. All we have to do is be the opposite of what we were. Sometimes this "works," but often such dramatic change is merely illusory and we resemble the weary Sisyphus, who hopes, in vain, to push that heavy rock over that steep hill. As soon as he reaches the top, the rock rolls back down.

Thesis and antithesis, myth number one and its opposite myth number two, speak the same language, share the same assumptions, and though the original family myth promises us love, or at least inclusion in the family drama, and our rebellion promises us self-fulfillment, both myths ultimately betray their promises and imprison us in a cage of unreality.

> The Tin Woodman knew very well that he had no heart, and therefore he took great care never to be cruel or unkind to anything.
>
> —L. Frank Baum, *The Wizard of Oz*

As a weightless Speck of Dust Laurel was her mother's favorite child, but she apparently suffered from the indignity of the myth that she was Nothing. Living that myth, she couldn't speak her mind, she couldn't feel pretty, she couldn't even take pride in her considerable intelligence. "Nothings" do not think or feel; they live only to make other people feel like Something. Such is the origin of the mythological identity of Pandora that has dominated much of Laurel's adult life.

Upon reflection, most of us can remember encountering people who equate being Trouble with being Real and who, consequently, *feel* alive only when they are having (or stirring up) trouble. As long as Laurel sees herself as that Thoughtless, Irrepressibly Curious female figure, an Eve who eats the apple and brings about the Fall, or a Pandora who opens the box and lets out all the evil spirits that plague mankind, she feels as if she is the cause of all the misery in the world, but she is *anything* but Nothing! In adopting this mythic identity, Laurel is transformed. Or is she?

Laurel had been invisible, but she became an ever-nagging presence, an irritant that could not be ignored. She had been an amateur psychologist, exquisitely attuned to the secret needs of others, but she became a social misfit, predictably abrasive and "inadvertently" offensive. As the Speck of Dust, Laurel is loved; as

Pandora, the Troublemaker, she is reviled. But the difference is the same, for in either case she is not fully human, and though the one identity is a welcome antidote to the other, she remains a mythic character and is thus obliged to squelch her actual potential.

Pumping life into her identity as the insidious Troublemaker, as if it were her true self rather than a betrayal of her self, Laurel ingeniously finds ways of confirming its reality. She went through a phase in her life when she would secretly gorge herself on junk food (hardly the weightless Speck of Dust) and then, feeling disgusting and unfit for human contact, would retreat shamefully into her solitary cocoon, just where a Troublemaker like her rightfully belongs.

Or, after neglecting her health, in a heroic effort to deny herself and live as a shadow and not a person, Laurel ended up in the emergency room of a hospital in the middle of the night in a state of "crisis" requiring more attention, in the way of medical intervention and family support, than she would have had she taken adequate care of her body in the first place. Laurel's mother was furious at being called out of bed at one o'clock in the morning to attend to her irritating daughter, whom she routinely accuses of being a hypochondriac. Didn't Laurel know that she didn't have any real medical problems but only invented ones (shadows aren't supposed to have bodies), and that, rather than demanding her family's time and money, she was supposed to be inconspicuous? Of course, Laurel knew only too well what her mother wanted her to be (that's why she had postponed getting treatment when she needed it), and she would swing the pendulum back and forth between complying with her mother's wishes and violently refusing to give in. When Laurel makes trouble, when she suffers the pain of rejection, she feels doomed and guilty, but she also feels as if she has finally been true to herself, and there is some vindication in that.

As the perennial Other Woman who "innocently" sabotaged her professional advancement, Laurel oscillated between an image of herself as self-effacing and an image of herself as boldly self-destructive. After she has listened patiently and sympathetically for months to Brian's tearful excuses as to why he can leave neither her nor his wife and kids, Laurel's stomach begins to turn—the double-talk she has swallowed begins to curdle. The Flattering Mirror of a person shatters in her lover's face, spraying painful splinters everywhere and earning her her reputation: she's no lady, she's a vindictive tramp!

Banished from "paradise" for breaking the rules and asking for more than what Brian or Marty or anyone is willing to give, this modern-day Eve guiltily but gratefully flees from what appears to be the threat of nothingness (Nirvana, where there are no feelings, neither good nor bad, and where she is Nothing).

But if Laurel is relieved to not be Nothing, her relief is short-lived. Her victory leaves her bleeding and threatens to cut her off from the "love" she thinks she needs. Compelled to stir up trouble in order to feel alive, she feels fundamentally unlovable. She does not trust herself and does not believe that others should trust her. Myth number-one is reconstituted as Laurel shamefacedly admits her guilt and tries to make amends, and the cycle begins again. A new job, a new man, a new chance to play the devoted slave and then start another bloody revolution. Condemned to pretense or else to a life of solitude, Laurel searches vainly for happiness, certain that, for her at least, it is, by self-definition, beyond her grasp.

Anna, whose fledgling efforts to stand on her own two feet at age one branded her as a willful little upstart with a "mind of her own" who said "to hell with the world," also flip-flops between images of herself as a Curious Troublemaker and the antithesis of this, which is a Selfless, Unassuming, and Good-Natured Friend of mankind. Her relationship with Elaine, that self-involved seaside companion who for years pretended along with Anna that Anna was not a person but her own personal security blanket, is but one example of Anna's efforts to transform herself and substitute one myth for another. Anna must pay for her vivaciousness, her curiosity, her critical thinking, qualities that only create problems. And Anna has committed herself to compensating others for the misery she imagines she has unleashed upon the world by just being who she is.

During adolescence and young adulthood, Anna faithfully fulfilled her family's prophecy, and when she wasn't being her parents' impetuous youngest daughter, gratuitously falling on her face so that her elders could scold her and put her back on her feet once again, they never seemed to notice anyway. She was the child of their middle age, whom they themselves had never planned for. Because her very existence was undeniable proof that they were sexual beings after all—despite her mother's superior attitude and stinging commentaries about "human nature," despite her father's unwavering optimism and good-guy persona—Anna was a constant reminder to her parents of their darker, less rational side, and thus her identity as an impulsive mischief-maker was fixed well before she was born.

Although many of Anna's classmates played hooky, drove eighty miles an hour, and smoked and drank in excess, she always managed to stand out as somehow different; at least that is how she experienced it. All the others were just going through a "phase," but she was living out her destiny, and she couldn't grow out of that. To prove that this was indeed the case, Anna would go just one little step further than her friends, making herself conspicuous in her rebelliousness. It was as if she were competing in a contest for the title of the most undomesticated young lady in her Midwestern suburban town.

As a result of her successful efforts to live up to her mythic image, by the time she had graduated from high school, Anna had already distinguished herself as unstable and untrustworthy, though when she was only eleven she began baby-sitting for three children every afternoon after school and prepared them their dinner each evening without any major mishaps. But somehow none of those responsible qualities of Anna's were ever entered into the equation, which was predetermined to add up to "near-disaster," and when it came time to apply to college, her parents simply assumed that she could not participate in the decision-making. How could Anna possibly know what was in her best interests?

According to the family myth, Anna needed careful supervision, and so, unlike her older and responsible brother and sister, she was informed by her parents which school she should attend (it had to be close to home) and what course of study she should follow.

Of course, precisely because Anna's parents never included her in their discussions about her future, and assumed that her judgment was faulty and her impulses were in need of curbing, Anna intensified her "rebellion," which in truth was no rebellion at all, just part of the grand design, and when she got to college she confirmed her parents' vision of who she was. Anna proved to be incorrigibly undisciplined in her studies, fundamentally inconsiderate in her dealings with her parents, who only had her best interests at heart, and doomed to mess up. She was even carted off to a psychiatrist at one point when she was caught in a "prank"—greasing the women's bathroom in her dorm with Vaseline at two o'clock in the morning.

After four years of sabotaging her parents' explicit program (they said she should get a degree in business administration and work in a bank), Anna decided to go east and to wander. She would take dance lessons, acting lessons, voice lessons, and would find herself. Ironically, life as a gypsy was the *real* program Anna's parents had written for her from the start, and her agenda to adopt an unconventional and unstructured kind of life, falling into debt that ten years later she would still be struggling to repay, was not entirely her own! Even when Anna was one year old, her mother could tell that *this* child would be a "free spirit," intemperate and irrepressible, that she'd cause mischief on account of her willfulness, and that she would always be her wearisomely active baby. (Miraculously, an aura of maturity enveloped her sister, Susan, even though she drank at least as much as Anna did and got herself pregnant in her junior year at college. As for Anna's brother, Mark, nobody questioned what went on beneath his beautifully sculpted mask—he was a Star, and the light emanating from his dazzling image was blinding.)

When I met Anna, however, she was nearly thirty, and I saw only faint traces of her identity as a Troublemaker/Wild Child. I would have never guessed, had she not told me, that once she had been considered the embodiment of Selfishness and Irresponsibility, or that she had once been greasing bathroom stalls at two in the morning in a college dorm. If anything, she seemed to err in the other direction, impressing me as a bit overly conscientious in her work and in her personal life, always exceedingly concerned with being fair and doing good.

It was true that Anna still hated to be boxed in by any relationship or nailed down to any one position, and that she undeniably cherished her freedom to pursue what she wished when she wished to. But the Anna I knew was always unusually careful *not* to trample on other people's feelings in the process of pursuing her personal goals, and perhaps this oversolicitousness, stemming from a hypersensitivity to other people's needs, is one reason she so enjoys her solitude and has remained single to this day.

Alone and self-directed, she does not feel obliged to muffle her responses quite so much as when she is with other people and unduly worried that she might offend somebody if she breathes too deeply. Self-supporting and romantically unattached, Anna can be free to be that untempered Pandora, whom she believes she is anyway, without anyone else's having to know about it or be hurt by it. She can express herself, pursue her whims, and even "steal" a bit of pleasure without anybody's balking. And if she is prone to self-recriminations, or falls on her face—well, that is her own private affair, and no one has to know that she's that naughty girl of the family myth.

Upon close analysis, it appears that, since Anna graduated from college and moved far away from home and family, she has simultaneously lived out the family myth and invented its counterpart, hanging on to her past but denying its hold on her imagination. Carrying on her early childhood legacy, Anna continues to defy (but subtly, and without all the commotion) anyone who attempts to rein her in and direct her life for her. Control is a big issue, and if she is going to "mess up" she wants to do it her way and then be the first to point the accusing finger. Nobody can put her down so much that she won't just "pop up" again.

But, contrary to the Anna of her youth, the new edition of Anna is careful not to ruffle any feathers, even if it means smoothing over differences, diluting her opinions, and clipping her own wings so that she can no longer fly high. Anna no longer drinks to excess, she has given up smoking (except, from time to time, she'll take a puff from a borrowed cigarette and enjoy it immensely), and she no longer drives above the speed limit. She is the kind of person who will telephone if she is going to be more than five minutes late for an appointment, and who, unlike her brazen alter-ego, will painstakingly consider all sides of an argument, anticipating all possible consequences before she takes any action. Ruminative Hamlet is more her model than tempestuous King Lear. Or at least *most* days.

Anna's well-earned trophy for being the most undomesticated young lady in her high-school class has been shoved to the very back shelf of the closet to make room for the trophy she has earned several times over for being the most well-meaning, most considerate of friends. Yet, although few people would guess that Anna was once considered Reckless or Selfish, *she* has not eradicated this image from her mind. And when, periodically, Anna the Selfless Healer rips off the straitjacket she has tied herself in, she sees Anna as the Willful Wrecker re-enter the arena. Myth number two retreats to the sidelines, making room on the stage for myth number one. She becomes argumentative and stomps off in a huff, and the battle for her identity begins anew, with Anna aligning herself with the Healer under the misconception that she is *really* the Wrecker.

Despite appearances and textual revisions of the original myth, Pandora has remained a constant if invisible presence in Anna's life. Why else would she feel so guilty about her ambitions, and take at least one step back in her career for every two steps she takes forward?

Anna has confided in me that she has the uncanny habit of losing money, though as a result of her youthful profligacy she can ill afford to lose more, being thousands of dollars in debt and often strapped for cash at the end of each month. There are three different characters in this drama as I see it: Anna, who makes the money; Pandora, who accrues the debt; and Pandora's mythic counterpart, who lives abstemiously in order to repay it. One need not be a strict Freudian to wonder at these losses whereby she takes away with one hand what she guiltily takes for herself with the other.

But Anna is determined to break out of this cycle—even at age one she kept popping up, despite her mother's efforts to put her back down. This will "to be" is no myth, and if Anna can learn to differentiate between normal self-expression and untempered narcissim, Pandora *and* her counterpart will resume their proper places as characters in mythology.

• • •

And then there is Kate, who had always been made to feel as if she were "too smart" (a smart aleck) because she helped her older brothers with their homework, "too selfish" because she didn't want to visit her father's grave with her mother *every* Sunday, and had a streak of the "devil" in her because, when her father was still alive, she preferred to ride with him and her brothers aboard his fire truck than to walk demurely with her mother (who everyone knew was beaten down with responsibilities) and help her out (as any good daughter would) as she laboriously went about her weekly errands.

Once Kate's father died—when she was seven—and left her mother widowed with seven children all under the age of eighteen, Kate attempted to salvage her reputation, prove her humility, and purify her soul by joining a convent after graduating from high school. There she discovered that, try as she might to disguise herself as a saint (and she did try, black habit and all), she could not change her "nature." She vomited up her food after each meal, literally unable to stomach the restrictions placed on her natural rebelliousness. And though she made every effort to defy her fate—she spoke not a word at table, and modestly averted her eyes during meals, maintaining the "custody of the eyes," as was required—it was to no avail. She was who she believed she was: a nonconformist and a gadfly, her mother's Crazy youngest daughter, who should have been happy sleeping in a crib alongside her parents' bed until she was nearly seven but wasn't; who should have been less squirmy when sleeping *with* her mother in her parents' bed once her father was no longer there but felt too claustrophobic.

Even today, forty-eight years old and more or less settled, Kate is an amalgam of contradictory images and impulses. A nursing supervisor in a small Catholic hospital and the mother of three teenage boys, Kate is a peculiar combination of a proper and prim matron and a mischievous imp who knows well when and how to hide her devilish grin. She comes into her therapy sessions with a litany of complaints about her boys, who are undisciplined and disrespectful, sometimes even physically abusive toward her. But she also enjoys making fun of the staid and self-righteous nurses and administrators she periodically locks horns with on her job;

then she sounds more like her sons than like their disapproving mother.

She is amused that her co-workers suspect nothing of her colorful past—that she has been hospitalized three times for psychiatric and alcohol-related problems—and yet also worries (or is it that she hopes?) that her cover will be blown. Maybe they will find out that she is not the pristine and virtuous woman she seems to be; what would happen then?

A paragon of responsibility most of the time, on occasion Kate still drinks too much, when she's had her fill of being a Tower of Strength, the embodiment of Temperance and Patience at work and a Disciplinarian at home. And when, after one of these "episodes," she is hung over and cannot go into work the following day, it is her secret act of rebellion, her reaffirmation of the mythological identity she mistakes for her real self. Once again she is the girl whose spirit cannot be broken, the thorn in her martyred mother's too thickly padded side. She is Pandora, who prefers to open the box and suffer the consequences rather than live harmoniously (and sanctimoniously) doing just as she is told.

Kate's family tells her that her psychiatric problems (as well as her failed marriage and her unruly sons) simply reflect her chronic unwillingness to take responsibility for her life. ("She thinks she knows it all, but she'll eventually learn her lesson!") Scorning the psychiatric establishment, they insist that Kate's not Mad, just Bad. And Kate is not sure what to think; she feels as if she has always been different from other people and knows that she has a fierce temper, which has gotten her into trouble on a number of occasions. But if she's not Good (and the experience in the convent proved that once and for all), and she is not Bad (despite her family's accusations), must she be Mad? This could have been a viable alternative myth, and some more biologically oriented psychotherapists, who adhere faithfully to the medical model of mental illness, might have encouraged her to adopt it—it would alleviate some of her guilt. (She's suffering from a disease; she's just "ill.") But to my mind that would mean substituting one false identity for another, and then the real Kate, who is in the process of creating a life here and now, would never see the light of day, would never receive the credit for the ongoing saga as it unfolds.

A person who has at one period been fanatically determined to be the greatest athletic hero, or war hero, may at another period become equally bent on being the greatest saint. He may believe, then, that he has "lost" his ambition. Or he may decide that excelling in athletics or in war was not what he "really" wanted. Thus he may fail to realize that he still sails on the boat of ambition but has merely changed the course.

—Karen Horney, *Neurosis and Human Growth*

Howard's life did not always look like a scene from an afternoon-television court drama, and Howard's mythological identities have gone through a number of permutations over the years, so that on first glance it appears that he has made some radical changes in his life. Yet, if we can see past the clutter and discover the inner dynamics that propel him first in one direction and then in another, we can see that all of the mythical identities he has assumed—the Nebbish and the Ne'er-Do-Well, the Underdog and the Shining Star, the Solitary Idealist and the Social Climber are variations on a theme of unreality in which he always figures as either bigger or lesser than ordinary human beings.

When he was a child, there was the myth of the Nebbish and the Bastard Son—both rejects, the one passive and ineffectual, the other aggressive and destructive. This was the family myth invented by his parents and internalized as his own. By the time Howard went off to college, the Shining Star of the Horatio Alger variety had usurped the place of the Nebbish/Bastard, as Howard infiltrated the "system" and tasted the forbidden fruit of worldly success. With a college degree and a debutante for a wife, Howard himself became an Exemplary Young Gentleman and Social Climber, and his former identity as an angry subversive was pushed underground.

But if the Nebbish/Bastard was no longer visible, as Howard enthusiastically played the part of the Underdog who ingeniously got out from under, it would not be long before a newer version of the original myth would emerge. It was only a matter of time before Howard began to suspect that, despite all appearances, he was still as inadequate and illegitimate as ever. After all, he argued, in the process of being transformed into an Exemplary Young Gentleman, he was forced to ingratiate himself (as his father had) and submit to the evaluations of others. Only a weak-willed little Nebbish would allow himself to be subjected to that, and only a bastard would manipulate the system as he had done so successfully (rumblings from underground).

Securely settled in his new life, Howard felt unsettled and uprooted. Having cut himself off from his "proper" identity, he felt not only dishonest but also disappointed in what that dishonesty was able to buy him in the way of self-respect. For one thing, he discovered that there were many Shining Stars up in the sky, and by becoming one he had lost some of his distinction. But, still worse, as an honorary member of the club that wouldn't have admitted him had he remained loyal to his original mythic image of himself, Howard felt cowardly and betrayed. He had found no magic cure for his self-loathing (the Bastard still sneered at him from the sidelines), and though he had latched on to a more attractive image, one that would have helped him navigate in the real world outside the family, this image did not deliver him from the myth of his ignominious self, or cure him of his addiction to mythologizing. He wanted more from life than just life!

Indeed, as the respected son-in-law of a respected member of society, married to a sweetly naïve and unsuspecting wife, Howard lived as an alien to himself, and squirmed uncomfortably in his new skin. He, Howard, was destined to be Hateful and an Outcast, and yet his wife and family and newly acquired friends insisted on praising him, not criticizing him; this couldn't be real, and if it was it wasn't what he had hoped for! Objectively speaking, the quality of Howard's life may have substantially improved, but *he* felt as if there were no substance to any of his experiences, and that the appreciation of his audience was more an irritant than a salve, exacerbating rather than soothing the constant raw and burning sensation that remained inside.

Howard became restless for another dramatic change, another treacherous undertaking that would promise to deliver him to his "true" and nobler self. Intolerant of those who believed that he was only human, no more no less, Howard retreated to familiar ground, proclaiming myth number one (the myth of the Bastard/Outcast) to be reality, and myth number two (the myth of the Exemplary Young Man) to be a seductive trap.

Mythological identities are weightless—they exist only in the imagination, without a center of gravity—and thus the pendulum is destined to swing back and forth and back and forth again. Just as Howard's first transformation was near completion, he was laying plans for another. Having assimilated himself into the mainstream culture, and having publicly established his credibility as a legitimate son-in-law, as well as a devoted husband and father, Howard prepared to wreck his "happy home" and to wreak havoc on his "bourgeois" marriage. He was that "ambitious." Re-enter the Bastard Son disguised as David, the unlikely slayer of the corrupt and monstrous Goliath.

The details of how Howard became derailed and his new life unraveled are not altogether clear, and I imagine that the "facts," were we privy to them, would not add up. The explanation that he offered for his downward spiral sounded reasonable (his wife was shallow, his in-laws' helpfulness was intrusive, his colleagues were lazy, and the bureaucracy he had to deal with at work was stultifying), but somehow it was not reason enough. What is clear is that Howard was the master planner of his fall from grace.

Although he often bragged to me of his conquests in the world of the rich and successful, and has let me know in no uncertain terms that he was not always how I saw him—an impecunious, aging, social nonentity—Howard has told me during moments of lucidity that he felt out of place during his foray onto the other side of the tracks. This, I believe, is the key to his reversal of fortune. Having made his way up the ladder, where he hobnobbed with the very society he had previously vowed to hate to his death, Howard felt "soulless," and more alienated than ever. Moreover, even as he related these feelings to me years afterward, there was very little sense that they were simply *feelings*, which may or may not be realistic. He was convinced that success meant selling his soul to the enemy and that thus, in being "successful," he was actually betraying his real self. To be Howard, Howard had to fight the system, not make peace with it.

So one day Howard just picked up his belongings (which did not make him feel as if he belonged) and left—not only his wife and child but everything, which included the house his father-in-law had generously given him the down payment for, his car, even his job. He returned east, to his home state, and burned all his bridges behind him, and in the conflagration the Promising Young Man without a soul turned once again into the Defiant Young Man with an ideal. A Modern-Day Don Quixote.

Planting himself firmly outside the system he had only recently participated in, Howard refused entry through the front door, despite the invitations. And then they stopped coming, the doors shut tightly behind him, and he had little choice but to remain on the outside peering in. That was all part of the grand plan, however. Howard preferred to bang his head noisily and disruptively, symbolically going through the motions of knocking down walls which were impervious to his attacks. Rather than discouraging him, the bruises he incurred inflamed him and inspired him to bang his head against the proverbial wall yet more.

As the Solitary Idealist, Howard is a defender of Innocence and Truth, and is eager to sacrifice peace and harmony in order to wage his battle against corrupt authority. While working in the school system, he described himself as the *sole* advocate of the children, whom he liked to characterize as victims of their teachers. In contrast to his bureaucratic colleagues, who cynically push papers and sheepishly follow "the rules" of the game, Howard has liked to see himself as the muckraker, the daring "whistle-blower" who alone has had the courage to defend the spirit and not just the letter of the law. This is a far cry from the people-pleaser/politician we would have encountered years earlier on the college campus!

In recent years, then, Howard's ambition has been to be pointedly *un*ambitious, at least in the common usage of the word. On principle, Howard scorns the wealthy, the ambitious, as well as the silent majority, who are neither wealthy nor ambitious but who compromise their ideals and submit to the filthy "system" without waging any protest. In Howard's universe, "who shall escape whipping?" By design, I suspect that there have been very few!

By attempting to outsmart adversaries who are bigger than life, Howard has hoped to forget that his spirit was crushed numerous times by mere mortals; he has hoped to turn the tables on the past. In the fairy tale, the frog must become a *prince*, not an ordinary person; and the spell must be broken through the deployment of supernatural powers—otherwise, how could the frog endure and justify his painfully long captivity? Unwittingly, Howard seems to have been living that fairy tale.

Howard's commitment to his mythic struggles has been expressed through a variety of symbolic interactions. For example, Howard is unfailingly fifteen to twenty minutes late for our psychotherapy sessions, and I am convinced that he is as compulsive about his tardiness as others are about being precisely on time. Being consistently late is critical to his latest version of his identity, or at least the image that he is trying to approximate. When I've offered the usual interpretation of unconscious anger as the reason for his lateness, it only falls on deaf ears, and I've come to the conclusion that this is because issues having to do with self-esteem, not anger, are sustaining the symptom.

Invariably, Howard apologizes for being late, makes excuses, which I suspect he believes no more than I do, and then looks at me abashedly, as if I were about to scold him, which of course I never do. But by arriving after the time we officially begin our session, Howard silently communicates that *he* does not conform to *my* structure (or any structure), nor will he submit to what he presumes to be *my* agenda, even if it means that *he* is the one to be short-changed in the end! He is *not*—I repeat, *not*— a Wimp!

But whether Howard is late or early, acts flirtatious or confrontational, one thing is constant: whatever Howard sets out to do, he does with a fervor that aims at proving himself exceptional, out of the ordinary, indifferent to the limits imposed by space and time.

Yet, even as Howard disdains the perquisites of power, and disclaims any interest in the pleasures of worldly success and interpersonal harmony, he conspicuously flexes his powerful muscles and speaks nostalgically of the days when he resembled Michelangelo's statue of David (the shepherd who later would become king). Those were the days when he was married to a veritable princess, and rubbed shoulders with the president of this corporation and the vice-president of that.

Though Howard's flexing of muscles is meant to be taken figuratively, referring to his self-congratulatory, even grandiose attitudes, in summer he does tend to wear sleeveless tee shirts which reveal his impressively massive biceps. Again, the message he sends through his nonverbal behavior is that he's no Sensitive Plant, no Nebbish, no patsy. His muscles are real, but they also serve as metaphors which communicate his aspirations as much as Julia's knee socks and ponytail tell us of hers.

After several months of therapy, during which time Howard began cautiously to peek out from behind the wall of his bravado, he related a dream that graphically expresses the significance of leading his life as he has. In the dream, Howard sees himself on a mountaintop overlooking a steep precipice. People are lined up in front of him, and as a man holding a staple gun staples each of them in the head, they fall over the edge to their deaths. Angrily Howard notes that the people in his dream passively submitted themselves to this assembly-line form of self-destruction, but when it came his turn to be staple-gunned he alone refused. Instead of dutifully obeying the powerful figure with the staple gun, Howard grabbed the weapon from him and threw him into the abyss.

The staple, an instrument that we ordinarily conceive of as a helpful tool that holds things securely in place and allows us to avoid confusion and loss, is portrayed by Howard in his dream as an instrument of destructive power. The order it imposes is not our own but one we submit to. If this is the case, as Howard seems to think it is, destruction of the Powerful, who try to order us, is the only path to survival.

Howard's disorderly life, his purported inability to control his impulses, his knee-jerk resistance to authority afford him protection against feelings of annihilation. This is the implicit message of the dream. He aspires to be the Wild-Eyed Hero who breaks the rules of decorum (comes late for psychotherapy, confronts his supervisors on their ineptitude, challenges his girlfriend's idealism) as he unrelentingly chips away the varnish that hides the blemishes of the existing order. If he suffers on that account, it is ennobling, for in his suffering he triumphs. The myth of the nebbishy little boy who broke no rules, won no battles, and deserved the contempt that was heaped upon him is exploded, and a new myth is born.

Within this myth, he can be heroic without betraying his original mythic self; he can be the Bastard child his parents imagined and yet be glorious at the same time. Thesis and antithesis, bad and good, inadequate and transcendent. Just as in the Greek myth of Prometheus, man's benefactor, who suffers for millennia on account of his courageousness (or is it his *out*rageousness?), Howard can feel both helpless and superior, he can be despised by his fellow men and yet the most deserving of men's love.

Can this ingenious myth survive? And can it provide sufficient consolation for the original blow to Howard's self-esteem, embedded in the myth of his inadequacy? That depends on other players and their willingness to cooperate and see things as he prefers to see them. I suspect that, in the world of myth, which by now is the world Howard is accustomed to, this myth is the best that Howard can do. Until the picture of the contemptible little boy is recognized for what it is, a figment of first his parents' and now his own imagination, Howard will be a committed mythmaker, conscientiously trying to undo the damage that was done him. One fairy's spell cancels out another's, ad infinitum.

> It is fateful and ironic how the lie we need in order to live dooms us to a life that is never really ours.
>
> —Ernest Becker, *The Denial of Death*

Having been exiled from her mother's home at an early age, Helen developed diametrically opposing images of herself which correspond roughly to the different households in which she alternately lived. By identifying herself as both part of and distanced from her chaotic mother's crazy home, Helen developed a mythical identity as a singular Lady amid a swarm of wild animals who both attracted and repelled her, who were her closest relations and her fiercest competitors for her mother, Eunice's affections.

When Helen was only five years old and her mother, Eunice, was only twenty-two and pregnant with her fourth child, Eunice decided one day, without advance notice or discussion, to transfer Helen's care over to an elderly great-aunt and great-uncle, a couple with whom Helen's mother had virtually no contact herself. They were avid churchgoers, respectable and pious, and their lifestyle could not have been more different from her own.

In stark contrast to Eunice's household, where expectations for the children were ambiguous and inconsistent, and life was lived on an impulse that changed from moment to moment, Helen's great-aunt valued orderliness and predictability above everything else. In her home, the rules governing behavior were inviolable and unchanging, if just as arbitrary as in Eunice's. As the newest and youngest member of this household, Helen was obliged to conform to these rules or risk yet another banishment. And what then?

From Helen's description, her great-aunt and great-uncle had little tolerance for the natural expressiveness of children, and they showed no desire to cultivate any. Their routines were not subject to modification, and Helen did not need to be told directly that she was expected to accommodate herself to them, no questions asked—it was simply understood. Helen learned quickly what was expected of her, and as a rule of thumb she knew she had to refrain from doing anything that might disturb the peace, which, retrospectively, Helen experienced as funereal. This meant no visits from friends, no loud games, no spontaneous actions, no voicing of opinions, no open displays of emotion. A good child was clean, obedient, quiet, and above all undemanding and appreciative, and Helen wanted to be Good. Resolutely she was determined to annihilate herself, and as a compensation be reincarnated as her mythological identity, which, after all, was more glorious than she could ever be.

Helen's great-aunt served as a model. She prided herself on keeping her house immaculately clean (even if it meant that many rooms were "off limits" and essentially unlived in), and she never raised her voice above a loud whisper. Helen has vivid memories of her great-aunt spending entire days laboriously washing by hand all the curtains in the house, and then, bent over the ironing board in the kitchen, she would instruct Helen in the virtues of hard work and Christian humility. She didn't want to turn out like her mother, did she? With no husband, countless children, and generations supported by welfare? A faithful apprentice, Helen tried hard to follow her great-aunt's example, and gradually she mastered the art of making herself saintly, sometimes disappearing altogether. Her experience at her mother's, though radically different, had actually given her good practice in pushing her feelings into a closet.

But, as might be expected, when real life tries to mimic fairy tales, contradictions arise, although they cannot be acknowledged without risk of destroying the entire system. So, when Helen's great-uncle furtively fondled her breasts as she sat perched on his lap in the evenings after dinner, while her aunt was tidying things up, Helen was discreet and pretended that it wasn't happening, just as her great-aunt pretended that her husband was loving and devoted to her, an upstanding member of the community, and a gentleman, though even Helen knew that he came home drunk every weekend, and had on at least one occasion lunged at her great-aunt wielding a kitchen knife.

If Helen didn't pretend, she'd spoil things for everyone; the elegant house of cards would come crashing down on her head (as well as on everyone else's). Helen discovered in her new home, as Julia and Kate had discovered in theirs, that she had only two or at most three alternative identities: she could be either Good or Bad or Crazy (the latter being a variation of Not Good). As it turned out, Helen was Good, Inconspicuous, and commended by all as an exemplary child and then as a Lady.

On the surface, life proceeded smoothly, but Helen had long since severed the connection between appearance and reality, between what was going on inside and what could be seen outside. Although she understood the difference between the mask and the person behind the mask, often it was unclear which of the two deserved her allegiance.

Faced with the glaring contradictions between her early- and her later-childhood experiences, Helen solidified her identification with a mythical Beauty figure (a Ministering Angel), and with it her attraction for the unhappy Beast, whom she felt destined to liberate. Instead of being torn asunder, or having to choose between the two worlds, her mother's and her great-aunt's, Helen vowed to unite them. Thus, in her imagination at least, she was loyal to both and did not have to fear exile from either one.

Before coming to therapy, Helen had not given up her quest to be included in the life of her mother's household, as much as she secretly reviled the characters who inhabited it. The tumult, the gossip, even the naked misery functioned as a peculiar kind of refuge from the deadly silence of her second home. Indeed, Helen's marginality inspired her to find various entry points that would admit her back into the familiar jungle, where she would invariably lose her bearings and then her mind.

Ironically, Helen found that her mythological identity as a Pure and Selfless Angel was what made her most welcome in both of her homes. In this form, she blended into the shadows at her great-aunt and great-uncle's home, and brought to her mother's dank apartment a breath of fresh air, sweetening the otherwise bitter atmosphere, so that hope had a chance of surviving.

As previously noted, family get-togethers and family crises continued into adulthood to supply Helen with an abundance of opportunities to try once again to accomplish her mission. Her nieces and nephews have now joined forces with her brothers and sisters, to live, as she describes it, lives of desperation. And as in childhood Helen plays her complementary role, soothing, commiserating, quietly absorbing the others' misery, and hoping to transform the Ugly into the Beautiful. But, predictably, Helen returns home from her various missions depleted, angry, and suspicious. She usually becomes depressed. Is she being used? (If only she would admit it!) Are they snickering behind her back? Is she contemptible rather than admirable? Or is she simply crazy, tormenting herself with all these morbid ideas? Of course, that would mean that she, more than anyone, was in dire need of a Ministering Angel to save *her* soul. The standard textbooks might describe what follows—the withdrawal, the incessant doubting—as "self-destructive" or "self-defeating" behavior, but in this state of mind Helen is more accurately described as one bent on destroying a beautiful but deadly myth.

The character who emerges from the rubble when Helen the Ministering Angel "self-destructs" is Helen the Dysfunctional Depressive—in other words, mythological identity number two. When Helen falls (or, better yet, dives head first) into a deep depression, she unhooks her phone, lets dishes pile up in the sink, sometimes even loses her job; there is little trace of the Lady she was. Sometimes Helen even explodes in a very unladylike fashion, so that her relatives call her "paranoid," urge her to rest in bed, and uncharacteristically begin to worry. Where is their ray of hope now?

Ashamed and contrite over what she has done, Helen pours her heart out to me, her psychologist, because I am the one person who is paid to listen to *her*. But a sympathetic ear is not all that she needs. Until Helen realizes that she does not need to become Selfish, Parasitical, or Insane, a Whiny Baby or a Manipulative Bitch, once she has denied the myth of the Ministering Angel, she will have created only an antithetical myth, which calls for yet another Ministering Angel as the family drama plods on inexorably. And will Helen try out for the part once again?

Bulimia is a disorder of antinomies. The powerful obsession with being thin is matched by an equally powerful obsession with gorging on food, and though this may appear paradoxical, it really makes perfect sense. The Greedy Beast who binges and the Purified Spirit who has been purged are both mythic characters who speak the same language and operate under the same assumptions.

Sometimes a young woman who is bulimic will speak as if her exaggerated interest in food is completely understandable albeit unfortunate, implying that her desire to overeat is some inherent aspect of her personality that she must learn to control but can never hope really to change. She *is* that Ravenous Beast, and her only hope lies in careful subterfuge! At other times, however, she will refer to her overwhelming desire to be thin as the "true" reflection of her nature, in which case her own fleshy body figures as an alien creature, and food is like a false lover who plies her with sweets and smothers her with flattery until she gags for want of fresh air. (She is that Pure Spirit who needs nothing but her ideals!) From this perspective, the bulimic's purges are in the service of self-realization, and the perfect body is her only proof that she has reclaimed her lost soul. (See Hilde Bruch's *The Golden Cage* and Mara Selvini Palazzoli's *Self-Starvation*.)

But I maintain that the bulimic's binge is no more an expression of her "real" self than her restrictive eating and her self-induced vomiting. As she purges herself of the Greedy Beast, she invents the Bodiless Spirit, which, not being viable, reinvents the Greedy Beast, and so on and so on. Starved, she proves herself piggish when she gives in to her tremendous appetite; stuffed, she proves herself the victim of her body's shameful desires when she discovers that she feels even more hateful full than empty. Thesis and antithesis, they feed off each other and are inseparable.

From early on, Sherry adopted both of these mythic identities, and though she was convinced that she was *really* a ravenously hungry Jellyfish, weak-willed and worthy only of contempt, she frequently appeared as a Snow Queen, poised and a bit self-righteous, as she patiently listened to her father's, her sister's, and her friends' naked confidences, which spilled messily onto her starched white apron. With a hint of superiority but without complaint, Sherry tidied up the mess, fed the hungry monsters, and secretly envied them their freedom to scream and cry and demand satisfaction for their various hungers. She ate nothing (at least not in public), she asked for nothing (except admiration), all the while pretending to be as coolly in control as her attractive though unexpressive mother.

But Sherry, if not her mother, suspected that the Bodiless Spirit was only an act. She was not really a Snow Queen, and her desires were not really frozen inside her. Indeed, her mother's aversion to feelings and her biting criticism of Sherry's imperfections ("She always said I had a flabby stomach and insisted that I join the high-school swim team even though I really wasn't much of an athlete") had always made Sherry feel as if she were not only physically grotesque but also "too hot to handle," a seething caldron, threatening to bubble over with unbridled emotions.

So, although Sherry exercised religiously to rid herself of her "bulge," made it to the pool three out of five afternoons a week, and never let her parents hear a foul word escape her lips, she secretly identified with her irascible, filthy-mouthed, but affectionate father, who was always watching his calories and cholesterol, always going off his diet, and always seeking solace for his hurt feelings.

As much as Sherry wished to match her mother's image of the ideal woman, and was pleased to see that she was thinner than anybody she knew (certainly thinner than her middle-aged mother), years of self-denial and semistarvation left Sherry feeling not only proud of her "accomplishments" but also angry and betrayed. Even though she ate like a bird and was five feet six and weighed only ninety-five pounds, her high-school boyfriend left her for another girl, who was louder and fatter than Sherry would ever allow herself to be, while Sherry stood by passively and watched, not deigning (or daring?) to voice a protest. And, watching her younger sister "sow her wild oats" and say and eat and do just what she wished, Sherry wondered who in fact was victor, when she herself received first prize in the contest of self-denial? Why couldn't she just be herself, like everybody else?

But Sherry mistook the myth of the grotesquely ravenous Jellyfish as a faithful rendition of her real self and, understandably, was deeply divided as to whether to defend this contemptible creature or to continue to bury it alive. Within this framework, binging and purging seemed to be the perfect solution—in private, Sherry could be herself (a disgusting pig), and yet the public would continue to see her as her antithesis.

Of course, the more she hid "the beast," the more she felt confined and bestial and terrified of being discovered and openly despised. So, by the time I saw Sherry in the hospital, she was binging and purging more than three times a day, and feeling fat and ugly and completely out of control. Myth number one was more real to her than ever, and she never doubted for an instant that she *needed* myth number two (she was addicted to purging as much as to the binge). If she didn't regularly purge herself, wouldn't her preferred identity be poisoned, and wouldn't she eventually explode? For deeper more permanent change, Sherry would have to purge herself of both images by realizing that both are illusory.

> You are my sunshine, my only sunshine,
> You make me happy when skies are grey,
> You'll never know, dear, how much I love you,
> Please don't take my sunshine away.
>
> —Jimmie Davis and Charles Mitchell

• • •

He dismantled himself to undo her projections, to spite her, in order to feel self-generated.

—Christopher Bollas, *The Forces of Destiny*

Imagine the burden of being someone's "only sunshine," and then imagine the dreary insides of that "someone," who begs you not to abandon him to the dismal grayness lurking within. A child living with such contradictory messages might well wonder whether it is better to keep on "shining," and join his parent in the battle to shut out the gray, or to turn off the light, open the floodgates, and force the rain to pour down upon the party.

When a parent projects a beautiful image onto a child it is no less a projection than any other image, and embedded within all projections are the seeds of their opposites. Beneath a parent's injunction to his child to be Joyful, Serene, or otherwise Outstanding is the unconscious fear that in actuality he and his child are doomed to be miserable, guilt-ridden, and fundamentally wanting. The narcissistic person, who is the likely product of such fantasy projections, is paradoxically "full of himself" and yet characteristically prone to feelings of anomie and emptiness.

In popular usage, the term "narcissim" refers to an excessive involvement with the self. We think of this narcissistic person as one who puts himself at the center of the universe and acts as if he were entitled to special treatment. We have all encountered Princesses and Princes who conduct themselves as if the ordinary rules that govern human action do not apply to them. At times we find ourselves envious of the narcissist's air of self-importance, his perfectionism, and his complete lack of humility. We wonder if he is not indeed worthy of the special treatment he claims is his due. At other times, however, we are enraged by his insensitivity to our feelings, and his unquestioned assumption that we exist only to mirror him, to reflect on his radiance. Though we happily tolerate his attitude in a young child (particularly when it is our own), we find ourselves becoming weary of being audience to his exploits, which demand our constant applause.

As his namesake, Narcissus, our modern-day narcissist is supposedly in love with himself to the exclusion of other people. But, then, if his own perfection is a myth and not reality (and we know it must be), he is really in love with a mythic image of himself, not his real self at all. His story is just like the Greek myth in which Narcissus died, wasting away for love of an elusive reflection in the pond. We have to ask: What is the fate of the self in this case? And what self-betrayals are implicit in the adoration of an insubstantial if beautiful image? Emptied of his real self, the narcissist becomes a Bottomless Pit, and no reflection, however beautiful, can fill the void.

Diana's history as her parents' Museum Piece is variegated. When she was first put on display, she enjoyed the attention and the admiration she received. Holding herself proudly, she looked down at her public below, sympathetic to their insecurities though somewhat impatient with their shortcomings. At that time, everyone seemed to nod in approval and to accept the definition of herself that she had naturally assumed had some basis in reality. She was poised, articulate, and charmingly precocious. The kernel of truth in the myth made it easy to embellish the beautiful picture her parents were determined to paint. She was a dutiful artist's model and restrained herself from the temptation to make any unexpected moves that might spoil the beautiful tableau.

But as time passed, Diana began to feel embarrassed and frustrated by her elevated position, which cut off possibilities of intimacy with others. Watching the crowds of people milling around her, laughing, crying, whispering, strolling arm in arm, she was, moreover, filled with envy and self-hate. Although she was surrounded by warm bodies clumsily jostling one another, she was too pristine to be touched and too polished to allow her true feelings to show through the glossy veneer. She assumed that nobody expected her to feel as ordinary people do, and that nobody expected to be able to touch—works of art are only to be admired from a distance. But even if she were to discover that there were people out there who did not subscribe to her myth, she was her own most exacting critic and would not tolerate any revisionism.

So, by the time Diana had graduated from college, before she had even turned twenty, life was becoming very troublesome, despite, or perhaps because of, her statuesque and exalted image of herself. Once brazenly self-confident, Diana was beginning to feel self-conscious and insecure, about her future and even about her mythical identity, which, as it turned out, could not withstand the test of adult reality. With lightning speed, she had gracefully jumped over life's hurdles to a round of thundering applause. But how was she, a presumed Goddess, going to negotiate everyday life and preserve her special identity at the same time?

Diana's razor-sharp intellect, with which she had indiscriminately if unintentionally ground her opposition into bits, was adorable in grade school and entranced her professors and a small coterie of friends in college, but outside the hallowed halls of the Ivory Tower it was not charming. Moreover, it only left her with "chopped meat" for company, and this was poor compensation for being so brilliant, so articulate, so daring. Everyone else her age was spinning romantic tales, or suffering from unrequited love, or joining the peace movement, or at least raising his or her consciousness!

Indeed, Diana was acutely aware that all around her people were falling in and out of love, getting passionately involved in sex and politics and sexual politics, and that, unless she stopped being the chaste Goddess of the Hunt, she was going to be left out. But in order for Diana to participate fully in life, she had to relinquish her mythic identity, and because she had lived it so long, this seemed virtually impossible—it had infiltrated each and every pore, it was essential to her. At times it seemed as if Diana did not recognize that the Goddess Diana was only an image that had been created for her, and that she could, if she wanted to, become a woman and live like other women. But at other times, Diana was painfully aware that she was not actually what she (and her family) had imagined her to be, and when, upon this realization, her fanciful identity began to disintegrate before her eyes, she felt *so* vulnerable, *so* diminished, that she was desperate to reconstitute it at any cost to herself. Although as she grew older Diana's inflated self-image engendered feelings of loneliness and isolation, she could not discard it without first creating a comparable substitute.

As Diana's childhood defenses cracked when her desires for intimacy intensified, she became increasingly uncomfortable with herself, and, by extension, with her body and her sexuality. Her body had always been a unique source of shame, a nagging reminder that she was penetrable and an object of other people's desires, not simply an agent of her own. Diana's intelligence may have threatened other people, but her female sexuality threatened *her.* (Could that have been the origin of the Greek goddess Diana's chastity?) Diana's father's overly enthusiastic appreciation of his daughter's "voluptuous" adolescent body is without doubt the significant factor here. According to his scheme, her very attractiveness left her open to attack. (Men were Beasts and beautiful women, particularly beautiful Goddesses, unleashed their bestiality.) Mixing his metaphors, George would compare Diana to the goddess Venus, of whom he was also a devotee, and, from what she described, he could scarcely keep his hands off her. She was a statue on a pedestal but, more significantly, she was *his* statue, and she dare not behave as if he did not possess her, body, mind, and soul.

Paradoxically, Diana's mythically exalted identity was the source of her vulnerability, and though it inspired her to scale new heights, it also sapped her of her vitality, souring her on love and sex. Eventually, she grew to detest the Goddess, and turned her on her head so that she would not have to look at her face to face in the mirror ever again.

So, to the extent that Diana felt "doomed" to be special, she also yearned to be unexceptional, wishing (futilely, she felt) that someday she might be able to tear herself away from her own reflection and happily lose herself in a crowd or in a lover. She longed for that "oceanic" feeling that Freud talked about in his later years, the feeling of oneness with the universe. She toyed with the idea of being more like her angelically inconspicuous mother, who seemed to disappear into the shadows cast by her husband's and daughter's expansive presences. Attracted and repelled by this alternative identity (her mirror image), one that promised to liberate her from her ego and its desire, Diana needed to arrive at a compromise. She would become a champion of the Selfless, a defender of the Disenfranchised, and thus be "one of the people" and a heroine at the same time.

Although by age thirty Diana evinced scarcely a trace of her earlier self, the precocious little girl who was destined to be the first woman president, she had found in her politics a new avenue through which to express her specialness. Heroics were in the name of the revolution, not in her own name anymore, and if Diana no longer aspired to Power and Status, she found that she could shine by *not* shining, rise to the top by violently rejecting the usual markers of fame and fortune. She could be a Goddess and "one of the people" at the same time. She could fulfill her parents' prophecy and yet appear not to, fight the old battles and yet march under a different banner and be convinced that she is free.

Leaving behind her the Ivory Tower of academe, where she had been captive for years, leaving the competition to be the First, the Best, and the Fastest among her peers, Diana began to teach grade school in the heart of a New York City ghetto, and for a while devoted herself to the underprivileged many, whose lives were as distant as possible from her myth of unique perfection.

An avid individualist up until then, Diana began to join groups—women's groups were among the first—and she gradually became deeply involved in politics—educational politics, city politics, feminist politics, and then, finally, international politics. Diana the elitist wiped out all visible signs of her elitism, an elitism that had left her gazing into the same pond, miserable and alone. She discarded Beethoven and Mozart and filled her shelves with reggae and the blues; Shakespeare and Jane Austen had to clear the way for Marx, Lenin, and the teachings of Mao, and Diana became a proponent of the Oppressed everywhere.

But even as Diana became a leftist guerrilla and a lesbian, she inadvertently fulfilled her father's vision, perhaps no less than had she remained a Marble Statue fixed upon a pedestal. They are opposite images, but both are aspects of the same mythology, in which she figures as his Most Exalted daughter or else his Most Debased self. As a revolutionary advocate of the "people," Diana expresses the rage and disillusionment that had inspired her father to turn her into an idol with whom he could identify and in the process nurse his wounded ego.

Ten years ago, Diana virtually disappeared. Under the auspices of working to help peasants in Mexico, she left home with no forwarding address, and cannot be located. From what I heard, George was enraged at his daughter's abandonment, "after I gave her everything she ever wanted." But he should have known that goddesses don't have to follow the rules. Mythic Diana does not need to report back to anyone as she goes off to the woods to hunt. In his last will and testament, George disinherited his favorite daughter, though in his final months he was known to call out her name, in what must have been a final plea for immortality.

For the rest of the family, Diana became only a memory, but as a memory she remained, as always, bigger than life. Being the goddess she was destined to be as long as she lived the family myth was intolerable, and she had to go very far out of her way to eradicate that identity and to convince herself and others that she was not the person she was presumed to be. If, in working with the peasants and workers, she repeats to herself again and again, "I am not special, I am not special, I am not special," I can admire her valiant efforts to break the spell, even if I am not convinced that she has.

If Diana is no longer alive and, like Narcissus, has met with a premature death (a victim of South American guerrilla warfare), it will be because she was trying to untangle the knot that kept her tied to an unreal image of herself, hoping that, by defending the rights of the peasant, she would also be defending her own right to be a human being too.

Julia, the sweet Ministering Angel and topless go-go dancer; Helen, whose family always called her Lady; and Jessica, whose parents and infinitely patient fiancé agree she "can do no wrong," also periodically "dismantle" themselves, to borrow a phrase from psychoanalyst Christopher Bollas (*Forces of Destiny*, p. 164), in an effort to retrieve a sense of reality. Like Diana, they strain against the myth of their own perfection, but in the process the "repressed" returns in the form of another myth. (Freud discusses the "return of the repressed" in his paper "Moses and Monotheism." Basically, his idea is that, despite our conscious intentions, those qualities and impulses that we have suppressed and overcompensated for eventually spill out in one form or another; nothing is lost to the Unconscious. R. D. Laing and other family-systems theorists such as Nathan Ackerman, Boszormenyi-Nagy, and Murray Bowen, discuss how the repressed impulses of one family member are often projected onto another, who expresses them for the entire family.)

Julia is proud of her tongue-twisting oral gymnastics, which can satisfy any man's sexual fantasies (she tells me of her ability to tie a knot in a cherry stem using only her tongue), but if this is defiantly *not* her or her mother's image of Beauty, then it is the image of the Beast, who, being an essential part of the fairy tale, is nothing other than an implicit aspect of her original mythological identity.

Helen's social withdrawal associated with her bouts of depression undoes the myth of Lady, the solicitous and selfless Angel of Mercy who untiringly ministers to other people's needs. Her "parasitic" family, her insensitive girlfriends, and her kind but sexually impotent boyfriend are suddenly jolted out of their childlike dependency, as Helen the Heavenly vanishes and Helen the Mournful "sad-eyed Lady of the lowlands" (Bob Dylan) assumes her place. Temporarily "incapacitated" by her "emotional problems," which are "out of her control," and which she cannot be faulted for, Helen is *unable* to fulfill her destiny. Her answering machine picks up her messages, her dishes sit in the sink for days unwashed, but Helen's life is still "on hold," as she once again sacrifices herself, this time to the cause of undoing the myth of self-sacrifice.

Jessica's tendency to magnify her own and everyone else's blemishes confirms *and* disconfirms the image of her as a perfect child. Perfect people are entitled to live in paradise with other perfect people and naturally are satisfied with nothing less. Her critical attitude is thus proof of her perfection. However, perfect people should also not be bitchy or indecisive, and the perfect woman certainly should be happily married by the time she has reached thirty!

As long as Jessica is vacillating endlessly and stringing other people along on her spirals of indecision, she proves that she is Difficult and Exasperating, and does not conform to her image of herself as the Apple of Someone Else's Eye (a not-too-distant cousin of the Apple Polisher). But as a Complicatedly Knotted Soul, Jessica is not much more "real" than when she's someone's Babydoll. In both cases, the question remains: What does Jessica think? What does Jessica want? What does Jessica feel? Jessica has created a new myth, but, just as in the old, she is still the center of attention and divorced from her real feelings. She may look different, but let's not kid ourselves—this is a far cry from self-fulfillment!

Miranda was to be her mama Miriam's Little Helper, and, just like her quietly domesticated mother, her job was to bring joy and simple comfort to her joyless family and fretful home. Her parents had slept in separate rooms for as long as she could remember, and since Miranda saw little trace of any affection between them, she concluded that her parents were joined together by shared feelings of despair, which they tacitly agreed would never be articulated except obliquely—the world economy was falling apart (not their marriage); a friend was suicidally depressed (not Miriam or Miranda's father, Elliot).

Indeed, before Miranda came of age, no one in the family ever cried out; they camouflaged their pain ingeniously as irritability and intellectual argumentativeness, in the case of her father, or fatigue and emotional numbness, in the case of her mother. But, whereas Miranda's mother rarely complained about anything (her eyes just went vacant, and she often fell asleep right after the dinner dishes were put away, positioned in front of the television), her father rarely stopped complaining. Usually Elliot focused on his wife's cooking, which was bland and unimaginative, or on the failings of his co-workers, which according to him were egregious; sometimes, however, the national economy or international politics was the target of his vitriolic tirades. But, whatever the issue happened to be, and there was always something to criticize, beneath all the words, frustration and sadness permeated the atmosphere. No wonder Miranda was enlisted to infuse the stale air that settled over the dinner table with sweetness and innocence. She had a purpose, and her family was depending on her.

In order to fulfill her role, Miranda was to be undemanding and cheerful, "seen but not heard," pretty but not that intelligent. Pollyanna was to be her heroine, or maybe Beth March from *Little Women;* her sister, Deborah, had already appropriated the role of feisty Jo, and her mother needed an ally to pick up on her cues and take over when, discouraged by life, she could no longer rally the enthusiasm required to recite the clichéd homilies that her family lapped up, though without ever listening carefully to their messages.

When Miranda was three or four, her father nicknamed her "Little Miriam," after her mother, and she recalls how cozy she felt when it was pointed out time and again that she had her mother's "high cheekbones," and pretty round face. When Miranda and her older sister, Deborah, talked babytalk and invented nicknames for each other, Miranda was designated by her name as her mother's girl, Deborah undeniably as their father's. Unpremeditatedly, the names they made up at age six and age nine reflected these not-so-covert family alliances. Miranda was called Poopy, a close relation to her mother's nickname Moopy, and, not coincidentally, her sister was Dunion Duna, a phonetic relation to their father's Dutcht.

According to the family lore, Deborah and her father were broadly classified as the melancholic and ruminative Intellectuals who, on account of the complexity of their thoughts and the tenderness of their feelings, were incapable of achieving inner peace. They argued loudly, they were both highly competitive, and, despite their air of self-importance, they were presumably doomed to be troubled to the end of their days. (They knew too much not to be!)

As part of the balancing act, Miranda and her mother, Miriam, were classified as contented, well-balanced souls—shepherdesses of the kind you see in storybooks, walking impassively up grassy slopes, seemed to correspond to the image she painted for me. These pastoral figures have no other aspirations than to tend their sheep and feed their families and then, on the weekends, to dance merrily to the strains of folk music.

The origin of this mythology can be traced to certain actual differences that existed between Miriam and Elliot in social class and temperament. Miriam, unlike her husband, had been born to rural poverty and forced to drop out of school in the eighth grade to help support her mother. Her "humble origins" and soft-spoken manner were the raw materials used to create the caricatured image that defined her in the family and threatened to envelop her daughter Miranda.

Purportedly uncomplicated by ambition, and presumably incapable of participating in her father's and older sister's esoteric musings about life and its meaning, Miranda as a mythic character was created to aid and abet her mother. Miriam, in collusion with Elliot, was trying to stifle her unarticulated feelings about her background, her aborted education, and her disappointing marriage, in which she figured as an afterthought. (Elliot never hid the fact that he had married her on the rebound.) Perhaps together Miranda and Miriam could find the courage to "whistle in the dark" cheerfully and scare away the ghosts. Together they could lull each other to sleep and dream away the bitterness and despair.

But, as much as Miranda savored the intimacy with her mother that her mythic identity brought her, lo and behold, she became her family's emotional barometer, and *not* their uplifting spirit. In the process, she embodied Misery, not Joy, and betrayed her mother's secrets rather than joining her in her presumed oblivion. Had she failed her parents, or was this *really* what they needed her to do? I believe she picked up her parents' subliminal message and actually fulfilled the prophecy of being Little Miriam, but she did it indirectly, not by mirroring her mother's false persona, but by peeling away at her façade and exposing her mother's darker feelings to the light of day.

Although Miranda continued to be called Little Miriam, by the age of five she was also told, repeatedly and with some amusement, that she was "oversensitive" and had her *father's* "worried look." Her grade-school teachers inquired why her eyes were red and rimmed with black circles, her classmates taunted her with "crybaby," and hotel proprietors apologetically requested that the family find other accommodations because Miranda's constant crying and fits of temper disturbed the other guests. Miranda was distinctly *not* a Ray of Sunshine; indeed, she was the very opposite, a black storm cloud.

Instead of following gaily in her mother's footsteps, Miranda took the lead from her mother, reversed directions, and pulled them both through gloomy alleyways. Sometimes she even got her mother to raise her hand to her in angry protest—quite an accomplishment, considering that Miriam was herself a committed pacifist.

Mama's Sweet-Tempered Girl had become a "sourpuss," a "problem child" (maybe she needed psychotherapy?), and though Miranda still enjoyed being cuddled and to that end could appear quite kittenish, she was convinced at a very early age that simple pleasures were not hers to keep. She, more than anyone in her family, was a "miserable sinner," a term she encountered in her prayer book that fit her evolving image of herself. She loved it when unsuspecting strangers continued to draw a parallel between her and her mother, and when high-school boyfriends mistook her for an all-American apple-pie kind of a gal, but it always felt like a sham, which she was bound by conscience to reject. She was too proud to reap any long-term profit from her deceit.

Her periodic attempts to distance herself from her mythological identity began almost as soon as Miranda recognized what that identity entailed. She recalled that, throughout much of her childhood and adolescence, she was crying or throwing herself on the floor in despair and rage. Anything was an excuse for another outburst. What could be less like her mother and less like a cheerleader than that? Her parents called her "spoiled," then wondered bitterly whether she wasn't "emotionally disturbed," and when Deborah wasn't trying to quiet down and comfort her pathetic but noisy little sister, she was accusing her of being a "wild tiger." Miranda's father sometimes warned her of the "discontent that casts a shadow grey upon the likeness of a summer's day," and it was evident that the myth of the lighthearted little Shepherdess (Wordsworth's golden daffodil swaying in the breeze) had backfired and been replaced by a variation of the myth of the Mama's Baby, the Sensitive Plant.

When she was a teenager, Miranda's promiscuity and emotional volatility consolidated her identity as a wild, immature, and desperately unhappy human being; as a young woman, however, Miranda found her image of herself as an exotic but Temperamental Tiger competing with her image of herself as a contentedly Domesticated Cat. She was uneasy when either identity was submerged entirely. In public, she exposed only her sweet, uncomplicated face (which was restored after adolescence) and was confident that people everywhere liked her (and they did, if we are to believe her, though for all the wrong reasons).

Sometimes she felt that this was who she really was, if only she could just allow it. But at other times she felt suspicious of her contentment, her sweet nature, and her apparent "good adjustment." Was she betraying herself by being lovable and undemanding? Would she become like one of the mythical sheep in the storybooks?

To counteract such dangers—in the privacy of her home, where nobody but family or the closest intimates could see her—Miranda continued to flare with anger over minor injustices, and fell into a heap of tears when she felt she was not listened to, waving the flag of authenticity in her defense. Suddenly the purring stopped and a caterwaul echoed through the air. The Tiger bared her fangs, and the Shepherdess was contemptuously pushed aside.

The mythic characters Miranda identified with complemented each other (just as her mother's Angel balanced out her father's Disillusioned Intellectual). But where was Miranda really when, crying uncontrollably, she thought she was being real? Myth number two, the Tiger in the cage, as much as myth number one, the Shepherdess on the grassy slope, her family's Ray of Sunshine, relegated her to the land of make-believe and distanced her from her true self.

Rebecca's virtue lay in her Maturity, and even at age eleven she was considered better equipped to care for her one-year-old brother than her more volatile and more anxious mother, Sophie. Indeed, Sophie relied on Rebecca as one would an older sister to bear the responsibilities of motherhood that she herself had little time or patience for. This arrangement would have been inconceivable were it not for the mythic qualities ascribed to Rebecca by both of her parents. Like Diana and Jessica, and even Miranda, Rebecca was to be her parents' Perfect child, but her "perfection" lay in the fact that she was so Independent and Self-Sufficient, that she scarcely needed any attention or affection from them. This is how, paradoxically, Rebecca became a Self-Sufficient Self-Starter to please her parents, ignoring her own self and all her needs in the process. No wonder that, when she was in her mid-thirties, she fantasized about "liberating" herself from her high-powered career to become a traditional housewife, with misty visions of being cuddled and taken care of prominently in the foreground!

Rebecca's father worked round the clock in the family hardware business that he had struggled on his own to build up over a lifetime. Her mother taught grade school and in her free afternoons volunteered in various community organizations, rarely getting home from work before six o'clock in the evening. But her "workaholic" parents never felt that they had to worry about Rebecca's grades, friendships, or emotional adjustment, since, according to the family lore, Rebecca was perfectly capable of handling herself, and then also caring for her younger brother on her own. She was just that Reliable.

Though Sophie acknowledged that she herself was going through an identity crisis at forty-five (this was discussed at the dinner table), it never seemed to occur to her or her husband that their adolescent daughter might also be experiencing some conflicts. Sophie had questions about her career and her sexual attractiveness (she was constantly on diets and taking continuing-education courses) but surely Rebecca did not. Indeed, when Rebecca was on the brink of becoming anorectic during her senior year in high school, Sophie appeared to her daughter to be less concerned about her emotional and physical welfare than jealous of her slender figure! "You're so thin" was immediately followed by "Do you think I look too fat in these pants?" Why should her parents worry about Rebecca? After all, she was one of those people who always sailed smoothly through life and never lost courage. This was why they admired her so.

Slavishly Rebecca applied herself to confirming the myth of her emotional stability; she was a Supergirl and then a Superwoman, self-contained and impervious to stress, and throughout college and graduate school there were no obvious cracks in the mirror. True, during her teenage years she became secretly obsessed with her weight, and then, during the spring semester of her freshman year in college, nearly dropped out after discovering that her best friend had decided to room with someone else the following year. But these crises passed, without anyone's suspecting the extent of her anguish, and the myth of the Mature and Independent Rebecca remained intact, all disconfirming data carefully tucked away in a conveniently inaccessible place within her mind.

Even after Rebecca married a man twenty years older than she, a professor she had met while getting her master's in business administration and working full-time in a bank, she continued to pride herself on her emotional reserve and financial independence. Committed to retaining her privacy and her freedom, even if it meant sacrificing a certain amount of romance and intimacy, she insisted on keeping her own separate bank account and dividing the household expenses evenly between them. Initially this put a strain on their relationship, and put her at a distinct disadvantage, since her income was considerably less than her husband's and she had to cut corners with her own expenses in order to keep up. But to Rebecca not having to ask anything of anybody was a sign of maturity, and so her self-denial was a source of comfort, not deprivation. She argued that she did not want to be accused of being a "gold-digger," but I believe it was more significant that she lived in fear of becoming a needy/whiny baby, and bent over backward in the other direction. Rebecca's only concession to her husband's desire to lavish her with gifts was the large diamond engagement ring she wore everywhere but, she admitted, with a certain amount of embarrassment.

Precisely because it would have been easier for Rebecca, now that she was a married woman, to slacken her resolve and lighten her heavy workload, she dug her heels in deeper than ever and took on more responsibilities at the office, hoping in this manner to guard against the temptation to betray her ideals. She feared that if she wavered even a little she might lose her balance altogether and stumble helplessly into who-knows-whose arms.

Rebecca would rather forgo that extra blouse, or a meal at a fancy restaurant, or a week-long winter vacation at the Bahamas, than take the risk of sliding into a dependency that would violate the assumptions of her mythic identity. As a mythic figure, she could not allow herself to soften too much, even with someone as warm and generous as Jesse, her husband. His fatherliness, so unlike her own father, made her nervous, but I suspect it was a major element in her attraction to him. Paradoxically, Rebecca seemed convinced that by walling herself off she became *more* self-possessed—though, as it turns out, this is a contradiction in terms.

When, however, Rebecca became a mother at thirty-six, her illusion of invulnerability and autonomy was cast into doubt. For the first time in her memory, she was unable to stem the flow of intense feelings of attachment and dependency, her son's as well as her own, and over the course of a few months they succeeded in steadily eroding away at the very foundations of her life as she had been living it.

For years Rebecca had distanced herself from her feelings of connectedness to others and her sense of responsibility for their well-being. Had she not pushed these feelings out of her mind at an early age, she would not have been able to sustain the image of herself as mature beyond her years and completely self-sufficient. This image served the purpose of the family drama—it was what her family needed her to be. But it also prevented her from being swallowed up by her all-too-dependent parents, who simultaneously pushed her to grow up before her time and tried to hold on to her so that she could take care of them.

This "matter-of-fact" approach to life worked reasonably well for Rebecca until there was a baby, who, brimming with emotion, didn't know the rules of her private game. Her son could not thrive in an emotion-free environment, and Rebecca discovered that she didn't want to anymore either, even if she had spent years courageously proving that she could.

As a daily witness of her baby son's normal neediness and dependency, and the primary recipient of his unabashedly naked displays of affection and anger, Rebecca became uncomfortably aware of aspects of her own personality that she had diligently shut out in pursuit of her identity, and felt both uneasy and delighted at discovering that she was not the mythic figure she had thought she was. The question remained, however, who she was.

Through her identification with her son, Rebecca began to see herself in a very different light, coming to the "radical" conclusion that all those years of hard work had been in the service of self-betrayal, and not self-fulfillment after all. With this, Rebecca began to wonder at her commitment to her career, and to re-evaluate her ambitions. She considered whether she wouldn't meet her needs better by dropping out of the rat race entirely (a race she had previously seen as Olympian) and staying home full-time with her baby son. What Rebecca had previously assumed to be essential to the fulfillment of her destiny, the status and achievement that she depended upon almost as an addict depends upon his fix, began to look like an empty diversion from her genuine desires, something that sapped her of her spirit rather than infused her life with meaning.

Jesse, who was more than willing to support the family, urged Rebecca to let him pamper her a little and indulge *him* in his admittedly paternalistic fantasies, which up until that time he had carefully censored. (He knew that within their household Knights in Shining Armor were *not* politically correct!) Before becoming a mother, Rebecca would never have allowed herself to consider taking him up on such an offer (and for this reason the offer would probably never have been made). Yet, as the ice within her began to thaw, she began to ask herself why she wouldn't allow herself this pleasure, and why it was against her "principles" to lighten up, be taken care of, and maybe even "waste" some time just living. Who was she trying to be, anyway, when she felt compelled to need nobody and nothing and do everything all herself?

Loving another person and being loved herself simply for being alive was formerly a forbidden pleasure (only babies can have this, and she was supposed *never* to have been a baby), but mightn't she now give herself permission? Nobody would squeal. Wasn't that part of being a good mother? Wouldn't the "baby" within herself and the real baby outside lose something if she did not get off the merry-go-round that was not making her merry but only frenetic and let go?

But letting go of her mythic identity as the Mature Self-Sufficient Career Woman/Supermom was not that simple, particularly since Rebecca began to substitute one unreal image of herself for another. Upon realizing that she was *not* made of stone and that she really didn't want to shelve her emotions or turn her back on her son's desires or her own, Rebecca erroneously concluded that perhaps she was really nothing *but* heart (and a child's heart at that), and, with this new image of herself in mind, she felt as dependent and as home-bound as her eight-month-old son. It was not surprising that Rebecca's newly distorted image of herself, one that was *opposite* the image she had previously held, triggered feelings of panic, not exhilaration.

When I saw Rebecca in psychotherapy, she was confused as to

who she really was and seemed to think that she had to choose between two completely antithetical identities. "I wish I could just drop it all," she said, referring to her work, and "let myself off the hook. Why can't I be like the other mothers I see in the park and just not worry about building a career or having money of my own or being productive? I *should* be happy to play all day on the floor with my baby and let go of all that other stuff; it only torments me." I couldn't agree more that Rebecca needed to free herself from the straitjacket she had tied herself into for so many years, but I also sensed that she was not altogether ready to untie the knots, fearing that her guts would spill out and she would be more incapacitated than ever, that one tattered fragment of a person would substitute for another.

By identifying so intensely with her son, Rebecca had invented a new myth of herself as a baby—and a deprived one at that. As the emotionally neglected baby and child that she had been but no longer was, Rebecca felt that she could not stand on her own two feet or venture far from home; she could only smile and cry and tentatively begin to make her way in the world, with a lot of help. Surely such a figure could not keep up with her work at the office, or juggle motherhood and career, as some women managed to do. Indeed, she cut a rather pathetic figure outside the world of childhood. "When I think of quitting work, I get a wave of vertigo, as if I were falling into an abyss and there was no bottom." Rebecca might have found the self she had buried long ago, but time had passed, and in actuality she was no longer the person she had been back then. This restored image of the forgotten child was no longer up-to-date, it was no longer "real." Thesis and antithesis alternate awaiting a new synthesis, without which Rebecca would no more be able to find herself in fantasies of idealized motherhood than she had found herself as she furiously climbed the "ladder of success" without regard for where it led her and what she was leaving behind.

In fairy tales, when a frog becomes a prince or a cinder-wench becomes a princess, we know that the transformation that has occurred is permanent and true. The wicked spell has been broken, and our hero or heroine is finally free to fulfill his or her true destiny. In real life, transformations are often deceptive, and just when we think we are forging ahead, we may find that we are merely going around in circles. The merry-go-round music is entrancing, but we eventually realize that, even if we manage to switch horses midway, the scenery remains the same and we are still going nowhere.

Breaking the spell of the self-fulfilling prophecy is in some ways more difficult a task than our fairy tales lead us to believe, but in other ways it is really far simpler. True, there is no magic on hand, but, as it turns out, we don't really need any. We ourselves are our own most unyielding adversaries, and so it is mainly ourselves that we need to win over in order to "wake up." Once certain that it is indeed *possible* to get off the merry-go-round horse that we have harnessed ourselves to without getting right back up on another, then it is a question of convincing ourselves of the value of doing just that. What harm, if any, is there in dismounting? And if we are still dizzy, is it humiliating if on occasion we stumble and fall? Whom will we be saying goodbye to as we wend our way out of the magical circle? And whom will we encounter beyond?

6

Breaking the Spell

> Is there a way, O Self, thou who hast known bitterness,
> To burst the crystal that the monster has profaned,
> And take flight, with my two featherless
> Wings—at the risk of falling through eternity?
>
> —Stéphane Mallarmé, "The Windows"

> The spontaneous gesture is the True Self in action.
>
> —D. W. Winnicott,
> *The Maturational Processes and the Facilitating Environment*

Transformations do occur, however, and spells can be broken; after all, the power of the self-fulfilling prophecy lies in our belief in its power. As soon as the Wizard of Oz is exposed as a charlatan, Dorothy and her friends are freed to discover their own capabilities, and when they do, they realize that they don't need the Wizard's false magic after all; they are sufficient unto themselves. When we expose the mythic elements in our identities, we challenge their power to shape our destinies. In the process, we rediscover "the spontaneous gesture," which is what psychoanalyst D. W. Winnicott calls the "True Self in action." Then, just like Dorothy, we too can begin the process of returning "home."

Stories such as "Beauty and the Beast," "The Frog Prince," "Snow White and Rose Red," and the numerous myths of the "birth of the hero," whose identity is mistaken in his youth for that of a mere commoner, express a universal human need to believe in a self that is nobler and truer than the one we live with daily, a self that is destined to emerge after a long period of confinement. Otto Rank documents the recurrence of this motif in myths from diverse cultures *(The Myth of the Birth of the Hero).* The hero in these myths is invariably of noble birth, but, on account of circumstance, he lives in obscurity until his "true" identity is discovered once his heroism becomes manifest.

In storybooks, love and sometimes extraordinary feats of courage are the magic required to liberate the forsaken self so that a person's appearance will no longer be at odds with his essential reality. In real life, however, love is "not enough," to borrow a phrase from the late Bruno Bettelheim *(Love Is Not Enough)*, and though insight into the origins and functions of our mythological identities is essential in order to break their stranglehold on our imaginations, we find, to our dismay, that insight alone is not a magical cure. We have all encountered people who offer us the most elegant interpretations of their own behavior and yet, despite their "brilliant" formulations, continue to act out the very conflicts they purportedly understand so well. And don't we often observe ourselves walking right into the same old familiar traps, time and again, even when we recognize the bait and could "easily" not bite?

Freud, a major proponent of "insight" as a tool by which to alleviate psychic suffering, addressed just such contradictions. He spoke in his later works of a "compulsion" to repeat the past and referred to the "adhesiveness" of our libido as he tried to figure out why intelligent and well-analyzed patients resisted "cure" and reinvented their conflicts, despite their presumed insight and the unpleasant consequences that they correctly anticipated would ensue.

In his paper "Analysis Terminable and Interminable," Freud proposed that "the adult's ego, with its increased strength, continues to defend itself against dangers which no longer exist in reality; indeed, it finds itself compelled to seek out those situations in reality which can serve as an approximate substitute for the original danger, so as to be able to justify, in relation to them, its maintaining its habitual modes of reaction."

But Freud's description of how we ingeniously construct our lives so that we can hold on to our customary ways of living and loving, as frustrating as they are, leaves many questions unanswered. It does not illuminate *why* we should remain wedded to the past when the past is no longer real but only exists in the form of memory. There is no glue, and we are not literally stuck; "adhesive libidos" seems an unfortunately passive metaphor to me. We are actively digging new holes and then falling into them.

In order to understand *how* to change ourselves and in turn our relations with other people, we need to understand our conscious thought processes as well as our unconscious motivations. Why are we convinced that we are fated to live our lives the way we do, when we are not? And when "fate" is no longer an issue for us, and new possibilities are opened up, what then is our *current* investment in continuing to pump life into our mythological identities? Without our constant support, these insubstantial figures would die a natural death. Do we have a stake in keeping them alive? In other words, it is critical to understand why, once we have separated reality from myth, we still continue to go whirling around, riding piggyback on our mythological identities "as if" we had no choice?

Originally, the distorted images of who we are were imposed upon us, unintentionally perhaps, but without our being aware enough to raise a convincing protest. Over the years, however, we have appropriated these false images for our own purposes, and though they betray some aspect of our humanity, they may seem closer to us than the "buried" self within, which is, after all these years, somewhat of an abstraction. We may believe theoretically in a "true" self, but since it is, in many cases, only a potentiality that has not yet been actualized, its existence is unproved, and so we are naturally skeptical.

A common source of confusion stems from the failure to distinguish clearly between what a person *does* and who he *is*. Though from an existentialist position one might argue that the two are, for all practical purposes, equivalent, and that in fact a person is nothing more than the sum total of his actions over the course of a lifetime, we can always change what we *do* but not who we are. Anyone can act like a Simpleton, a Snow Queen, a Rebel, or a Martyr (though some of us are better suited to certain parts than to others), but when one actually *is* such a character, the future is predetermined and there is no freedom.

By the time the Charmer/Adorable Baby is sixteen or even six, she may no longer feel as if the caricatured qualities ascribed to her are foreign or even acquired; indeed, they feel self-generated, and by that age they are. Psychoanalysts refer to these qualities as "ego-syntonic," and argue that, precisely because they are not experienced as alien to ourselves, they are the most invulnerable to change. Thus, despite the limitations this identity imposes on Lisa's life as a professional woman, she subtly resists any attempts to tamper seriously with this persona. It is as if she herself were being deconstructed, not a mythological image, and as if without these identifying characteristics she might end up being colorless, devoid of content, paradoxically unauthentic.

Even in fairy tales, characters need courage to break spells; typically, the women in these stories patiently endure tremendous hardship, and the men slay dragons or other fearsome creatures. Some of us try to follow their example. We call such women "saints" or "martyrs" and sometimes label their behavior "masochistic." Such men we call "daredevils" or "heroes," and label their behavior "reckless" or "courageous," depending on the outcome.

But the courage *real* people, as opposed to fairy-tale characters, need if psychic change is to occur is of a very different sort. To break free from the self-fulfilling prophecy, we must be willing to lose our footing temporarily as we embrace the truth about ourselves and others and life in general. This means not only that we must question our most basic assumptions about who we are, but also that we must admit that the wrongs of the past cannot be undone, or even compensated for. We cannot expect to receive special treatment, now or in the future, to make up for the time we have lost. It is gone, whether we like it or not.

Psychoanalyst D. W. Winnicott suggests that the "True Self" "comes from the aliveness of the body tissues and the working of body-functions, including the heart's action and breathing" (*The Maturational Processes and the Facilitating Environment*, p. 148). Ironically, it was in an effort to protect this True, precious, but fundamentally unmysterious Self that we constructed a False, disposable self and pledged to live unspontaneously as mythological figures.

But if this is the nature of the "monster" that has kept us in thrall, then we need no miracles or heroes to break out of our trance and come alive again. We are our own prison guards. Once we are *truly* convinced that the benefits of being real and seeing clearly outweigh the liabilities and risks, and that ordinary unhappiness, which can never be eliminated entirely, is preferable to neurotic misery (to paraphrase Freud, "Studies on Hysteria," p. 305), we will naturally rediscover "the aliveness" that is and always has been there, even though it has been hidden and gagged and we have been accomplices in the crime against ourselves.

Psychologically, however, this is no easy task. It means acknowledging that the defenses we so painstakingly built are now obsolete and ecologically unsound. (They *were* necessary when we were growing up, but now they are depleting our psychic resources!) After we spent so much time and creative energy constructing our elaborate armor, it is a bitter pill to swallow to think we should throw it all away and start anew. Understandably, many of us hesitate before taking such a monumental step.

Changing patterns of behavior often sounds simple on paper, and there are a myriad of "self-help" books on the market that suggest this is so. But if it were actually the case, we would all divest ourselves of our false identities as soon as we had identified them as impostors, and as a general rule we do not. We hesitate before finally sentencing the "criminal," wishing to be certain that we have gotten the right guy. *He* continues to plead innocent of any crime, maintaining that he is our most loyal subject, and a kindred spirit no less, and that we would be foolhardy to exile him from our lives. But even when we are convinced that we have been deceived, we are often loath to give up our customary ways of being, though they constrict our lives or, worse yet, force us to re-experience our most dreaded nightmares. There are a number of reasons why.

For one, real life is not a rose garden (as the psychoanalyst in Hannah Green's novel, *I Never Promised You a Rose Garden*, cautioned her schizophrenic patient), and even if we can live more spontaneously, as soon as we are real people we must face the fact that we can never recover our lost childhood innocence, never have a different mother or father, and, despite our past disappointments, will not grow up to live happily ever after. What is done is done, and having suffered doesn't mean that we are immune to suffering again. Only fairy tales can promise us the gift of paradise, and only mythological identities allow us to pretend that fairy tales are true.

Moreover, after years of life as a "character," life as a person may seem wanting in excitement or drama; feeling bigger or lesser than life is definitely distinctive, and there is even a peculiar satisfaction to be derived from failing to live up to one's potential—there is always the promise of a glorious tomorrow, or the dream of what we could have been.

After identifying himself with the Responsible Citizen for most of his life, John found it distasteful to live with the idea that he had any weaknesses of character, any hidden sorrows, any ungenerous impulses. After all, he was not supposed to, and he assumed that people loved and respected him because they believed he was who he appeared to be. Moreover, since he had always been praised for his "maturity" and broad-mindedness, his own good opinion of himself hinged upon his ability to approximate this ideal, and for the most part he succeeded. He had, for all intents and purposes, become what he originally imagined himself to be, so why now unravel an identity that he had so carefully woven together with only the very best materials? (How frustrated and disappointed his mother would have been had he been just a boy at thirteen, and not her surrogate husband, and how frustrated and disappointed he would be as an adult were he to lose this claim to specialness, after so many years of tedious labor and self-sacrifice.)

Even though John "knew" intellectually that the image he projected was not entirely true to his inner reality (he might appear integrated, unsentimental, and unfailingly logical, but there were pieces missing in the picture), and in confidence has stated explicitly that he wanted to be more spontaneous and less exacting with himself, judging by his behavior, he was actually quite reluctant to let go of his persona, which, after thirty-five years, was more than skin-deep. Unfailingly Responsible, he would one moment criticize himself for not enjoying his life enough, then berate himself for being too distractable and too undisciplined. How would he ever make a name for himself in his profession and *really* fulfill his potential if he continued to fritter away his time with trivialities? In this fashion, John oscillated between reproaching himself for living his mythic identity and reproaching himself for not living it faithfully enough. He wanted to loosen up and "free" his creativity, but only so that he could be more perfect!

John complained of his confinement, and yet, like many of us, he confined himself. As long-term prisoners learn devious ways to use the system to their advantage, John too learned to extract pleasure from living an unauthentic, unspontaneous life. He felt proud that he was in control of all his messier feelings, and though he envied those "less responsible," morally flabby individuals who, to his way of thinking, were evidently not, he also felt smug and superior, as any self-denying martyr would. Moreover, after years of holding himself rigidly in place, John would have felt terribly awkward, maybe even bashful, if he allowed himself to move through life more fluently. According to his scheme, this would make him "boyish," and that was too steep a price to pay for a little pleasure. To put it crassly, where were the dividends?

From our distanced perspective, John is a victim of his own mythology, his own distorted images of himself and others. However, from his perspective, he is not only a victim but a master of deception—euphemistically speaking, a creative artist. After all, by shutting down his own internal monitoring devices so that neither he nor anyone else knows who he really is or what he really feels, he has managed to conquer reality and preserve an illusion of control. If John regarded his inhibitions and his compulsive perfectionisms as a burden, and he did, he also valued these qualities; his "character" was his most precious possession. This is why John, the quintessential Rationalist, was really not leading a very rational life at all, cutting himself off from his potential and stifling his spontaneity in pursuit of a dream.

There are still other hidden advantages to continuing to live in character, be it the Clown, or the Ne'er-Do-Well, or the family Brain, even when it has outlived its usefulness. By remaining loyal to our past, we deny that our precious time and energy have been wasted and our selves betrayed. Moreover, there is some consolation in the belief that what was and what is simply *had* to be, and some pleasure to be derived from withdrawing from the battle and surrendering to our "fate." (We shrug our shoulders and declare, "That's just the way I am," overtly expressing our regrets, but covertly heaving a sigh of relief at not having to take responsibility for the future.) However, this method of conflict resolution has obvious limitations. As long as we continue the deception and insist that it is no deception at all because this "character" is who we really are, we do not undo the damage done us, but only rename it so that we can live more comfortably with it.

Whereas some people stubbornly ally themselves with their mythic characters, others vehemently reject them and sentence their families to a lifetime of reproach. Sometimes they mistakenly assume that the purpose of psychotherapy is to shift the burden of guilt from their own shoulders onto the shoulders of their parents and siblings. They condemn the past, yet at the same time hold on to it by blaming it for their present anxieties and insufficiencies. This pointing the finger may be cathartic, and initially may be experienced as truly liberating; ultimately, however, it does not inspire renewal. By proclaiming that other people, who were but are no longer formidable presences, are the cause of our current misery and responsible for who we are today, we live the myth of the Victim, and as such are forever tied to our presumed victimizers. This does not break the spell but, rather, affirms its power over us.

Finally, our mythological identities shield us not only from the truth about ourselves but also from the truth about the human condition generally. When we get off the stage, we are forced to admit that we are indeed only human, and that consequently much of life is beyond our control. We are limited (and always will be), and, besides, other people are not entirely predictable, nor are they always as we would have them, since they are only human too! All this may seem obvious, but in the world of "as if" we live "as if" it were not so. This "existential" reckoning can be liberating or terrifying, depending on how important it is to feel in *total* control of our universe, and how important it is for us to deny the human realities of life and loss and death. (See Ernest Becker's

Denial of Death, in which he discusses the existential dilemma that faces all human beings because of our dual physical and spiritual nature. We are animals, and hence must endure the limitations imposed by physical reality, but we also have the capacity to imagine transcending the human condition, though in actuality we never can.)

When Anna decides not to play the part of Pollyanna, her friend Elaine stops calling her and she realizes that she has lost her longtime summer-holiday companion. Anna will have to find new ways of spending her vacations now that she is no longer jockeying to remain in Elaine's orbit, and she will have to decide whether or not it is sometimes better to be alone than with someone who is not a *genuine* companion. Of course, Anna can always find another Elaine—there are a plethora of them out there. But, having taken the first step toward rediscovering her own substance, Anna cannot go back and reconstitute the original friendship; it has lost its "charm," just as being Elaine's satellite has lost its magical appeal. The merry-go-round has temporarily come to a halt, but it will be up to Anna whether she wants to stop spinning and get off, or buy another ticket and sway to the music.

When Helen stops pretending to have orgasms and pretending to herself that she doesn't mind not having orgasms, her devoted lover of twelve years freezes, becomes impotent, and then runs in terror back to his wife. But when he returns to Helen three weeks later, more passionate and more respectful of her feelings than before, the question remains: Can she tolerate that? What will he expect from her in exchange? Will she *have* to have an orgasm? Does this mean she must descend to his level and give up her role as the Ministering Angel? There are advantages and disadvantages to being of this world and therefore being not quite so Pure, so remote. By stripping away her disguise, Helen has admitted that she wants something from someone—in this instance sexual gratification—and though this means she is not entirely sufficient unto herself, as she would have liked to believe, she may just get some of what she wants after all!

And Maia wonders what her mother would do were she not constantly giving her something to worry about. Would her mother begin to fall apart? Would she go into therapy herself for chronic agoraphobia? If Maia were not the Irrepressible Wild Child, would her mother still be her mother? She can't be sure. Before anyone decides to take such a giant step and disrupt the status quo, he may well ask himself whether it is worthwhile to give up his familiar illusions and take the risk of seeing clearly what life really has to offer. Or, as poet Stéphane Mallarmé put it, "risk . . . falling through eternity."

SOME BENEFITS AND RISKS OF DECLARING THAT THE GRAND PROCESSION SHOULD END BECAUSE THE EMPEROR REALLY HAS NO CLOTHES

> There is an urge to articulate the true self, and I name this the destiny drive which I link up to the force of the true self to elaborate personality potential.
>
> —Christopher Bollas, *Forces of Destiny*

> Why should I see
> whose vision showed me nothing sweet to see?
>
> —Sophocles, *Oedipus the King*

As we become attuned to the assumptions that we un-self-consciously make concerning our own and other people's identities, we are less apt to be seduced by partial truths (damning and flattering) or tranquilized by facile explanations for our behavior. Moreover, as our individual mythological identities begin to crack, the overarching myth that we are passive onlookers in our own lives also begins to crumble.

But if, once we have discovered that we are not all that we appear to be and that what we appear to be is not all of what we are, feelings of helplessness or, if you will, "fatedness" dissipate, this is just the first step toward getting off the merry-go-round. Though the "spell" may be broken, we may find that we prefer to act "as if" it weren't, and to continue as we always have, living with others within our shared mythological world.

If it is true, as many psychologists would have us believe, that there is a natural thrust toward self-expression and self-fulfillment, it is also true that there are opposing forces within the psyche that actively maintain the self-deceptions that keep us as shadows living within the shadows. We will never stop reinventing our personal fairy tales until we acknowledge both impulses—the impulse to see clearly and speak honestly in the uncertainty of the present, and the impulse to live buffered from uncertainty by the clouds of the past.

So the question to pursue at this juncture is not so much how to break the spell of the self-fulfilling prophecy as *what* keeps each one of us from doing so once we have the wherewithal to be disillusioned and to live outside the family orbit. The continued running of the family drama depends upon our *active* participation, so why, once we have denounced the play and identified ourselves as one of a cast of characters, do we continue to betray our "true" selves and insist on living life in a role, "as if" we could do no differently?

After we have gained insight into the nature and origin of our distorted self-images, what typically follows is an extended period of experimentation and self-examination as we assess for ourselves the actual and imagined consequences of discarding these images in favor of being real. Only then can we make an informed choice between living life as the child we were and living life as the adult we potentially can be. Despite our fantasies, outside the world of myth it is a choice that is only ours to make.

Laurel has the power of eliciting blame but also envy from her family and lovers when she is an Irrepressible but Abject Messmaker. As long as she sees herself in the image of Pandora and acts accordingly, she is guaranteed a special place in their imagination and hopes not to suffer from the feelings of invisibility which originally inspired her to stir up trouble all too visibly. Incurable Messmakers need not ever worry about being forgotten like a Speck of Dust. They are not unanchored, floating, or threatened with disintegration.

By willfully disregarding the consequences of her actions, Laurel has managed to preserve a shred of dignity (*she* can't be tamed). Moreover, by believing that she is the source of all the misery in the world (the bad apple that spoils the entire bushel), she can feel extraordinarily powerful. Her more conventional brother, Ethan, surely does not have such an impact on his environment!

Laurel and Anna and Maia and Kate are all ambivalent about betraying this false but perversely "noble" identity (or relinquishing their claim on Pollyanna, Pandora's mirror image and antithesis). Bidding goodbye to all the troubles these mythological identities bring with them means also bidding goodbye to the illusion of control that they engender. Consider Laurel's dilemma.

Laurel waits by the phone, uncomfortably aware of the passage of time. It is a Monday evening, and before Brian went away for the weekend with his wife and children, they had made plans to have dinner together. No specific arrangements had been made, which was typical of Brian, who intimated that it would be unreasonable of Laurel to expect him to commit himself to a definite time or place, given the complicated state of his affairs. "We'll have to play it by ear," he had said, which meant that he'd call her when he had a chance. All she had to do was just be there.

Laurel was to be Brian's Bohemian mistress, with whom he could feel impulsive, undomesticated, and potent, and in return he would be hers forever. Though Laurel knew that such "plans" would leave her in a state of limbo, she suppressed any qualms she may have felt and silently acquiesced. This was not out of naïveté but by design. She had not *wanted* to raise a protest at that moment, because she wished to prove that she was Understanding, Flexible, Carefree, and, unlike Brian's mythologically suffocating wife, willing to indulge him even if it was at her own expense.

But rather than leap to unfounded conclusions and label Laurel "masochistic," as her brother, Ethan, was known to do with dramatic flourish, it is important to see that her "self-denial" was part of a larger picture in which she figured as an inveterate Troublemaker, whose feelings were by definition petty and troublesome. And by denying herself, Laurel knew that she was creating for Brian the illusion of perfect harmony and unburdened sexuality, and that this was her allure. How, given her defiled self-image, could she deny herself *that* power?

Multiplying the one incident tenfold, Laurel could project herself into the future and anticipate that Brian would grow to depend on her and her indulgences. Then she could pretend that his addiction to her adulation of him was true love. The part that Laurel played in Brian's life demanded self-control in addition to self-denial, but it was familiar to her: she had learned it years before at her mother's side. It was also, however, the overture to the grand entrance of Pandora, the Instigator, the Destroyer of the Peace, the flip side of the sexually liberated Free Spirit.

And so, on this Monday evening, after a long and productive day on her new job, which she got despite her hard-earned reputation, Laurel found herself wrestling with a not-unfamiliar feeling of suspended animation. Here she was once again consigned to waiting "passively" on someone else's desires, her own temporarily stifled. As seven o'clock passed without her hearing a word from Brian, Laurel began to feel a tightness in her chest and an overwhelming impulse to disrupt his happy "party" in the most outrageous fashion imaginable. She would call him at his home, which was the one thing he had expressly forbidden her ever to do, and then, after exposing him to his wife and children, she would watch guiltily (and gleefully) as the house of cards that she herself had carefully built along with Brian collapsed upon their heads. After a stint of being Pollyanna, she would reaffirm her identity as a Brazen Troublemaker, unrepressed and irrepressible.

Laurel's long-standing allegiance to her identity as a Pandora-like figure is understandable when placed in context. Why would she want to give up that image of herself if the only alternative image is that of a Speck of Dust, someone else's Flattering Mirror? After biting her tongue and denying her desires, Laurel finds it a welcome relief to lash out indiscriminately, stirring up the waters and breaking all the rules. By serving as a vehicle for Unbridled Passion, Laurel assumes the blame for life's misery and suffers the consequences of her rash actions, but it feels worthwhile if she can retrieve her humanity and assert her existence. It is a pleasure, if only fleeting, to unmuzzle herself and boldly yell out "the truth"!

Originally the myth of the Troublemaker served as a kind of compensation for Laurel's experience of invisibility. Later, however, there were still other benefits that she accrued by living out the myth of her Incorrigibility, and before she could discard it she would have to agree to give these up. By seeing herself as a jealous, grasping, and bitchy Homewrecker/Jobwrecker whom nobody could possibly love, Laurel preserved the illusion that she had only herself to blame for her chronic state of unhappiness, and that she and nobody else was the master of her fate. Ironically, Laurel felt more in control of her life when she defended and rationalized Brian's (or Marty's, or her mother's) insensitive behavior toward her than when she acknowledged that she was being treated insensitively and that her demands for consideration fell repeatedly on deaf ears.

In order to break out of this cycle, and truly become master of her "fate," Laurel would have to give up being the Flattering Mirror, and that was not as simple as it sounds. This identity had evolved out of her experience of herself as insubstantial and thus totally dependent, but it became the vehicle by which she hoped to gain surreptitiously the power she assumed she "naturally" lacked. Of course, the more she played the part, the more she was pigeonholed, and the more she believed that it was the only one she *could* play. This is the knot we all find most difficult to untangle.

As a Flattering Mirror, Laurel was confident that she could remain indefinitely Brian's (or someone else's) most treasured object, and since she lacked a sense of her own subjectivity, being such an object was her only chance of being loved and feeling in control. As long as she doubted that she had anything inside herself to latch on to (no center of gravity, no substance of her own), she could not risk losing that hook into another person's insides. She'd float away, disintegrate.

As Laurel began to recognize that she was a real person with needs and desires of her own, she also realized that as such she had no guarantee of being able to secure herself a central position in another person's life. If she inhabited her own body, she could not very well live inside someone else's. This was both wonderful and terrifying. Her mother had exiled her from the "inner circle" for the crime of being a separate person, and only as Pandora, the guilty messmaker, was she able to gain readmittance, having suffered and done penance. But, then, of course, as a real person who is no longer her parent's dependent child, Linda wouldn't need to hold on for dear life to another's insides—only mirrors are vacant when there is nobody there to reflect.

Let's return now to that anxious Monday evening, an evening that would be a turning point in Laurel's life. By eight o'clock, Laurel was in state of deep reflection; her anger had abated somewhat, but her mind was racing and her heart was beating fast. She knew that she was very hungry, and that this passive waiting by the telephone could not go on indefinitely. When she finally decided to go out and get herself something to eat, however, rather than call Brian at his home, precipitate a crisis, and stir up the usual sort of trouble that had won her her reputation, there was far more at stake than simply satisfying her need for bodily nourishment.

Had Laurel postponed her dinner indefinitely, she was certain to be ravenously hungry and uncontrollably angry when Brian finally did call. Then what would happen next could be easily predicted. There would be the customary scene, in which Laurel would end up figuring as the hysterical and unreasonable Other Woman, who not only ruined a happy marriage but also spoiled what could have been a lovely evening and a beautiful romance. And then, after the tears and threats, there would be promises and entreaties, and the Flattering Mirror/Speck of Dust would reappear to cap off the performance.

Now an interested spectator in her own life drama, Laurel declined the opportunity to get up onstage and assume one disguise or another. She betrayed *both* of her mythological identities as she walked out onto the street, with no thoughts of revenge, and reentered the world as Laurel—a woman, not a Temptress or an inanimate, weightless piece of matter. She didn't know whom she would encounter at the local restaurant she chose for her dinner, nor did she know how she would spend her time after she ate. Her horizons had opened up, she was on her own, and she was free to act spontaneously.

Being an Innocent Beauty had been Julia's dream since she was a child; it was her mother's necessary fiction too, and even though periodically it turned into a nightmare as she found herself abandoned first by her husband and then by her lover, she couldn't bring herself to wake up just yet. At least as Beauty Julia could be purified of the ugly emotions that real people have to live with all their lives. And *her* love, unlike the love of ordinary people, promised to work miracles—if only she were patient and loyal to her image, she would have the capacity to transform Beasts into handsome Princes. What power! What transcendent hope! What a reprieve from the sterility of life in her mother's immaculate house and passionless marriage!

To an outsider, the actual losses Julia incurred in her pursuit of this fantasy image may seem to far outweigh the actual benefits. But this is because an outsider sees only Julia the adult, not Julia the little girl, who, like any little child, contorted herself to gain love and security, and then prided herself on her ability to adapt. It is this childhood Julia who demanded compensation for her early sacrifices and who will not be satisfied to grow up and lead just an ordinary life and be an ordinary woman, not a kind of fairy-tale character. The little girl Julia was the one who refused to let go of the myth of being Beauty (it had been and still was her only solace), and it was *she* who threatened Julia, the adult, with the return of the Beast were she to become real. (That little girl felt positively bestial when she wasn't in character.) Let us briefly examine how this internal struggle between myth and reality manifested itself in her adult life.

Julia had always wanted to be a writer, and there was good reason to believe that her aspirations were not unrealistic. She had graduated with honors in English from a prestigious university, served as editor-in-chief of the student literary magazine, and, according to her own timid admission, been an exemplary student all of her life. But after such a promising beginning, Julia's life took a very different path, and her literary talents were shunted to the side. I attribute this largely to Julia's undying allegiance to her mythological identity as a kind of Ministering Angel figure, an allegiance that even supersedes her loyalty to her "self." One might argue that her talents have been channeled into the creation of her ongoing life drama and are unavailable for other work.

Although Julia argued convincingly that as a single mother struggling to make ends meet she had no time to pursue any intellectual or artistic interests of her own, minimizing their significance with a studied shrug of the shoulders, Julia *had* managed to devote boundless time and energy to rescuing her near-destitute alcoholic lover, Peter, but this of course was because *that* activity was an essential part of her myth. He, she insisted, was *really* a very talented if hitherto unrecognized artist, and she adroitly steered most conversations to his life and away from hers, as if her fate were identical with his. (In the fairy tale it was.) Personal ambition of the sort that commanded public attention did not fit with the image Julia had adopted for herself, and so Julia muzzled her *self* and turned her back on her "destiny," in order not to jeopardize the myth she so "ambitiously" had constructed.

Indeed, at one point, when I naïvely offered my enthusiastic support for her literary ambitions, I discovered that Julia was mistrustful of people who did take an interest in the person behind her beautifully crafted mask. Ironically, she felt more at home when her real self was being ignored, or, better yet, not seen at all, and Peter, as well as others before him, have done this service for her. She tended to fall in love with men who pretended along with her, and by her sweetness she systematically kept everyone else at arm's length.

Julia indefinitely postponed her dreams of self-fulfillment until "tomorrow," rather than take the risk of losing her special identity by fulfilling herself today, but she sacrificed her self-esteem in the process, and was chronically tortured by feelings of inferiority that were only the natural outgrowth of the self-abasing, diminutive identity that she was intent on assuming.

Julia is a perfect example of how intellectual insight alone is not sufficient to motivate a person to stop doing what she knows she does best. Having read the popular books on "codependency" and on self-destructiveness, Julia "knew" that she was addicted to her role of "rescuer," and was even willing to agree with the "experts" that this was not real love but only a simulation. Moreover, having been in psychotherapy for more than eight months, she claimed to have "understood" the childhood origins of her distorted images of herself. Yet Julia remained terrified of the demons that might have been unleashed were she to have "articulated" her true self, as psychoanalyst Christopher Bollas put it (*The Forces of Destiny*, p. 280). She did not realize that the so-called demons were but another aspect of the same myth of being Beauty, and that, if she were to consent to be a person and live outside the myth, those "demons" would no longer seem so demonic or feel so out of control. As long as she did not permit herself to express anything other than the *prettiest* of feelings, she reinforced her image of herself as secretly monstrous, and her investment in being unreal continued to grow.

Julia left therapy precipitously, and just at the point at which she seemed to be making "progress," which was only evidence of how subjective the experience of "progress" can be. She had not been in contact with Peter for more than six weeks, and in their last encounter she had been uncharacteristically unsympathetic when he offered the usual excuses for not returning her phone calls or keeping their appointments. Angry but well focused, Julia had described herself, albeit bashfully, as more confident than ever of her rights and his failings. As she began to take her own life into her hands, she made plans to go away with her daughter on vacation, and had even contacted a neighborhood newspaper to inquire into the possibility of future writing assignments. Beauty was fading into the background, and the Beast had been tamed and identified as no Prince at all.

But even though Julia was clearly proud of her newfound "autonomy," I had a suspicion that change was coming too fast, and that she was still not all she appeared to be. Julia knew very well how to be the "perfect patient" (compliance was her specialty), just as she knew how to be the perfect daughter and the perfect lover, but she always had her own secret agendas. She was willing, with my help, to test the waters and see how life felt outside of her myths, but just in case life didn't "work out" as planned, she was ready to beat a hasty retreat and was quietly preparing to find a new Prince/Beast so that she could begin her familiar story over again.

Once Peter and the mythology that went along with him were expunged from Julia's life, she experienced a noticeable vacuum. Where was her purpose now that she was no longer his Ministering Angel but, rather, was looking at him from across the table and seeing him for the first time with all his blemishes? And how could she distinguish herself when she no longer suffered unduly at his hands? Her contact with the newspaper had yet to generate anything exciting, and it was only a neighborhood publication, so, "naturally," she was uninspired. Having surrendered her mythological identity before establishing a viable, self-respecting alternative, Julia panicked and withdrew from me and from therapy, that dangerous mechanism of change.

During our last session, Julia casually let drop that her former husband, whom she had previously described as infantile and impulsive, was expressing renewed interest in reconciliation. She was evasive about her feelings and minimized her previous skepticism about his "reformed character," but I saw the wheels had been already set in motion as she contemplated a new "project" to substitute for the now defunct Peter. Julia's ex-husband's sudden reappearance on the scene led to talk of her past promiscuity, her brief "career" as a topless go-go dancer, and her sexual prowess. This conversation proved revealing.

Julia's eyes sparkled as she spoke of her past sexual escapades, and, far from feeling exploited or pained by these memories, she seemed temporarily to gain strength from them. Julia exulted in imagining herself as a veritable Femme Fatale, because her sexual charms as that mythological figure gave her the power to bring men to their knees, or so she believed. Though others may have regarded her with sympathy or contempt, as the mere object of men's desires, Julia *felt* as if she were finally in control when ensconced in this identity.

Julia's sexual attractiveness assumed mythic proportions and was as much her magic as her Innocence and Modesty. The myth of the Sex Queen and the myth of the Innocent Virgin served similar psychic functions for Julia, and as we can see, one can be substituted for the other. Each identity holds out the promise of omnipotence, which is something the real Julia can never attain. No writing assignment, no contract, no flesh-and-blood daughter can give her that. The illusion of total power is something that all mythological identities foster. Julia will only "break the spell" and become her "real" person when she has agreed not to want to cast spells of her own.

Larry suffers inordinately because of his "sensitivity" and his presumed inability to adapt to real life. He wishes that he were undaunted by trouble and that he were as "thick-skinned" as everyone else. But as the Mama's Boy and the Sensitive Plant, Larry winced whenever he heard a scratch in a record and politely refused to eat a slightly overcooked steak. A harried wife or a homeless beggar, a patronizing doctor or a critical boss could spoil his good humor for an entire day, and there was nothing a Sensitive Plant could do except rage against his fate and dream that someday someone would deliver him from this imperfect world. How, then, could Larry possibly be expected to live with a seizure disorder that destroyed his career as a commercial artist at age fifty-four?

When, as a result of his disability, Larry's charmed life unraveled before his eyes, he was forced to confront his earliest, most shameful feelings about himself, but he mistakenly assumed that these darker feelings were nothing other than the "true" reflection of his character. Insisting that everything positive in his life was merely the product of illusion, Larry rediscovered his original damaged identity, and though he was repelled by what he saw, he embraced it queasily, as one would a bedraggled old friend.

As Larry's psychotherapist, I was convinced that exploding the myth of the Sensitive Plant, which in his case was related to the myth of the Insatiable Mama's Boy and was the impetus for the now defunct myth of the Ladies' Man, was going to be crucial in order for Larry to adjust to his objectively unfortunate condition. When I met him, Larry was suicidal, so this was going to be a matter of life and death. Psychotherapy could not cure his seizure disorder, but it could alleviate some of the shame and self-loathing that were associated with it. Living with seizures that render one periodically disoriented is bad enough, but when these seizures assume symbolic meaning and are taken as proof of an essentially flawed identity, they become intolerable.

From the point of view of an outsider, Larry's life as a Hothouse Flower/Spoiled Child seemed distinctly unrewarding, and one might have thought that he would have been the first to want to deconstruct the image and leave behind the shame and anxiety that it engendered. After all, if he were not doomed to be quite so sensitive and quite so demanding, then he would have been able to endure his own as well as other people's imperfections. He would have discovered, moreover, that he was really *not* going to crumble like a beautifully preserved dried flower outside of its picture frame, even if he was handled roughly and life was filled with disappointments.

But as it turned out, Larry was far from eager to hear alternative interpretations of his "faulty" character, interpretations that held out to him the possibility of psychic change. Instead, Larry initially defended his "cursed" identity as if he were defending his mother's virtue and his father's virility. Indeed, in order to preserve his image of his mother as Mother Teresa and his father as the sexy if ill-fated Casanova, Larry had to blame himself for their deficiencies as human beings and as parents. So he believed that *he* wanted too much, rather than consider that his mother had given him too little; and he painted himself as a Wimp, rather than indict his father for his sexual inconstancies and his gross insensitivity toward his mother. Larry's myth of himself was but a fragment of the entire family mythology, and naturally he hesitated before destroying his image, which, in the world of his imagination, still served the purpose of protecting his family's good name.

But I adduced that there were even more important reasons why as an adult Larry was reluctant to challenge the mythology he had lived by. Through the years, Larry had artfully constructed a world in which his weaknesses were transformed into strengths. This being the case, Larry had a personal stake in preserving his illusions, despite their potentially unflattering implications.

As long as Larry conceived of himself as a Sensitive Plant, an Anomaly of Nature, he felt entitled to special treatment, and less guilty when he failed to "measure up." His delicate constitution (which he would claim was the bane of his existence) *deserved* pity and reverence, tenderness and understanding, and in this he found solace. What's more, beginning with his very own mother, Larry had found that the world was filled with women who loved the image of a poetically melancholic little boy—indeed, loved that image more than they would ever love his real self. Larry has often served as their reprieve from the world of macho men (a world represented by his father and brothers), and when he doubled as the free and easy but exquisitely sensitive Ladies' Man, he scored a secret victory over his antagonists, and beat his father and brothers at their own game!

Indeed, out of an image of weakness and inadequacy, Larry created a network of relationships in which he could feel like a Prince, and in which there were clear advantages to not being earthy and resilient like everyone else. Larry's emotional intensity and childlike dependency on women became the basis for his romantic charm, and during those thirty-odd years when Larry cut a handsome figure as a captivating Ladies' Man, it never occurred to anybody that his sexual "insatiability" was an outgrowth of his early image of himself as a perennially frustrated Mama's Boy. Larry's idealism and hypersensitivity were recast as evidence of his intelligence and refinement, and, far from being contemptible, these qualities set him above, not below, your average, practical guy.

So when, suddenly, what Larry had always dreaded would happen did happen, and Larry was the first to taunt himself with "I told you so's, he was also the one who put up the fiercest resistance to revising his age-old perception of himself. And then, invoking Charles Darwin to suit his purposes, Larry maintained that, since only the fittest could and should survive, he, being constitutionally "unfit," would be better off "giving up the ghost." In his fantasy, that was all he was anyway, since he was his mother's shadow or a mere parody of his macho father and more virile older brothers!

Yet, despite all the evidence Larry drummed up, he wasn't able to convince me that the way he was was the way he always had to be, even though he played his usual parts impeccably and let me catch glimpses of both the Charmer and the Sensitive Plant/Mama's Boy. Stubbornly, *I* couldn't relinquish the idea that this was his myth. So, gradually, Larry realized that he had two choices: he could dismiss me entirely, in which case he could either drop out of therapy or simply go through the motions of self-examination, hoping to seduce me into pampering him as he had seduced others before me, or he could join me in my skepticism, seriously reconsider the "facts" of his life, and begin to write a new narrative.

After months and months of melancholic reminiscing about his childhood, his "perfect" mother, his awesomely dictatorial father, and his failures in love and marriage, even Larry began to grow weary of chastising himself for his "weaknesses." The story was monotonous and actually, on numerous retellings, hardly credible—there were too many missing pieces and too much black and white. So Larry slowly fleshed out the characters that had previously been one-dimensional and became receptive to fresh interpretations of motives and plot.

As the broken record was tentatively set aside, Larry's mind was set in motion, and he began to look less like a puppy dog in need of a home, and more like an intelligent man of fifty-four who was understandably angry and disappointed, both with his present condition and with his former life. The cloud was lifting.

Anger and disappointment need not be paralyzing. It all depends on who is experiencing these feelings. To a Sensitive Plant or a Mama's Boy, they are overwhelming; to a Debonair Ladies' Man, they are humiliating; but to one who is neither "fragile" nor "specially entitled," these feelings can serve as an impetus for change. As Larry took action to improve his life and uplift his spirits, and challenged his image of himself as a frail, dependent child, his mythological identity began noiselessly to disintegrate, opening up new possibilities and closing off some old ones. It is difficult, though not impossible, to sustain an image of oneself as dysfunctional and on the brink of wilting when new, contradictory evidence keeps mounting and it is publicly acknowledged. This was the reward (or liability) of being in therapy and acting on insight gained!

By placing limits on his siblings' unhelpful helpfulness, which only left him feeling more helpless than he really was, Larry not only shook the entire foundation of *their* relationship, but also revealed an inner strength that he had always assumed did not exist. By getting involved in community politics and returning to his noncommercial artwork, which had been neglected while he compulsively and flamboyantly pursued women and career, Larry found that he was capable of leadership, and even capable of initiating his own pleasure, and then change led to more change in a kind of snowball effect. What Larry had assumed was impossible for him to do was not (he could manage and even manage well), and so he was forced to reconceptualize who he was and what was essential to his identity.

Once Larry saw that he existed outside of his reflection, the spell was irrevocably broken, and though he could always reinvent the myth in order to find solace in a sense of entitlement or a dream of rescue, now that it (as well as its antithesis) was exposed as sham, he would never be the same again.

Howard's skirmishes with authority have drastically limited his professional opportunities and consumed his time and energy, and he frequently complains bitterly about how he struggled (to no avail) to uplift his fellow citizens from the moral degradation in which they were presumed to have lived. Yet, when confronted, Howard confessed that the conflict he stirred up everywhere was stimulating to him, and that he had depended on this "shot in the arm" for his feeling of aliveness. Without a good fight, Howard had always felt as if he were nothing and life were meaningless. Little battles, ones that he had a chance of winning, held little attraction for him: if he were actually to vanquish his "enemy," he would lose the very basis for his identity.

Mythological identities are always, in some fashion, spin-offs of reality, and as a child Howard was literally the "little guy" who fought in vain to depose his seemingly all-powerful parents. By identifying himself as an Underdog Soon-to-Be-Hero, Howard reproduced his family drama but also transformed himself into its hero (in fantasy, if not in reality). Like the Greek hero Prometheus, who dared to defy the edict of the chief god, Howard was attacked for his feats of heroism (Prometheus is tied to a rock and vultures tear at his liver), and yet he still could sustain the hope that his courage would not go unnoticed and that in the end he would be vindicated. Life as a martyr, an underdog, a social pariah was amply compensated for in the specter of Eternity.

Were Howard to give this life up now, what could he expect to get in exchange? A decent and steady job in his chosen profession? Perhaps, but, then again, perhaps not; he had already burned many of his bridges behind him, and it may have been impossible to rebuild amid the rubble. Could he hope for a stable relationship with a woman? Maybe, but again there were no guarantees—he was middle-aged and twice divorced, and his financial situation was tenuous at best. Friendship? Probably, but we must remember that this pleasure was entirely foreign to him and he might not know its worth. As his mythological character, Howard had not been one to consider friendship when assessing a person's value to him, and would need to introduce new measuring rods in order to assess the value of reciprocity, tenderness, interest. What Howard would be certain to gain would be a sense of his own inherent value independent of images, and with that the freedom to live more or less spontaneously in the present, without gnawing regrets or "delusive hope." But, as is true for everyone, only Howard could decide whether this was a fair exchange.

Howard liked to see himself as a radical who lived life stripped of illusion. He believed, moreover, that he, unlike his timid and conventional wives, lovers, and colleagues, was not afraid to look reality squarely in the face. He was eager to point out how often he had dared to expose hypocrisy and insincerity and corruption, even when it cost him a marriage or a job. Yet Howard had never "dared" to challenge the myth of his own martyrdom, which was created in compensation for the myth of his own vile inadequacy; this myth was sacrosanct and kept him self-righteously spinning his wheels in never-ending frustration.

The Solitary Idealist, the Iconoclast, and the Marginal Man I encountered was nothing more than a latter-day version of Howard's parents' original myth of the Bastard/Alley Cat, and Howard proved to be less of a revolutionary than an expert at covering lies with new lies. Over the course of therapy, however, Howard began to recognize that for nearly thirty-five years he had been the one tuning into the same action movie, and that he and nobody else had the power to turn off the projector and turn on the lights. Far from being evidence of his "free spirit," Howard's righteous indignation was studied and unspontaneous, and his explosive rage, which won him a psychiatric diagnosis of "borderline personality disorder," was more an expression of his childhood experience than a noble response to anything in his current life. He came to realize that it was *he* who was relentlessly reinventing the family drama, and, rather than purging himself of a past that he claimed to despise, he had become its foremost promoter as he played producer, director, and leading man in the ongoing saga. By enlisting countless others to play the familiar supporting roles, Howard had justified what Freud called his "habitual modes of reaction" ("Analysis Terminable and Interminable," p. 238). Far from being a radical, he upheld tradition far more than he had ever wanted to admit.

Howard had stopped his clock a long time ago, and was pretending (though he had not realized it was pretense) that he had the power to make time stand still. He had figured that if it stood still long enough he could make that little boy he believed himself to be stop feeling so impotent and so sad.

But all Howard's insight into his past would have been for naught had not Howard also recognized that his life, as he was living it, was not an epic drama but a personal tragedy which was now largely of his own devising. Facing this truth meant facing not only that he had wasted his creative energies for many years but also that there would be no "happy ending" at all unless he tore off the mask, and even then there would be a big question mark, simply because there always is. This is the human condition, which the existentialists tell us can make cowards of us all.

Tentatively, and therefore not at all like an epic hero, Howard started to try out other forms of feeling alive and worthwhile, experimenting with new ways of relating to men and women. He became self-conscious about his choices of sexual partners, and uncomfortably aware that in the past he had gravitated toward the very women who could never really satisfy him, women who looked to him to fight their battles for them and do the outrageous things they would never have done themselves. Having acknowledged that he had been most at ease when he could play the familiar role of advocate and daredevil, Howard also recognized that, when he ended up feeling exploited after the initial glow of heroism had dwindled and then died, he was largely responsible. He had scanned the field for two-dimensional women who desired nothing more than a two-dimensional man, and so he, no less than they, had created a two-dimensional relationship that was ultimately empty and uninspiring.

As Howard ceased to feel compelled to act out his mythological identity, he no longer needed to find "inadequate" women who could fit into his grand design. Consequently, he felt less victimized, and also less smugly patronizing, as he approached women who wanted to relate to a man, not a mythic character. But there were some not-so-obvious drawbacks. Howard was less in control in these more substantive relationships, and thus felt more vulnerable. Without the distraction of the bright lights, the make-believe set, and the canned music that accompanied his dramatic performances, Howard found that he really cared about some people and really did not care for others; this made him anxious.

Howard was not used to being a human being among other human beings, having believed for so long that his only choices were to be either a worm amid gods, a god amid worms, or a hero temporarily disguised as a humble peasant. The pleasures and pains of "just" living were new to him, and he was still a tourist awkwardly negotiating in an alien tongue.

His spell had also been broken, and though Howard, like Larry and Laurel, was still free to *choose* to play his usual part—stirring up the usual sorts of crises, and secretly dreaming of glory—he could choose not to. The magic being gone, he was on to his own tricks, and his pleas of martyrdom were no longer credible. (Karen Horney discusses the different imaginary "paths to glory" that we devise to compensate us for our basic feelings of anxiety. See *Neurosis and Human Growth.*)

Had she not become a mother, Rebecca might never have questioned her life's goals, or wondered whether she was actually happy being as Self-Sufficient, Unsentimental, and Ambitious as she was, or at least appeared to be. By most standards, Rebecca was a great "success," and there was no reason to challenge the status quo. She was attractive, she had been offered an executive position in a prestigious company immediately after having received her degree in business administration, and she was married to a wealthy man who respected her "independence" and yet provided her with a context in which she could be "taken care of" if she was so inclined. People admired her for her achievements, and envied her her composure. So, in a way, Rebecca was able to have her cake and eat it too, having made a life for herself in which she could proudly refuse to be pampered.

The life Rebecca had was the life she had striven for since she was a young child, with herself cast in the role of the Perfect Daughter, and these were her values—or so she believed. If she was missing something by leaving little space or time for intimacy with her husband or friends, working until eight o'clock most evenings, she was not aware of the loss.

As perfectionistic as every "perfect" child is doomed to be, Rebecca had always been her own worst critic. Yet, before becoming a mother, she had never berated herself for being too serious or too driven or too self-involved. If anything, she had faulted herself for not being serious or driven or selfish enough. She had been determined to balance on the narrow pedestal she had been placed upon years before, and had not been conscious of any major problems with the mythic character she struggled to embody.

Then Rebecca had a baby and became a mother, which posed a problem, because her mythic character could not mother—she had no tender feelings and she never allowed anyone to interfere with her schedule! But Rebecca's baby, like all babies, was not so scheduled or so standoffish, and though Rebecca had managed to find a husband who would accommodate her, and friends who wanted little in the way of intimacy (or if they did she did not hear of it), her baby's pressing needs could not be easily ignored. His piercing cries and joyous smiles pried open a window into a secret world that Rebecca had previously shut out, having for years worn thick blinders everywhere (even to bed). Bombarded by her own forgotten desires to love and be loved, to care for others and to be taken care of herself, Rebecca felt rejuvenated but also dizzied by her emotions, which she categorized as childish. She was easily brought to tears, happy ones and sad ones. Moreover, and this was perhaps most disturbing, she had what seemed to her to be a dangerously rash impulse to abandon herself (or at least the person she had believed was herself) and the profession and life-style that she associated with her.

Whose life was she living, anyway, by compulsively denying herself time for intimacy and leisure in her quest to excel? And why was she obliged to tear herself cold-bloodedly from her home each morning, gulping down her black coffee, to spend long hours at the office, researching various advertising strategies, when her heart was not in it and money was not realistically an issue?

Instead of laboring over voluminous financial reports and mollifying impatient supervisors and ingratiating subordinates, she fantasized about spending her days playing endlessly with her son, cross-legged on the floor, going to the park, chatting with other new mothers about teething and "separation" and educational philosophies. And when her husband came home at six o'clock, they could have "real meals" together, not just prepackaged ones. Perhaps they could get a puppy. And what prevented them from not doing anything in particular at all—just "nesting"?

But Rebecca's head began to swim whenever she seriously contemplated making these changes in her life, and this made her pause to consider her motives. I believed that as a child Rebecca had never been properly "hatched" but, ironically, had incubated for so long within her mythically invulnerable identity as the Self-Sufficient Woman of the World that she was uncertain what she would look like were she finally to peck her way out of her protective shell. Would she be full-grown? Or would she still be a baby herself? After all, her imperviousness and her "maturity" were turning out to be illusory. Which was the false image, the cool, capable woman, or the sweetly naïve and weepy baby? These questions plagued Rebecca, and she had to find out.

As time went on, Rebecca was no longer convinced of the reality of her mythic character, but for months she held on for dear life to the well-worn images of herself as Mature, Rational, and completely Independent: although the spell had been broken, she was still vulnerable to emotional blackmail. This was because, as always, the counterpart to the myth of perfection is the myth of fundamental inadequacy. She was either the Independent woman of one myth or a contemptibly Dependent little girl in the other. Although Rebecca no longer believed in her statuesque invulnerability, she still believed that her real self was weak and undignified, "babyish," and that without the artifice life would be intolerably unstable, she being beholden to everybody. (Babies *are*, without their knowing it.)

For a while, Rebecca romanticized motherhood and envied nonworking mothers their "freedom" and presumed spontaneity. But this was no more real than glorifying a vice-presidency in a Fortune 500 firm. Both images were traps that confined her and denied the complex and multifaceted nature of her personality. Only as Rebecca began to accept the reality of herself as a woman who was neither hermetically sealed over nor gushing with emotion, neither all for herself nor all for other people, all "grown-up" nor all the "baby," could she agree to her own liberation from the world of myth and jump down from the pedestal that had won her so much acclaim but cost her her spontaneity.

Rebecca decided to take a leave of absence from her work in order to spend more unstructured time living and playing with her baby, but she could do this only after she knew that she was not doomed to become Silly Putty as soon as she made friends with her more tender feelings. Then the alienated pleasures of the past (the admiration, the illusion of being in total control) could no longer compete with the pleasures of being real, pleasures Rebecca rediscovered watching her baby as he un-self-consciously expressed his desires and wrestled with his own and life's limitations. Her future is a question mark (she knew that she didn't want to play on the floor every day indefinitely), but now at least it is *hers* and she is living in time.

REDEFINING INTIMACY

> . . . and though they neither of them dealt any further with fairies and their magic, they learnt more daily of the magic of Love, which one may still learn, although fairy magic has fled away.
>
> —"Dorani," in Lang's *Olive Fairy Book*

As we begin to revise our distorted images of ourselves, we naturally seek confirmation and support from others. Not only do we want recognition for our labors, but we also wish to share our discoveries with those closest to us and in the process reassure ourselves that our journey out of the world of myth is not a solitary one. Often, however, we do not immediately find the responses that we are looking for, as our parents, siblings, friends, mates, and even our own children resist changing their mental pictures of who we are and stubbornly refuse to acknowledge us without our familiar disguise.

Although Laurel no longer saw herself as doomed to be an underachiever and a social misfit, her mother continued to speak to her as if she were, ignoring all evidence to the contrary. Anxiously she urged Laurel to snatch up any job she could find, and dismissed the possibility that her daughter might actually be offered a plum position in a top publishing house that had already shown her some interest. *That* was fanciful thinking, according to Laurel's mother, not Laurel's hopelessness or diffuse guilt.

When Laurel tried to modify this archaic image of herself as an Outcast, her family's Orphan, she came up against what seemed like an immovable wall of resistance. On one occasion, when she was feeling uncharacteristically optimistic, she telephoned her mother, eager to report on how well her latest job interview had gone, thinking to reassure her that she would probably *not* be evicted from her apartment as the two of them had feared, when her mother would not hear of it and replied in what was her characteristic manner: "Did they ask you in the interview why you left your last job?" And then, with a chuckle: "See how ridiculous these interviews are. Nobody can ever find out in an interview whether a person is really qualified, so they may as well be picking names out of a hat!" Thus Laurel's mother reminded her of her lack of "real" qualifications, and attributed Laurel's success in the interview to her ability to camouflage herself temporarily as an acceptable candidate for the position. She followed up her remarks with a soulful plea to Laurel not to get her hopes up too high, explaining all the while that she just wanted her to be "realistic."

In the past, Laurel would have silently concurred with her mother's message and, instead of becoming angry at her for bursting her bubble, she would have simply become depressed over what was apparently an honest appraisal of her and an accurate foretelling of her future. Perhaps in her next job interview she would even have done something to fulfill her mother's prophetic vision of doom and destruction, and so have proved herself to be her mother's loyally unhappy daughter.

However, Laurel was beginning to feel frustrated and misunderstood by her mother's not-so-subtle deprecations disguised as insights. She began to regard the false image of herself that her mother reflected back at her as she would an alien creature, and it required a stretch of the imagination to locate herself in that funhouse mirror. Because her mother continued to insist that this was who she was, Laurel found herself feeling more distant from her mother as she became closer to her self. Sometimes this was troubling, and she longed for the "good old days," when they saw things eye to eye and were merged as one.

Or take, for example, Lisa, the younger of two sisters, who was always seen in her family as the Charmer. Whereas her older sister, Judith, was her father's protégé—wise, thoughtful, level-headed, and virtuous—Lisa was flirtatious, frivolous, and flighty, characteristics more closely resembling her mother, at least according to the family lore. Although she was only two years younger than Judith, she felt, even as an adult, as if she were her sister's daughter. She looked up to Judith, resented her authority, and felt uneasy speaking seriously in her presence, fearing that she would only trip awkwardly over her words. (Did her speech really become garbled, and did she really appear empty-headed? I don't know, but neither does she!)

When, as an adult, Lisa returned home for holiday dinners, she would be greeted accordingly—never mind that she had, in the last few years, shown herself to be a competent and dedicated student, and had gained respect on the college campus for her social activism within the surrounding community. *En famille*, she continued to be addressed as if she were fluff: "How's your love life?" "Have you managed to twist your professors around your little pinky yet?" "I was always against coeducation, because as a young man I would get too distracted when there were pretty women in my classes." "I hope you are learning something practical, because nowadays even a beautiful young woman like you might have to get yourself a paying job and earn a little money when you graduate." Lisa's parents continued to relate to her in terms of her charm, her looks, and her purported flightiness, and Lisa was invisible.

Lisa's father in particular liked to tease her about her romantic conquests (real and imaginary) and to let her know that he suspected her of all sorts of mischief. By his conspiratorial glances in her direction, he implied that he knew her better than anybody else (they always had a special bond) and that for this reason she should not "pretend" to be anything other than what he thought she was. When Lisa objected to her father's implicit formulations of her character, she was accused by the entire family of being oversensitive: "Come on, we only tease you because we love you. You know we wouldn't want you to change one bit." Lisa could not argue with that! She had come to the conclusion that this was indeed the case, though they didn't fully understand the implications of what they said!

On these family occasions, nothing more than a passing reference was ever made to Lisa's volunteer work at a shelter for battered women, or her academic accomplishments, which she characteristically minimized so as not to put a damper on the family fun. Neither her parents nor her sister seemed to notice that she dressed rather conservatively, and no longer called long-distance for more spending money. They made the same tired jokes about their "hippie" daughter who lived on whole-grain bread and imported cheese but liked smoked salmon and expensive wines when she came home for a visit.

In Lisa's family, as in most, reunions conformed to a set pattern; after the initial banter, Judith and her father would launch into their usual heated political debates, which, as tradition would have it, excluded her mother and Lisa. Eventually they retreated into the kitchen (as would be expected of the more "feminine" members of the family) and exchanged intimacies, filling each other in on the latest "gossip." Everyone felt "at home," not least of all Lisa.

Yes, Lisa had played her part artfully—smiling coyly when her dad would refer seductively to her irresistible sexual charm and impractical relationship with money. She even remembered one occasion on which she had enthusiastically embellished his portrait of her, in a kind of seductively incestuous "dance," by relating an incident in which she figured as the naughty nymph she was expected to be. And after all, despite her frustration at being excluded from the ongoing debate in the living room, Lisa admitted that she loved that time alone with her mother sharing confidences. But was it worth it? She was no longer sure.

Invariably, such family gatherings left Lisa with a sour taste in her mouth, feeling vaguely disappointed with herself and her loving family. She envied her sister's unquestioned dignity and her presumed intelligence, but found that, when she tried to interject an opinion about the economy or the breakup of the Soviet Union, nobody paid any attention, and her remarks were politely disregarded (heard but amiably dismissed, as if they were the free associations of a cunning but naively ignorant young child). She was certain that her parents loved her, but she realized that they saw only half of her person; though the other half had been content to go to sleep, she was waking up now and resisted being gently rocked back to the land of dreams, to the tune of the family anthem.

When we discard our familiar portraits of ourselves, we are bound to experience a sense of loss, if only because we are leaving behind some flavor of our childhood. But the feeling of personal loss is compounded when our internal psychic changes threaten to disrupt our present-day relationships. Embedded in each of these relationships are rules governing intimacy, and naturally we fear that if we break these rules we will be abandoned and cast aside as traitors by those very people who presume to love and value us the most. If we alone change and they do not, then the show will go on without us, and we will have lost the magic that made us feel protected, that told us we belonged.

So, for example, Julia's relationship with Peter was founded upon her selfless devotion to his recovery; they felt close only as long as he depended on her and her alone to rescue him with her unconditional and purifying love. His involvement in Alcoholics Anonymous, with its emphasis on recovery through self-help groups, coupled with her demands for an increasingly personalized commitment to her (marriage and children), violated both of their definitions of how to be intimate. She was not being selfless, and he was not depending upon her for his salvation. As a result, their relationship was in serious jeopardy as both of them stepped out of character.

Howard, on the other hand, suspected that Christina's attraction to him would quickly wane were he to be less combative and more conventional, a reasonable guy and not a ticking time bomb. Moreover, he found her less appealing as she succeeded more and anguished less in her career as a "struggling" photographer. If she ceased playing the part of a naïve and vulnerable maiden lost in the maze of the big, ugly city, he wondered what would keep them from drifting apart.

For Jessica, intimacy with her fiancé, Michael, rested upon the illusion of her little-girl perfection, which included her indecisiveness and "free-floating" anxiety. She foresaw a life of solitude whenever she contemplated not being his adorably impractical Princess, whose penchant for introspection made her so dizzy that she *had* to lean on him to steady herself, and keep from getting lost in the fog. She had contempt for Michael's blind devotion to her image, but hesitated to disillusion him or herself. Who would love her then? And who would vanquish the dragons if they turned out to be real, as her parents' overprotectiveness had implied?

Larry also intimated that his relationship with his latest girlfriend, who was twenty years younger than he, was founded upon false premises. He anticipated, and well he might, that he would lose her admiration and respect were he to reveal to her the extent of his disability and stop pretending to be the carefree, charming Ladies' Man she had fallen in love with just one year earlier. She loved to be his Playboy Bunny and would most likely have recoiled from being a comforting companion, let alone a nurse or social worker! Middle-aged and terrified of being rejected by younger women for being a Mama's Boy and Hothouse Flower, Larry found that, by playing the part of the charming playboy for so many years, he had trapped himself in unreality, where his relationships rested precariously on his continued ability to deceive.

As each of these "characters" experimented with being human, they were forced to confront the possibility that other people dear to them were invested in perpetuating their mythic identities. Of course, logically speaking, as long as we live as characters, it is impossible to establish any *real* intimacy with other people. But in that case the illusion of intimacy that comes with participating in a shared dramatic performance may be all that we know or hope to attain.

As children, we were forced to accept whatever terms our families offered us. If we felt obliged to sever our connections with certain aspects of ourselves in order to build connections with other people and participate in the family drama, wouldn't it be understandable that we would readily assume this obligation as we grow older?

Although mythological identities originate in early-childhood relationships, they are sustained and nourished by our current interactions, and we are as responsible as anyone else for creating the conditions in which they can continue to survive and flourish. The "spell" under which we have been cast can only be broken in the present. Our insights into the power of the self-fulfilling prophecy have no practical significance for our lives unless we translate them into action. The self-righteous martyr who continues to behave like a martyr and feel victimized even though he knows that he has orchestrated the entire performance, is still committed to betraying himself, and still convinced of the benefits of not being true to who he is.

Although there is never any guarantee that other people will agree to see us as we are, and surely no guarantee that they will prefer us to our mythic selves, we can certainly make it clear that *we* are taking off our various costumes and getting down from the stage so that we can *live* out, not *act* out, the rest of our lives. When we do this, we may actually inspire others to follow suit, just as the little boy in the fairy tale "The Emperor's New Clothes" inspired his fellow villagers to join him in his bold declaration of the truth, which they all knew deep inside but were too timid to admit: "The emperor has no clothes." What a relief finally to say it, and then maybe even to stop the wearisome charade!

INTERPERSONAL STRATEGIES FOR BREAKING THE SPELL

Reality Testing: Making the Implicit Explicit

Identifying unsatisfying patterns in relationships is the first and most obvious step to take in attempting to break the spell of the self-fulfilling prophecy. But even the most elegant and most thorough descriptive analysis of what transpires between two or more people will have no practical effect on their future behavior unless, in the process of describing what *is*, we challenge the implicit assumption that this is the way it must be. This means recognizing that the status quo does not necessarily reflect innate and hence unchangeable aspects of one's own or another's personality or ability. And that, even if we repeat ourselves endlessly, it does not mean that we *cannot* do otherwise.

As soon as we publicly acknowledge that nobody has genes programming him to become a Mama's Boy, or a Troublemaker, or a Marble Statue, or a perennially Innocent Child, we are free to reverse the seemingly irreversible. (Even exceptional intelligence, beauty, and sensitivity, which are to some degree inborn, are not psychic equivalents of being the mythological Shining Star or Sensitive Plant or what-have-you.)

As we enlist our family and friends to "test reality" with us, we will reveal that no one is consistently any of the stock characters that we are frequently mistaken for; if we look carefully, we are sure to discover that psychic life is always filled with contradictions and gray areas, and potentialities which have never been met.

In the process of testing reality, Lisa might point out to her family that her life has included more than her romantic exploits, and she might add that their fantasies have little relationship to what she is actually doing when she is away at college. Since her family prides itself on being close and loving, she can point out, moreover, that their exclusive focus on her looks and "charming" personality leaves her feeling hurt and invisible despite their "good intentions." When they accuse her of being defensive—and they have—she can tell them that she is indeed defending who she is, and then she might undefensively ask why she shouldn't. If she is confident that this is indeed what she is doing, she need not waver from her position or explode in frustration when her family fails to see her from a fresh perspective. The more she is convinced that they have no magic power over her, the less their distortions will disturb her, and the more persuasive she will be. Her seriousness will astonish her fellow actors far more than any dramatic display; a "fluff" can be hysterical, but she cannot be resolute.

Laurel's mother never stated explicitly that Laurel was doomed to fail on account of her obnoxiously aggressive personality, but this was what she implied when, with a roll of her eyes or a sidelong glance at Laurel's brother, Ethan, she dismissed the possibility of Laurel's getting and keeping a job (or a man). Nor did Laurel's lover Brian tell her directly that she was merely his Flattering Mirror, but he communicated just that by demanding her rapt attention and refusing to reciprocate her interest and admiration.

When messages are conveyed by innuendo, their meaning is more easily denied, so, to break the spell, this oblique mode of communicating must be avoided at all costs. We must not agree to be naïve, even though feigning innocence can make us feel cozy and protected, as if we were still children, nor can we allow someone else to "save face" by splattering egg on ours. Laurel might question her mother's deflating response to her successful job interview and offer her an uncensored interpretation of it. (As long as she pretended, along with her mother, that her mother's cutting remarks were innocuous, even well intentioned, she only fed the myth.) Why did she think that Laurel's success hinged on her ability to pull the wool over the interviewer's eyes, when in fact her résumé was objectively very impressive and there was no tangible reason to doubt her ability to do the job? Indeed, her last position demanded even greater responsibility. Did her mother believe that she had a personality problem? Well, Laurel might concede that she too had shared her mother's concerns about her "social skills," then say she had found, to her astonishment, that she *could* be quite likable when she was convinced that this served her purpose. Laurel's mother might squirm uncomfortably when confronted with the implicit message hidden beneath her euphemistic language, and she might tell Laurel that she was imagining things when she thought that her mother wished to undermine her. But in either case the cards would have been laid out on the table, and the pact of secrecy would have been forever broken.

When Brian sulked one evening after Laurel had stated a clear preference for Chinese rather than Mexican food for dinner, she took the opportunity to address more fundamental problems in their relationship. Did Brian expect her not to have her own preferences? Or were her feelings always supposed to correspond with his? And why was her desire for a discussion about dinner experienced as nagging and intrusive? Had he hoped she would have no opinions when he rescued her from her mess of a life? All fighting words perhaps, but ones that would strike at the very heart of their mythological relationship. Food is certainly not the issue! What is at stake is how intimacy is being defined and at what expense.

Shared reality testing requires some consensus as to what is reality (as opposed to one individual's take on reality) as well as which elements of a shared reality are immutable and which are not. As we gently confront our family and friends with their misrepresentations of us, we must be aware that partial truths easily masquerade as the Entire Truth, and by this maneuver we are rendered powerless. If we find ourselves fumbling for words as we try to defend our newly acquired insights into our characters, this does not mean that "they" are right and we are wrong. As in the ancient tale of the six blind men who describe an elephant as either just like a snake, or a tree trunk, or a spear, or a rope, or a wall, our friends and family are bound to draw very different conclusions about the nature of things, depending on the slice of reality they have at their fingertips. Therefore, if we wish our relationships to reflect our updated images of ourselves, we must make sure that these fresh images are in sharp focus and available for all to see. Until we highlight what is really essential, we cannot expect others to understand that they have been cuing into what is really peripheral.

Paradoxical Approaches: Transforming the Drama into the Theater of the Absurd

Unfortunately, mythological identities are not the product of reason and are therefore often invulnerable to rational argument. Maia's mother's belief in her daughter's Wild Incorrigibility expressed her own unconscious need to feel beleaguered, and her own unarticulated fear of losing control. Nicole's husband had a personal investment in relating to Nicole as if she were an exotic Delicate Flower, because if this was who she was then he could feel both powerful and tender as he played opposite her in the role of her protector and participated vicariously in her emotional storms.

Consequently, merely identifying a disturbing interpersonal pattern and amassing evidence that it is based more on fantasy images than on reality may not alter what has become habitual. Nicole may point out again and again to Frank those situations in which she has proved herself to be both competent and resilient, and yet, as long as Frank wishes to preserve his image of her as fragile and unworldly, he may just nod his head in feigned agreement and continue to see her as the naïve little child he always has.

Through bitter experience with fruitless discussion, most psychotherapists come to the humbling realization that often it is futile to argue with someone else's illusions, and that it is itself an illusion to think that logic must prevail and that truth must reign victorious. When people have a strong emotional investment in holding on to their beliefs, they will do so even if they ignore disconfirming evidence. Indeed, when our insights and diplomatic confrontations lead to no visible change in our relationships, we may be left feeling more frustrated than ever, as if we have been foolishly running in place alongside someone else's merry-go-round horse and getting nowhere fast. When this happens, we may question our own revised perceptions of ourselves and begin to wonder whether or not we "protest too much" and why. (If you can't fight them, join them.)

Insisting that one is *not* an Adorable Baby or a Loser or a Responsible Guy sometimes has a kind of boomerang effect whereby, in frustration, the Baby begins to feel like throwing a temper tantrum, the Loser is tempted to fall messily on his face and splatter every disbeliever with his blood, and the Responsible Guy sighs in quiet resignation and agrees once again to cease ruffling feathers and accept the foibles of those less responsible than he.

This is the point at which other strategies for change might prove to be more effective. Family therapists speak of "paradoxical interventions," in which, instead of trying to impose change upon a resistant family, they encourage the family members to continue doing precisely what they have been doing, only more so. (See Jay Haley, *Problem-Solving Therapy*, or Mara Selvini Palazzoli, *Self-Starvation*, for discussion and case illustrations of paradoxical interventions in family therapy.) For example, if a child is school-phobic because he senses that his mother has her own conflicts about his growing up and separating, the therapist using a paradoxical approach will support the child's desire to stay home and the mother's unconscious fear of letting him go. Rather than prodding the mother and child to give up their dysfunctional behavior, the therapist "goes with the resistance," plays devil's advocate, and in this manner subtly forces the family to re-evaluate what they are doing now that it is magnified tenfold. The child will be instructed for one week *never* to leave his mother's side, even for an instant, so that he can be extra sure that she is safe, while the mother will be encouraged *never* to let her child out of her sight, since without him she might not be able to make it through the day. If the undesirable behavior is exaggerated to the point of absurdity, even the most rigid patterns begin to bend and break, as family members cannot help becoming self-conscious about the drama they are enacting and uneasily aware of their complicity in keeping it going, despite their protests.

Similarly, when honest confrontation fails to reap tangible changes in our relationships with others, and we find that, despite the contradictory evidence, we are persistently treated as if we were our mythic characters, then we too can resort to paradox. For a variety of reasons, it may prove more effective. Most people do not like to feel pressured into changing their beliefs or behaviors, particularly by friends or relatives. They may experience the mildest instruction as a kind of criticism, or even a challenge to their intelligence or loving good intentions. Moreover, if they feel that their freedom to choose how to act or what to believe is being infringed upon, they may resist changing precisely because they are being asked to. Paradoxical approaches allow people to draw their own conclusions and preserve their dignity, since there is no overt struggle for power. I understand that some Oriental methods of self-defense operate according to a similar principle—one does not attack head on but allows one's opponent to topple under the weight of his own resistance.

By appearing to withdraw from the battle and exaggerating the characteristics that are ascribed to us, we ingeniously render our "character" and the entire drama in which we are participating ridiculous. When the mythological underpinnings of a relationship are thus highlighted and are no longer obscured in euphemism and innuendo, the myth of who we are explodes. The heat gets too intense, and the pot *has* to boil over, and then, if we are to eat the same meal, we must begin preparing it all over again. This takes time, and with time we may pause and reflect; we may even decide to change the menu and try something new.

An example of this approach would be if Lisa the Charmer/Airhead picked up where her father left off and, rather than arguing with her father's sexualized two-dimensional image of her, carried it to its logical extreme. "I agree, coeducation is a terrible idea! Whenever I walk into a classroom the men fall over in their chairs and begin to pant. Nobody ever gets any work done when I'm around, because they're too busy trying to hide their erections. I guess there is not much I can do about it either." And, "I've got my professors so tightly wrapped around my little finger that they routinely assure me—in confidence, of course—that I'll get A's in all my classes even if I fail to hand in a single paper the entire semester! What power!"

And imagine how surprised Jessica'a fiancé would be were she to support explicitly his image of her as his personal Goddess, his helplessly confused Princess, and his image of himself as a Man of the World. What would he say were she strenuously to *agree* with him that he undoubtedly finds a simple solution to every seemingly complicated problem, and that, although she knows nothing, she is nevertheless perfect, a treasure that deserves nothing less than a castle in the sky? What would he do if she were to exaggerate her "dizzy-dame" qualities to the point where she begged him to accompany her to work each morning because she couldn't possibly navigate the complex subway system on her own? Though Michael has never framed their relationship in such caricatured terms (he speaks like a man even if he feels like a character in a fairy tale), and has only implied that she is worthy of his idolatry and needful of his firm guidance, she can take the lead and do it for them. In the process of explicating the myth that they have shared, Jessica will make it difficult for them to continue to relate to each other "as if" the myth were real.

In Jessica's case, a paradoxical approach to myth-breaking might sound something like this: "You can't get angry at me, or demand that I be more considerate of you and stop my vacillation, because you know that I am perfect, and, like a glass figurine, so fragile I might break. If I can't make a decision about whether or not to marry, you can't blame me. Anyway, it only enhances my mystery and makes me more adorable and exciting. It's okay if I don't know what I want, because naturally you know better than I what is good for me. And life would be so very dull if both of us were as practical and levelheaded as you, and so very frightening if both of us were as misty-eyed and slippery as me." This sounds preposterous, perhaps, but that is the point: it might just jolt Michael out of his trance.

And, finally, Laurel may find that a paradoxical response to her family's deprecatory remarks preserves her sense of dignity. As soon as she stops defending her character and stops trying to persuade her family that she is really not a loser who is worthy of their contempt, she feels less guilty of the crimes they accuse her of.

Woefully she reported that her brother, Ethan, verbally attacked her one evening for being a "masochist" and for having allowed her lover to "kill her" (metaphorically speaking, of course). Rather than curling up like a wounded animal or protesting angrily and joining Ethan in the self-righteous histrionics he indulged in at her expense, Laurel might have disarmed her brother by responding in this manner: "Yes, I am being beaten daily. Didn't you know that I wear long sleeves so that nobody can see my bruises? I am in awe of your perceptiveness; you have discovered my darkest secret. I can see now that Brian is a veritable Monster. Can I be *your* slave?" Or "Yes, I agree, everyone takes advantage of me and I get sexually excited from being abused, just like the masochists in the textbooks. I even enjoy your attacking me this very moment. Yell louder; please, berate me for my weakness; I deserve your contempt. And, please, maybe you can call me every evening, and perhaps once during the day at the office too, just to check up on me and see if I'm all right."

There is an important distinction to be drawn between the use of sarcasm and the use of paradox. Paradox, as a therapeutic tool, rests on the assumption that people are often unaware of the extent to which *they* create their own reality and unconsciously choreograph their lives. We make love, we fight, our emotions soar and then plummet, we move about restlessly and then fall back languidly into oblivion, and sometimes it all feels inevitable. When the lights in the auditorium are dim, we cannot see the strings that jerk us and the other characters in our lives in one direction and then another, nor can we see the people behind the screen who are in charge of pulling the strings. We don't even realize that we are simultaneously the puppets *and* the puppeteers! But turn up the lights, and we expose the complex mechanisms behind the elaborate performance we put on each day as we move in perfect time to the scarcely audible, yet constant, music. The drama may continue as always, once the characters have regained their composure, after squinting their eyes to adjust to the harsh lights, but as members of the audience as well as players on the stage, we can never again be tricked into believing that the action is spontaneous.

There is no assurance that a paradoxical approach will succeed in changing people's minds or forcing them to revise their faulty images of who we are, but it is bound to disrupt the even flow of interaction that lulls us into living with our lies. By loudly applauding our dramatic performance, we call attention to the artifice and interrupt the endless "tape" that threatens to drown us in monotony.

Recognizing That It Takes Two to Tango

No child can be faulted for participating in his family drama, even if it means that in the process he has sacrificed large portions of his personality and committed himself to a life of deception. Nevertheless, without blaming the child for his necessary compromises, it would be a misrepresentation to describe him as a *passive* victim of circumstance. As children, we play an *active* role in creating and sustaining our mythological identities, which are conglomerations of our own and other people's skewed images of who we are and who we should be.

As adults in pursuit of the "real self," we must recognize and acknowledge our continuing role in perpetuating the habitual relationship patterns we claim to abhor. If we are consistently treated like an adorable baby or a schlemiel, a troublemaker or a martyred saint, in all likelihood it is because we are acting the part and feeding everyone the right cues. Though it is an illusion to believe that we can have *total* control over other people's responses to us (the "power of positive thinking" has real limits), it is an act of self-deception to believe that we have no control over their responses whatsoever! Only in fairy tales are characters either helpless or invincible, cast under a spell or capable of transcending human limitation. (Of course, this does not apply to extreme situations in which power relationships are politically based and role relationships are enforced by threats of punishment. A black person living under apartheid or a prisoner in a Nazi concentration camp cannot be accused of personally contributing to his oppression. We must not fall into the trap of blaming the victim.) When we decide to leave that magical world, we are obliged to challenge the myth of the innocent victim, embodied by the image of the captive princess in the tower, just as we challenge the myth of the Knight in Shining Armor and the promise of "happily ever after."

Lisa may bemoan her family's stubborn refusal to recognize her accomplishments or, for that matter, her insecurities, but unless she stops chattering girlishly about frivolous matters and dares to introduce a more serious tone into her conversation, she must assume some responsibility for cultivating their image of her as their charming little Nymph/Airhead with not a care in the world.

Laurel complains that she has never been accepted by "corporate" America, that her mother treats her like bacteria, and that Brian treats her like a stray cat (he leaves out some food for her from time to time but never lets her enter the inner sanctum of his home). And yet, if we look carefully, we see that Laurel is the artist who is creating the image, and that her boss, her mother, and her lover only embellish what is there.

So, for example, although Laurel has closets filled with pretty clothes and money in the bank, she often makes a point of dressing like an orphan, in drab, shapeless blouses and too-baggy jeans. Her downcast eyes and her caved-in chest, her tendency to speak in a plaintive little voice, add up to a portrait of the quintessential Outcast, everybody's Stepchild, who, having rejected her own body, is naturally going to be rejected by society as well. Until Laurel decides to stop projecting this image, it is unfair of her to feel victimized when it is reflected back at her in the eyes of other people.

What is true for Lisa and Laurel is true for all of us. If Anna does not want to be considered a nuisance and an upstart, she must stop apologizing every time she takes a deep breath or her older, "perfect" brother sneezes. Her constant apologies imply that she *is* the guilty party. And if she is *always* willing to pinch herself in so that she can slip smoothly into someone else's life drama, isn't she sending out a message that she can (and should) be bent out of shape at whim, since she has no natural shape to call her own? We must not blame the victim, but we also must not see ourselves as victims and deny responsibility for the fairy tales we tell and the "games we play."

If Helen wants to lose her reputation as the family Lady, the "goody-good," the Saint, the embodiment of virtue, she will have to stop sponsoring those family barbecues in which she ends up spending her money and depleting her energy by cooking and serving and cleaning up everybody's mess. If she faithfully carries the wood to the stake of her own execution, she should not be surprised if a fire is lit and she becomes the sacrificial lamb.

As long as Julia behaves as if she has no self, no other interests apart from Peter, he will treat her as if she were simply his personal fairy godmother, whom he can conjure up when he needs to and leave behind him without a thought about what she is doing now that she has pulled him out of his cave.

John, the rock of Gibraltar, alias Responsible Citizen, Husband, and Friend, will always be weighted down by other people's burdens if he continues to offer his shoulder and his ear indiscriminately to every flustered passerby. Can he admit that he is sometimes bored by other people's problems and yearns to cry and yell and laugh without constraint? His friends will be less dependent, and his wife will be less temperamental, once he has taken off his mask and stops offering solutions to everyone's problems but his own.

And, finally, Larry the reluctant Hothouse Flower/Mama's Boy must know by now that when he refuses to take care of himself—drinks only black coffee for breakfast and lunch and smokes three packs of cigarettes each day—he will be pampered and scolded and taken under some woman's wing. Sure, he is smothered and patronized and robbed of his freedom, but within Larry's honest protests that he is a man and not a little boy, there rings a false note. If he groans loudly under the weight of ordinary life pressures, how can he deny his complicity when people rush to relieve him of his burden and save his life?

Antiquated images of the self and others invariably fade slowly, but unless we introduce new, more vibrant pictures into our present-day lives, they will not fade at all—we'll touch them up, add color—because they will be all there is to see and all we will have to sustain ourselves.

LEAPING OFF THE PAGE

> If I do not do for myself, who will do it for me? And if I care only for myself, what am I? And if not now, when?
>
> —Rabbi Hillel, "Ethics of the Fathers"

Spellbound, we feel compelled to live out our mythological identities. But as the fog slowly clears and we see past the power of the self-fulfilling prophecy, we are suddenly brought face to face with a difficult choice. Once we see clearly, it is ultimately up to each one of us to decide whether we prefer to dig our heels in deeper every day and affirm our false identities as we grow old, or cut our losses now and move on, regretting but nonetheless accepting the sorry facts that time cannot be recaptured and lost opportunities cannot be reclaimed. The present is ours to shape, but our hands are crude instruments and we have no magic wands to help us out.

In examining *our* lives and the lives of others, we must ask ourselves a number of questions: What are the benefits of recognizing that a personal mythology was but is no longer necessary? What imaginary glory must we give up if we decide to stop twirling and "just" be real? And what changes will have to occur in our relationships with other people when we no longer live the myths that they are accustomed to living with us? These questions are the work of psychotherapy, but also the work of every person who believes that it is preferable to live boldly in broad daylight than to hibernate in the protective shadows of the past.

BIBLIOGRAPHY

Ackerman, N. *Treating the Troubled Family*. New York: Basic Books, 1966.

Adorno, Theodor W.; Frenkel-Brunswik, Else; Levinson, D. J.; and Sanford, R. N. *The Authoritarian Personality*. New York: Harper, 1950.

Andersen, Hans Christian. "The Real Princess." In *Favorite Tales from Grimm and Andersen*. London: Orbis Publishing, 1983.

Artiss, K. L., ed. *The Symptom as Communication in Schizophrenia*. New York: Grune and Stratton, 1959.

Bank, S. P., and Kahn, M. D. *The Sibling Bond*. New York: Basic Books, 1982.

Baum, F. L. *The Wizard of Oz*. New York: Parents' Magazine Press, 1964.

Becker, Ernest. *The Denial of Death*. New York: Free Press, 1973.

Berne, E. *Games People Play*. New York: Grove Press, 1964.

Bettelheim, Bruno. *Love Is Not Enough*. New York: The Free Press, 1950.

Bollas, C. *The Shadow of the Object: Psychoanalysis of the Unthought Known*. New York: Columbia University Press, 1987.

———. *Forces of Destiny: Psychoanalysis and the Human Idiom*. London: Free Association Books, 1989.

Bosormenyi-Nagy, I., and Spark, G. *Invisible Loyalties: Reciprocity in Intergenerational Family Therapy*. Hagerstown, MD: Harper and Row, 1973.

Bowen, M. *Family Therapy in Clinical Practice*. New York: J. Aronson, 1985.

Bruch, H. *The Golden Cage*. New York: Vintage Books, 1977.

Bruner, J. S. "Myth and Identity." In *Myth and Mythmaking*, edited by Henry A. Murray. New York: George Braziller, 1960.

Chodorow. N. *The Reproduction of Mothering: Psychoanalysis and the Sociology of Gender*. Berkeley: University of California Press, 1978.

Cooley, C. H. *Human Nature and the Social Order*. New York: Schocken Books, 1902.

de Beaumont, Madame. "Beauty and the Beast." In *European Fairy Tales*, compiled by Dagmar Sekova. New York: Lothrop, Lee and Shepard, 1971.

Dylan, Bob. "Sad-Eyed Lady of the Lowlands." Dwarf Music, 1966.

Erikson, E. *Identity, Youth and Crisis*. New York: W. W. Norton, 1968.

Festinger, L. "A Theory of Social Comparison Processes." *Human Relations* 7 (1954): 117–140.

Flaubert, G. *Madame Bovary*. Translated by Mildred Marmur. New York: Signet Classics, 1964.

Frenkel-Brunswik, Else. "Intolerance of Ambiguity as an Emotional and Perceptual Personality Variable." In *Else Frenkel-Brunswik: Selected Papers, Psychological Issues*, edited by Nanette Heiman and Joan Grant, vol. 8, no. 3, monograph 31. New York: International Universities Press, 1974.

Freud, A. *The Ego and the Mechanisms of Defense*. Revised Edition. New York: International Universities Press, 1966.

Freud, S. "Analysis Terminable and Interminable." In *The Complete Psychological Works of Sigmund Freud*, translated under the general editorship of James Strachey, vol. 23. London: Hogarth Press and The Institute of Psychoanalysis, 1964.

———. "Moses and Monotheism: Three Essays." In *The Complete Psychological Works of Sigmund Freud*, vol. 23.

———. "On Narcissism." In *The Complete Psychological Works of Sigmund Freud*, vol. 14.

———. "On Negation." In *The Complete Psychological Works of Sigmund Freud*, vol. 19.

———. "Studies on Hysteria." In *The Complete Psychological Works of Sigmund Freud*, vol. 2.

Girard, R. *Deceit, Desire and the Novel: Self and Other in Literary Structure*. Translated by Yvonne Freccero. Baltimore and London: Johns Hopkins University Press, 1965.

Green, Hannah. *I Never Promised You a Rose Garden*. New York: Holt, Rinehart and Winston, 1964.

Haley, J. *Problem-Solving Therapy: New Strategies for Effective Family Therapy*. New York: Harper Colophon Books, 1978.

Henry, J. *Pathways to Madness*. New York: Vintage Books, 1965.

Hillel (Rabbi). "Ethics of the Fathers." In The Mishna, chapter 1, *Metsudah Siddur*. Ed. Rabbi Abraham Davis. New York: Noble Offset Printers, 1982.

Horney, K. *Neurosis and Human Growth*. New York: W. W. Norton, 1950.

Ibsen, H. *Hedda Gabler and A Doll's House*. London: Faber and Faber, 1989.

Klagsbrun, Francine. *Mixed Feelings: Love, Hate, Rivalry and Reconciliation Among Brothers and Sisters*. New York: Bantam, 1992.

Kundera, M. *Life Is Elsewhere*. Translated by Peter Kussi. New York: Penguin Books, 1986.

Laing, R. D. *The Divided Self*. New York: Pantheon Books, 1969.

———. *The Politics of the Family and other Essays*. New York: Pantheon Books, 1971.

Laing, R. D., and Esterson, A. *Sanity, Madness and the Family*. London: Penguin Books, 1970.

Lang, A., ed. "Dorani." In *The Olive Fairy Book*. New York: Dover Publications, 1907.

Luthi, M. *Once Upon a Time: On the Nature of Fairy Tales*. Translated by Lee Chadeayne and Paul Gottwald with additions by the author.

Bloomington, IN: Indiana University Press, 1976.
McAdams, D. P. *Power, Intimacy and the Life Story: Personological Inquiries into Identity*. New York: Guilford Press, 1988.
McDougall, Joyce. *Theaters of the Mind: Illusion and Truth on the Psychoanalytic Stage*. New York: Basic Books, 1985.
Mallarmé, Stéphane. "The Windows." In *The Complete Works of Stéphane Mallarmé*, translated by Henry Weinfield. Forthcoming.
Miller, A. *Prisoners of Childhood: How Narcissistic Parents Form and Deform the Emotional Lives of Their Gifted Children.* Translated by Ruth Ward. New York: Basic Books, 1981.
Mosel, A. *Tikki Tikki Tembo*. New York: Scholastic Book Services, 1968.
Mother Goose: The Classic Volland Edition. Chicago: Rand McNally, 1976.
Ovid. "Narcissus." In *Metamorphoses*, translated by Frank Justus Miller. Cambridge: Harvard University Press, 1921.
Ovid. "Pygmalion." In *Metamorphoses*, translated by Allen Mandelbaum. Forthcoming.
Palazzoli, M. S. *Self-Starvation: From Individual to Family Therapy in the Treatment of Anorexia Nervosa.* Translated by Arnold Pomerans. Northvale, NJ: Jason Aronson, 1981.
Proust, M. *Swann's Way.* Translated by C. K. Scott-Moncrieff and Terence Kilmartin. New York: Random House, 1981.
Rank, O. *The Myth of the Birth of the Hero.* New York: Vintage Books, 1964.
Schafer, R. *Language and Insight.* New Haven: Yale University Press, 1978.
Shakespeare, W. *Complete Works.* Edited by W. J. Craig. London: Oxford University Press, 1905.
Shaw, G. B. *Pygmalion.* In *The Works of Bernard Shaw*, vol. 14. Great Britain: R & R Clark, 1930.
Shelley, P. B. *Poetical Works.* Edited by Thomas Hutchinson. New edition corrected by G. M. Mathews. London: Oxford University Press, 1970.
Sophocles. *Oedipus the King.* In *The Complete Greek Tragedies*, edited by David Grene and Richard Lattimore, vol. 3. New York: Modern Library, 1942.
Sullivan, H. S. *Interpersonal Theory of Psychiatry.* New York: W. W. Norton, 1953.
Travers, P. L. *Mary Poppins Comes Back.* New York: Harcourt Brace and World, 1935.
Tyler, A. *Dinner at the Homesick Restaurant.* New York: Alfred A. Knopf, 1982.
Vaihinger, H. *The Philosophy of "As If": A System of the Theoretical, Practical and Religious Fictions of Mankind.* Translated by C. K. Ogden. Great Britain: Lund Humphries, 1924.
Vaillant, G. E., and Vaillant, C. O. "Natural History of Male Psychological Health, XII: A 45-Year Study of Predictors of Successful Aging at Age 65." *American Journal of Psychiatry.* 147, no. 1 (January 1990): 831–837.
Watzlawick, P.; Bavelas, J. B.; and Jackson, D. *Pragmatics of Human Communication: A Study of Interactional Patterns, Pathologies and Paradoxes.* New York: W. W. Norton, 1967.

Winnicott, D. W. *The Maturational Processes and the Facilitating Environment: Studies in the Theory of Emotional Development.* Madison, CT: International Universities Press, 1965.

Wordsworth, W. *Poetical Works.* Edited by Thomas Hutchinson, revised by Ernest De Selincourt. Oxford: Oxford University Press, 1936.

Yeats, W. B. *The Poems of W. B. Yeats.* Edited by Richard Finneran. New York: MacMillan, 1983.

INDEX

INDEX

INDEX